THE MULTIVALENCE OF BIBLICAL TEXTS
AND THEOLOGICAL MEANINGS

Society of Biblical Literature

Symposium Series

Christopher R. Matthews,
Series Editor

Number 37

THE MULTIVALENCE OF BIBLICAL TEXTS
AND THEOLOGICAL MEANINGS

THE MULTIVALENCE OF BIBLICAL TEXTS AND THEOLOGICAL MEANINGS

Edited by

Christine Helmer

with the assistance of
Charlene T. Higbe

Society of Biblical Literature
Atlanta

THE MULTIVALENCE OF BIBLICAL TEXTS
AND THEOLOGICAL MEANINGS

Copyright © 2006 by the Society of Biblical Literature

Library of Congress Cataloging-in-Publication Data

The multivalence of biblical texts and theological meanings / edited by Christine Helmer ; with the assistance of Charlene T. Higbe.
     p. cm. — (Society of biblical literature symposium series ; no. 37)
    Includes bibliographical references and indexes.
    ISBN-13: 978-1-58983-221-3 (pbk. : alk. paper)
    ISBN-10: 1-58983-221-3 (pbk. : alk. paper)
    1. Bible—Criticism, interpretation, etc. 2. Bible—Theology. I. Helmer, Christine. II. Higbe, Charlene T. III. Series: Symposium series (Society of Biblical Literature) ; no. 37.
    BS511.3.M85 2006
    220.6'01—dc22   2006013717

14 13 12 11 10 09 08 07 06   5 4 3 2 1
Printed in the United States of America on acid-free, recycled paper conforming to ANSI/NISO Z39.48-1992 (R1997) and ISO 9706:1994 standards for paper permanence.

Contents

Acknowledgments

The origins of the biblical-theological discussion documented in this book go back to the Society of Biblical Literature International Meeting that took place at the University of Cambridge in July 2003. Since then, the volume has taken shape in conversations that have manifested the goodwill of all contributors, as well as the willingness of each to risk the secure confines of his or her own particular discipline and to build bridges across terminological, conceptual, and methodological divides. I have discovered that biblical theology is a discipline of risk. In an age characterized by the distance between the empirical and the conceptual disciplines, there is a risk in conceptualizing anew the intimate relations between the real and the ideal in view of epistemological and substantive concerns. This risk is met not only in the concrete wrestling with the terminological, conceptual, and methodological difficulties presented by the subject matter. It is also met by the willingness of dialogue partners to respect the ethical mandates governing any conversation, especially those conversations that strive for truth and knowledge. I thank all of the authors for participating in this biblical-theological discussion, for their enthusiasm in contributing to this volume, and for their risk-taking that challenges the biblical and theological disciplines to think anew about their relations to each other.

Two gracious colleagues helped in the production of the manuscript. I am most grateful to Charlene T. Higbe, who lent the manuscript the finest eyes to detail, the kindest words at the most intense times, and the most heartwarming joy to the editing task. It was also my especial pleasure in working with Brenna Moore. I thank Harvard Divinity School for providing the funding to support their work.

The discussion in this volume would not have taken place if it had not been for the leadership of Kristin De Troyer and Matthew Collins in making room on the SBL International Meeting's program in 2003 for the Biblical Theology Group. For their support of biblical theology and of this volume I am most grateful.

I thank Christopher R. Matthews, Series Editor of the SBL's Symposium Series, and Bob Buller, Editorial Director of SBL Publications, for accepting the volume for publication in the Symposium Series, for their kind enthusiasm for the project, and for their earnest dedication in bringing all aspects of the manuscript to completion.

My conversations with Robert A. Orsi have challenged me to think through the many ways in which theology can and must be brought down from the heaven of speculative possibility to the earth of embodied reality. Yet life is breathed into reality by transcendent glimpses of heaven, and it is to Robert that I owe those many real presences that birth joy and hope.

ABBREVIATIONS

PRIMARY SOURCES

4QPsJub^a	*Pseudo-Jubilees*
Abr.	Philo, *De Abrahamo*
Aen.	Vergil, *Aeneid*
Balb.	Cicero, *Pro Balbo*
Bell. Cat.	Sallust, *Bellum catalinae*
Carm.	Horace, *Carmina*
Cher.	Philo, *De cherubim*
De arch.	Vitruvius, *De architectura*
Deus	Philo, *Quod Deus sit immutabilis*
Dom.	Cicero, *De domo suo*
Ep. mort. Ar.	Athanasius, *Epistula ad Serapionem de more Arii*
Fast.	Ovid, *Fasti*
Flam.	Plutarch, *Titus Flamininus*
Fug.	Philo, *De fuga et inventione*
Gen. Rab.	*Genesis Rabbah*
Geogr.	Strabo, *Geographica*
Jub.	*Jubilees*
J.W.	Josephus, *Jewish War*
L.A.B.	*Liber antiquitatum biblicarum* (Pseudo-Philo)
Leg.	Philo, *Legum allegoriae*
Leg. man.	Cicero, *Pro Lege manilia* (*De imperio Cn. Pompeii*)
m. Yad.	Mishnah, *Yadayim*
Migr.	Philo, *De migratione Abrahami*
Mith.	Appianus, *Mithridatica*
Mor.	Plutarch, *Moralia*
Nat.	Pliny the Elder, *Naturalis historia*
Nigr.	Lucian, *Nigrinus*
Or.	Dio Chrysostom, *Orationes*
Or. Bas.	Gregory of Nazianzus, *Oratio in laudem Basilii*
Peregr.	Lucian, *De morte Peregrini*
Phil.	Plutarch, *Philopoemen*

Pis.	Cicero, *In Pisonem*
Pomp.	Plutarch, *Pompeius*
Res gest.	*Res gestae divi Augusti*
Sest.	Cicero, *Pro Sestio*
Somn.	Philo, *De somniis*
Trin.	Augustine, *De Trinitate*
Vesp.	Suetonius, *Vespasianus*
Vit. soph.	Philostratus, *Vitae sophistarum*

SECONDARY SOURCES

AB	Anchor Bible
ABD	*Anchor Bible Dictionary.* Edited by D. N. Freedman. 6 vols. New York: Doublday, 1992.
ACCS	Ancient Christian Commentary on Scripture
ANRW	*Aufstieg und Niedergang der römischen Welt: Geschichte und Kultur Roms im Spiegel der neueren Forschung.* Edited by H. Temporini and W. Haase. Berlin: de Gruyter, 1972–.
AOAT	Alter Orient und Altes Testament
ATD	Das Alte Testament Deutsch
AThR	*Anglican Theological Review*
Bib	*Biblica*
BibInt	*Biblical Interpretation*
BibInt	Biblical Interpretation Series
BThSt	Biblisch-theologische Studien
CBQ	*Catholic Biblical Quarterly*
ChrÉg	*Chronique d'Égypte*
CWS	Classics of Western Spirituality
EvTh	*Evangelische Theologie*
EZW	Evangelische Zentralstelle für Weltanschauungsfragen
FCB	Feminist Companion to the Bible
FOTL	Forms of Old Testament Literature
HBT	*Horizons in Biblical Theology*
HRWG	*Handbuch religionswissenschaftlicher Grundbegriffe.* Edited by G. Kehrer and H. G. Kippenberg. 5 vols. Stuttgart: Kohlhammer, 1988–2001.
HTR	*Harvard Theological Review*
IBC	Interpretation: A Bible Commentary for Teaching and Preaching
IDB	*The Interpreter's Dictionary of the Bible.* Edited by G. A. Buttrick. 4 vols. Nashville: Abingdon, 1962.
Int	*Interpretation*

JAC	Jahrbuch für Antike und Christentum
JBL	*Journal of Biblical Literature*
JR	*The Journal of Religion*
JRS	*Journal of Roman Studies*
JSHRZ	*Jüdische Schriften aus hellenistisch-römischer Zeit*
JSNT	*Journal for the Study of the New Testament*
JSNTSup	Journal for the Study of the New Testament Supplement Series
JSOTSup	Journal for the Study of the Old Testament Supplement Series
JSP	Journal for the Study of the Pseudepigrepha
JSR	*Journal of Scriptural Reasoning*
KuD	*Kerygma und Dogma*
Mod Theol	*Modern Theology*
NAB	New American Bible
NCBC	New Century Bible Commentary
NIB	*The New Interpreter's Bible*
NICOT	New International Commentary on the Old Testament
NovTSup	Supplements to Novum Testamentum
NRSV	New Revised Standard Version
NTL	New Testament Library
Numen	*Numen: International Review for the History of Religions*
NZSThR	*Neue Zeitschrift für systematische Theologie und Religionsphilosophie*
OBT	Overtures to Biblical Theology
OTL	Old Testament Library
RGG	*Religion in Geschichte und Gegenwart.* Edited by H. D. Betz et al. 4th ed. 8 vols. Tübingen, 1998–2005.
RVV	Religionsgeschichtliches: Versuche und Vorarbeiten
SBLSymS	SBL Symposium Series
SCrHier	Scripta hierosolymitana
Scriptura	*Scriptura: International Journal of Bible, Religion and Theology in Southern Africa*
SHR	Studies in the History of Religions (supplement to *Numen*)
SJOT	*Scandinavian Journal of the Old Testament*
SNTSMS	Society for New Testament Studies Monograph Series
StPB	Studia post-biblica
TRE	*Theologische Realenzyklopädie*
TSAJ	Texte und Studien zum antiken Judentum
VTSup	Supplements to Vetus Testamentum
WBC	Word Biblical Commentary
WMANT	Wissenschaftliche Monographien zum Alten und Neuen Testament

WuD	*Wort und Dienst*
WUNT	Wissenschaftliche Untersuchungen zum Neuen Testament
ZKG	*Zeitschrift für Kirchengeschichte*
ZThK	*Zeitschrift für Theologie und Kirche*

Introduction: Multivalence in Biblical Theology

Christine Helmer

1

The famous definition of biblical theology that Gerhard Ebeling formulated in 1955 identified the fundamental ambiguity haunting the field. Ebeling contrasts two meanings of the term *biblical theology:* "the theology contained in the Bible, the theology of the Bible itself" ("die in der Bibel enthaltene Theologie, die Theologie der Bibel selbst") and "the theology that accords with the Bible, scriptural theology" ("die in der Bibel gemäße, die schriftgemäße Theologie").[1] By "the theology contained in the Bible," Ebeling means a historical description of the theology that is implicitly presupposed or explicitly articulated by the text or the theology structuring the text. This is reached by employing primarily historical and literary strategies in order to contextualize the text's theological claims as historically situated claims. By "theology that accords with the Bible," Ebeling means the theologically normative claims resulting from conceptual-theological analysis that can be verified as congruent with the Bible, although not necessarily historically contextualized by the Bible. The contrast between the theology of the Bible and scriptural theology is, as Ebeling designates it, provisional: "Even if we take these contrasts as a merely provisional characterization, yet it is clear that we cannot be content only to distinguish the two meanings of 'biblical theology.' "[2]

Ebeling's contrast has convincingly set the conceptual parameters for biblical theology. The contrast between historical and theological methods, between the object as described historically and the object of theological construction, exposes the braided trajectories of biblical theology's two foun-

---

1. Gerhard Ebeling, "The Meaning of 'Biblical Theology,' " in *Word and Faith* (trans. J. W. Leitch; London: SCM, 1963), 1:78; translation of, "Was heißt 'Biblische Theologie'? (1955)," in *Wort und Glaube* (3rd ed.; Tübingen: Mohr Siebeck, 1967), 1:69.
2. Ebeling, "Meaning of 'Biblical Theology,' " 80; "Was heißt 'Biblische Theologie'?" 70.

dational disciplines. Yet the contrast reflects an ambiguity in the German term for *theology*—theology "in the broad sense" includes both the historical and conceptual fields—that is not adequately captured by the smaller radius that the word *theology* designates in the English-speaking world. Ebeling acknowledges that the term's ambiguity strives for resolution that the discipline's future is driven by the creativity inherent in tension. The English term, however, drives history and theology into sharper contrast than the original German. Theology in English is cast more narrowly as a conceptual discipline; its proclivity to normativity is underlined and consequently contrasted with historical description. If, however, the English term could recapture a hint of the German provisionality, then perhaps the blunt edges between history and theology could be blurred somewhat in order to create a productive tension.

It is the intention of this volume to blur the distinction between historical and theological approaches to biblical theology in order to explore the many ways in which biblical texts are related to theological meanings. A historical investigation into a specific text inevitably notes its multivalence. The text is perpetually embedded in a history of interpretative work. Whether it bears the traces of redactional modification, such as the Deuteronomistic Historian, or whether it exists in a final form waiting to be interpreted, such as the Pauline epistles in the New Testament, the text presents different historical layers for interpretation. With each historical layer, different possibilities for theological meaning are conveyed. The theology of Mark as an early historical layer of the Synoptic Gospels, for example, bears the messianic secret to its bitterly short ending, while the later theology of Luke does not hesitate to make overt claims about Jesus' central significance in history.

The key to blurring the history-theology distinction relies on the double presupposition that history is interested in theology and that theology is a historically located conceptual discipline. Ebeling's definition of biblical theology as a "theology contained in the Bible" presupposes that the biblical texts are interested in making claims, potentially transhistorical claims, about the relations of persons to others in community and personal relations in community to God. The historical analysis of texts includes the description of the claims that the text makes about theologically significant relations. Ebeling's understanding of a "theology that accords with the Bible" suggests a theology that is constructed outside the Bible and that can be shown to be articulated within specific parameters set by scripture. On a closer look at the ways in which theological theories are formed in the Bible, particularly through tradition-historical and canonical approaches, Ebeling's "scriptural theology" can be seen to be an intrabiblical phenomenon as well. Scriptural theology at both its locations involves the application of the criterion of "accordance" that is itself the result of a community consensus that can change with time. The historicization of scriptural theology blurs any clear and static boundary between history and theology. If this book's aim is the blurring of history and theology as a potentially creative resource, then it should not immediately raise the specter of dogmatic imposition. Nervousness around the potential dogmatic-theological distortion of the historical text arises quite probably in a conceptual framework pitting an ahistorical theology against the historically responsible study of texts. The claim of theology's historicity can alleviate this anxiety. By deliberately rooting its claims in history, theology frees historical studies to be strengthened by its conceptual analysis.

The aim of this book is to show how historical and theological approaches are mutually reciprocal in the study of the relations between biblical texts and their theological meanings. This is framed by the presupposition that the biblical texts are theologically underdetermined. As points of reference for ongoing religious traditions, biblical texts are given to be redacted, rewritten (*fortgeschrieben*), contextualized, actualized, and interpreted in places at a distance from the original composition. Theological claims are made and continue to be made through processes of the texts' recontextualization and reconceptualization.[3] The formations of theological theories, whether intrabiblical or extrabiblical, whether uniformly consistent or radically different from each other, are answers to the texts' invitation to explore their textuality, historicity, and referents. Why and how biblical texts are open to a variety of possible theological meanings is the issue at the heart of this volume.

The question concerning the relation between text and theology builds on the results of its predecessor volume, *Biblical Interpretation: History, Context, and Reality*.[4] The *Biblical Interpretation* volume looks deliberately at the relation between text and the claims about reality that the text makes. Text interpretation cannot evade the question concerning reality; the understanding of a particular text involves an analysis of the historical and metaphysical commitments that the text claims. The formation of theological theory, as is argued in the various chapters of *Biblical Interpretation*, is intimately related to historical and metaphysical questions. Historical context shapes the relevance of theological standpoints. The third-century controversy surrounding God's body, for example, resulted in theological decision-making that had an enormous impact on the Christian tradition's understanding of divine

---

3. I find this distinction proposed by Rolf P. Knierim to be very helpful (*The Task of Old Testament Theology: Substance, Method, and Cases* [Grand Rapids: Eerdmans, 1995], 84–85).

4. Christine Helmer, with the assistance of Taylor G. Petrey, eds., *Biblical Interpretation: History, Context, and Reality* (SBLSymS 26; Atlanta: Society of Biblical Literature, 2005).

incorporeality.[5] Historical processes determine the appearance or erasure of theological content and detail; the emergence of transcendental Idealism in nineteenth-century Berlin, for example, contributed to the rise in Trinitarian speculation and ultimately to the early twentieth century's proclamation of the Trinity as the systematic key to Christian theology. Philosophical questions concerning the reality of being, specifically the reason for existence and freedom's choice for evil, are questions forming the ground on which theological concepts are conceived. Furthermore, the text's metaphysical and historical claims to reality exercise hermeneutical constraints on theological interpretation. A Leibnizian power-appearance metaphysic, for example, shapes Schleiermacher's philosophical commitments, which he uses to interpret the soteriology of Col 1:15–20 in a universalist direction.[6] Issues of historical context and metaphysics presupposed both by the text and its interpreters are fundamentally significant to hermeneutical issues concerning theological claims about reality. If theology lays claims to the status in reality of its subject matter, then it must work together with those disciplines that provide accounts of reality.

The historical and philosophical emphasis of the predecessor volume leaves open the question concerning multiple possibilities for theological commitments that are themselves a function of textual multivalence. Biblical texts by virtue of their redaction and incorporation into larger genre sequences lay claims at different textual layers to different theological meanings. Canonical arrangement of books contextualizes the biblical text's final form for theological purposes, while preserving other distinct witnesses to its subject matter, to use Brevard Childs's terminology in view of the Christian Bible.[7] For some texts, early layers witness to an original *Sitz im Leben* from which traditions and liturgies grew. The Psalms, for example, have an original cultic location that is then transposed into another theological key when cited in relation to the New Testament passion narratives (e.g., Matt 27:46's allusion to Ps 22:1). Later layers as written stories catch glimpses of both their earlier oral sources and the processes of their dissemination. The books attributed to

5. See Karen Jo Torjesen, "The Enscripturation of Philosophy: The Incorporeality of God in Origen's Exegesis," in Helmer and Petrey, *Biblical Interpretation*, 73–84.

6. See my essay, "The Consummation of Reality: Soteriological Metaphysics in Schleiermacher's Interpretation of Colossians 1:15–20," in Helmer and Petrey, *Biblical Interpretation*, 113–31.

7. Childs distinguishes between "the Old Testament's witness to God's redemptive will in the context of the history of Israel" and "the New Testament's witness to God's redemption through Jesus Christ in the context of the early church." See Brevard S. Childs, *Biblical Theology of the Old and New Testaments: Theological Reflection on the Christian Bible* (Minneapolis: Fortress, 1993), 91, 93.

Israel's prophets, for example, contain prophetic words in direct speech, yet extensive historical information is brushed out in the process of transmission. Erasure in the final form allows the prophet's message to find addressees in communities other than the original group for which it was intended.[8] Textual multivalence can also be a function of the text's final form. The challenging question concerning the relation of the Hebrew Bible to the Christian Bible, which is composed of two Testaments, is the question concerning the possibilities inherent in the Hebrew Bible for different theological meanings. Those meanings are carried by possibilities in the text's content and form. The question of Jewish-Christian relations, then, is the question concerning the recognition of multivalence within one's respective religious tradition. It is scholarship on the Bible from both historical and theological perspectives that again and again challenges the tendency to unified interpretation by carefully drawing distinctions, classifying text material, and ultimately keeping open the plurality of interpretative options.

The view that only one theological meaning is generated by a particular biblical text is earnestly challenged in this volume. It is this view that is related to a supersessionist strand in Christian theology, yet has other manifestations, particularly framed by a Christian theological fascination for singular truth obtained by revelation. One challenge to this view looks at the nature of theological abstraction from the particular: theology's task is to abstract the universal from the particular, an action that is an inevitability of conceptual processes of making sense of the world and of communicating that sense in linguistic terms. Speech is itself constituted by the particular and the universal, thereby making interpersonal communication presuppose at least a minimum of conceptual abstraction. This kind of abstraction is most evident in biblical-theological projects that explicitly gather up concepts serving as orienting focal points, as in the search for the center of scripture (technically in German, die *Mitte der Schrift*), or in a theology of the New Testament that presupposes a high level of abstraction to claim a theology coherent and consistent across the diversity of Gospels and epistles. The reduction of predicative diversity is not in and of itself a problem in theology—abstraction requires a certain blurring of the particular in order to offer the orientation that only uniformity of meaning can provide. A problem occurs when theological abstraction negates particularity, as is the case with the anachronism that has lost contact with original meanings. A problem arises when theological abstraction imposes conceptual unity on a text. The traditional supersessionist reading of the Christian use of the Old Testament in semantic

---

8. Ibid., 170–71.

identity with the New Testament is a case in point. A theologically underdetermined canon that is open to theological possibilities is a perspective that
requires a carefully balanced understanding of theological abstraction in view
of determination by particularity.

One key aspect to the text–theology relation is the tailoring of a particular method to tease out the complexity of the text in relation to a theological
position. Christian A. Eberhart's chapter on Gen 22 shows, for example, that
theological decisions sometimes associated in the tradition with a text are,
on closer look, a function of a process of theological concept formation that
involves many steps of abstraction from the alleged foundational text. The
analysis of this process involves redaction history in addition to text-criti-
cal issues. A strict philological analysis—a careful look at the text's grammar,
syntax, verb tense, and distinctive terminology—is required when the text
contains the hermeneutical parameters for theological interpretation. Luther,
for example, translated the "ascension Psalms" (2 and 110) in a Trinitarian-
theological direction only after studying the passage's grammatical and syntactical features in Hebrew more deeply.[9] The analysis of a distinct passage
within a larger canonical segment also demands a sensitivity to theological
pluralism in addition to historical-critical study. The history of Christianity
can be read as a history of interpreting salvation from two perspectives, from
the Matthean perspective of a "secondary conditioning of salvation" and from
the Pauline perspective of "justification by faith."[10] If the canon includes vastly
differing opinions on one of its central themes, then theological pluralism too
can be entertained.

Textual multivalence keeps the canon open to theological possibility, yet
even multivalence has its limitations. Hermeneutical parameters, such as the
reality to which the text refers, the range of possible meanings presented by
the actual text, and the theological frameworks shaping interpretation, are
constraints that limit the interpretative possibilities of the text. The formation
of a theological claim inevitably requires artificially restricting the text's multivalence, yet such a restriction can also be accountable to canonical diversity
by a position infused with modesty. This point is illustrated by David Carr in
his chapter, "For the Love of Christ: Generic and Unique Elements in Chris-

---

9. See my "Luther's Trinitarian Hermeneutic and the Old Testament," *Mod Theol* 18
(2002): 49–73.

10. On the contrast between the Matthean perspective that stipulates works in addition
to the personal salvation given by Jesus and the Pauline elimination of works, see Christof
Landmesser, *Jüngerberufung und Zuwendung zu Gott: Ein exegetischer Beitrag zum Konzept
der matthäischen Soteriologie im Anschluß an Mt 9,9–13* (WUNT 1/133; Tübingen: Mohr Siebeck, 2001).

tian Theological Readings of the Song of Songs." Carr shows how particular aspects of the semantic potential in the Song of Songs are actualized in consistent ways. Interpretations range from the interpersonal erotic relationship to the marriage between the collective and God, yet the range is distinctly focused by a particular conceptual-theological lens. The claim of the text's theological restriction is, furthermore, an interpretative act that requires transhistorical cultivation. So Stephen T. Davis shows in his chapter, " 'Who Can Forgive Sins but God Alone?': Jesus, Forgiveness, and Divinity," that the traditional Chalcedonian reading of Mark 2:1–12 persists in its ability to logically and theologically persuade new generations of Christians of its correctness. Multivalence and meanings interact in forming a vibrant theological history. This volume attempts to demonstrate this vibrancy—the dynamic interplay between both elements without prematurely reducing complexity, even allowing different meanings to co-exist in tension with each other. The blurring between the historical and the theological, while admitting the relevant distinctions, can move biblical theology to be in a position to study the theologies arising in the processes of text formation and from the texts as they are read in later religious traditions.

2

Biblical theology's status as a bridge-building discipline is wonderfully poised to address both the historical and the theological dimensions of biblical texts. This volume presents contributions by scholars interpreting the text–theology relation by integrating both aspects. The analyses reflect a common commitment to the specific determinations of particular texts in relation to their respective generation of particular theological meanings. By this concentration on precise relationships, the contributors aim to anchor theological abstraction in the specific grammatical, semantic, and historical understandings of the text and, conversely, to relate particular aspects of the text to the conceptualization of its theological dimensions.

David Carr begins the volume with his chapter, "For the Love of Christ," which addresses the power of the Song of Songs to generate multiple meanings in both Jewish and Christian traditions. Carr demonstrates that the Song's interpretative multivalence in traditions of Jewish and Christian accounts of the divine–human relationship contrasts surprisingly with the literal level's erotic story of an interpersonal relationship. Carr shows how the story is transformed by interpretations that explore the text's semantic potential at multiple levels. The power of the text is gained when its different layers are opened up by interpretative processes.

The relation that C. R. Seitz chooses to focus on in his chapter, "Fixity and Potential in Isaiah," is that between the embeddedness of particular biblical passages in a larger literary whole and the potential of the stabilized passage for a plurality of interpretations. Seitz concentrates his argument on the example of the messianic prophecies in Isa 9, 11, and 7:14 (the reference to the עלמה and her child Immanuel). Who is the referent of these particular passages? Seitz compares his interpretation to the work of Brevard S. Childs and Marvin A. Sweeney and shows that the interpretative decision for the referent—either a historical or an eschatological figure—is theologically shaped by the text's final form.

Christian A. Eberhart's contribution, "The Term 'Sacrifice' and the Problem of Theological Abstraction: A Study of the Reception History of Genesis 22:1–19," deals with the question whether theological abstraction, while itself a necessary process, adequately captures and represents the meanings of biblical texts. Eberhart focuses on one of the most well-known biblical texts, the story of Abraham and Isaac in Gen 22, and on the story's key concept of sacrifice. He claims that the concept is ambiguous. An original cultic meaning is only marginally relevant to the story of Gen 22 and its reception history in Judaism and early Christianity; a secularized metaphorical meaning seems best to explain its meaning in those traditions. The result for a Christian theory of atonement is, as Eberhart concludes, that any soteriological claims concerning Christ's sacrificial death require a text warrant other than Gen 22.

A distinct focus on the way in which language moves its hearer to come to new theological understandings is offered by Lincoln E. Galloway in " 'Consider the Lilies of the Field…': A Sociorhetorical Analysis of Matthew 6:25–34." Galloway argues that theological meaning is a function of the rhetoric of the Sermon on the Mount, analyzing how the rhetorical patterns of the Sermon, its aesthetic devices, and its rhythms, all call attention to the contrast between an ideology of striving for material glory and an ideology that places God as the sole focus of striving. Galloway also shows how the movement toward a greater appreciation for God's sustaining of all human life is effected by the speech's linguistic questions, declaratives, injunctions, and imperatives. Multivalence is a feature of the speech's rhetoric that lends itself to a particular theology of universal divine care.

Gary Gilbert describes the literary and political relation of Luke-Acts to the Roman world in "Luke-Acts and Negotiation of Authority and Identity in the Roman World." Gilbert acknowledges the multivalence in the New Testament concerning political relations and shows that specific narrative tropes and theology constructions of Luke-Acts are decisively shaped by the political relation of dominant to subordinate group. Subtle strategies of resistance characterize this relation that can be read in Luke-Acts only when the historical layer is carefully compared with political features of the Roman Empire and the Second Sophistic.

John Barton focuses his contribution, "The Fall and Human Depravity," on Martin Luther's interpretation of Isa 64:5–12. Luther argues in his refutation to Latomus (1521) that this biblical passage, particularly verse 7 ("all our deeds are like a filthy cloth"), is to be interpreted to mean the depravity of human nature. Barton reconstructs Luther's interpretative method as a particular move of theological abstraction for the dual theological purpose of maximizing sin and maximizing grace. Barton also entertains an alternative reading more in line with modern exegesis in order to show that the same text can yield a different theological anthropology.

In his chapter, " 'Who Can Forgive Sins but God Alone?': Jesus, Forgiveness, and Divinity," Stephen T. Davis analyzes the meaning of forgiveness in relation to Mark 2:1–12. This story of the paralytic healed and forgiven by Jesus is paradigmatic for looking at the relation between the divine prerogative to forgive and the christological question regarding the divine nature of Jesus. Davis shows that this passage has presented, in the history of Christian interpretation, both minimalist and maximalist explanations for why Mark attributes forgiveness to Jesus. A maximalist and the traditional Christian orthodox reading attributes the divine prerogative to forgive to Jesus, which Davis argues is the most convincing reading. The argument for the philosophical meaningfulness and theological truth of the divine aspect in Jesus as the explanation for his capacity to forgive sins upholds the traditional Chalcedonian interpretation of this passage.

Kevin Mongrain focuses his chapter, "Worship in Spirit and Truth: Louis-Marie Chauvet's Sacramental Reading of John 4:21–24," on the contemporary Roman Catholic liturgist's reading of Johannine theology as a whole and John 4:21–24 in particular. Mongrain argues that Chauvet's pneumatic-liturgical interpretation of this passage preserves the multivalent dimension of its sacramental theology, while correcting some of its possible misinterpretations. According to Mongrain, Chauvet does not reduce biblical multivalence when determining theological meaning but preserves a multiplicity of meanings. One key dimension of this theological retention of multivalence is, as other authors also address in this volume, the insistence upon the historical and theological continuity of Christianity with Judaism. Mongrain looks at this relation in Chauvet's reading of the phrase "worship in spirit and truth" (John 4:24), which he sees preserving the original connection between the cult and ethics in Christianity and Judaism while pointing out a discontinuity between the two religions.

Bernd Oberdorfer analyzes the difference between Eastern and Western conceptual frameworks determining to a certain extent the readings of particular biblical passages with different Trinitarian theological results. Oberdorfer's chapter, " '...Who Proceeds from the Father"—and the Son? The

Use of the Bible in the *Filioque* Debate: A Historical and Ecumenical Case Study and Hermeneutical Reflections," thematizes the millennium-old question regarding the place of the Spirit in the inner-Trinitarian relations, an issue that continues to divide the two main churches of Christianity. Oberdorfer argues that the difference in articulating the inner-Trinitarian relations stems from different views of how the literal level of the biblical text reveals those relations. The future direction of ecumenical dialogue between East and West can be reoriented by retrieving a broader biblical text basis that reveals the inner-Trinitarian relations to be more complex and reciprocal than the one-way relations of origin.

In my own concluding chapter, "Recovering the Real: A Case Study of Schleiermacher's Theology," I address the issue of multivalence by reconstructing a theory about reality based on the New Testament texts. I use Schleiermacher as a resource to understand how the New Testament is related to the reality of multiple authors and how the many experiences of Jesus recorded in the New Testament categorize their subject matter in terms of the theological correlation between the person of Jesus and his work. The reality of authors and their subject matter also informs the way in which theological concepts are formed. Multivalence is necessary for theological conceptualization because it anchors the theological process of concept formation in reality.

Each chapter demonstrates that the relation between biblical multivalence and theological meanings is complex. In investigating this complex relation, biblical theology can reflect on the complexity of the reality of human religion that moves between openness and constraint, conflict and harmony.

For the Love of Christ: Generic and Unique Elements in Christian Theological Readings of the Song of Songs

David Carr

The Song of Songs (hereafter "the Song") is an excellent example of a text with a plurality of meanings that has served as a theological touchstone for both Christian and Jewish readers.[1] The quote attributed to Rabbi Akiba about the Song of Songs being "the holy of holies amidst the writings" (*m. Yad.* 3:5) is well known, and it well characterizes how many Jewish interpreters understood the Song to be a wellspring of language of praise of the God revealed as Israel's savior in the Torah. Though early Jewish interpreters tended to mine the Song for fragments related to broader discourses, later Jewish interpretations focused more on the Song of Songs as a depiction of the relationship between God and God's people, aspects of the godhead, between passive and active intellects, or the passion of the soul for God.

From an early point Christian interpreters developed overarching interpretations of the Song as a reflection of one or more layers of love relationships. Starting in the third century with literary homilies by Hippolytus and Origen and reaching white-hot intensity with an explosion of commentaries in the thirteenth century, many Christians have understood the Song to be a depiction of various divine–human loves. Generally, such interpreters have taken the Song to be first and foremost a depiction of the history of the love between Christ and the church, but they have often focused as much or more on other (related) love relationships, such as the love of the soul for Christ or the love of Mary (as an image of the church) and Christ. As will be suggested below, these Christian interpretations certainly build on the tradi-

---

1. Portions of this essay were presented at the History of Interpretation Section of the 2001 Society of Biblical Literature Meeting and as the 2005 Joseph Jackson Memorial Lecture at Garrett Evangelical Theological Seminary. Thanks go to the hosts and participants of both loci for their help in improving this work.

tion of creativity of Jewish exegesis, and they may have been shaped partly in response to early rabbinic exegesis. Nevertheless, Christian interpretations of the Song have more distinctiveness and originality vis-à-vis Jewish interpretations than is typically acknowledged. These interpretations represent a unique unfolding of the Song on multiple levels, using the Song to construct the believing community (and believers in it) as *lovers* of Christ.

The plurality so typical of both Jewish and Christian interpretation of the Song of Songs contrasts with the focus of much historical scholarship on specifying and narrowing the Song's meaning. Most scholars working on the Song with a historical-critical methodology have attempted to link the Song with a particular context and frame of reference, while (often) undermining older theological approaches to the Song.[2] A particularly apt example of this historical rejection of both multivalence and theological reinterpretation of the Song (often imprecisely designated as "allegory") comes from the author of one of the most extensive recent commentaries on the Song, Marvin Pope:

> The flexibility and adaptability of the allegorical method, the ingenuity and imagination with which it could be, and was, applied, the difficulty and virtual impossibility of imposing objective controls, the astounding and bewildering results of almost two millennia of application to the Canticle [the Song], have all contributed to its progressive discredit and almost complete desertion.[3]

This comment by Pope is illustrative of a much wider attitude shared by historical critics who have approached the Song. Further, recent feminist and womanist interpretations of the Song often have intensified this critique of theological use of the Song. For example, after a brief summary of theological approaches to the Song, Renita Weems asserts in contrast: "Today more and more interpreters are willing to read the [Song] as a collection or anthology of love lyrics that capture the joys and sufferings of intimate relationships and of sensual love. The book chronicles one woman's journey to find fulfilling

---

2. The term *theological* is meant to designate approaches that see God as a character in the Song. Various other terms could be used, such as *allegorical, nonliteral, spiritual,* and the like, but each has its liabilities. One could argue, of course, that this use of the term theological is inadequate because it ignores the potential theological character of readings focusing on love between humans. For the purposes of this essay, I would assert that no terminology is perfect, that approaches focused on human-human relationships can be theological, and that my use of the term theological to focus on past interpretations featuring God is only a provisional attempt to get away from the inaccurate use of other, yet more problematic terminology that has been used for these interpretations in the past.

3. Marvin Pope, *The Song of Songs* (AB 7C; New York: Doubleday, 1977), 90.

love with a man."[4] Weems's summary accurately characterizes much recent scholarship on the Song. Although some voices have urged reconsideration of the theological/sensual divide that has plagued both ancient and contemporary interpretation of the Song, the bulk of critical work on the Song has emphasized its human-sensual character and ignored or critiqued past theological approaches.[5]

This essay explores the uniqueness of Christian interpretation of the Song of Songs considered first in relation to parallel phenomena in other religious traditions and second in relation to elements of the text itself. The ambitious scope of the essay means that many topics must be treated cursorily. There is no space here for detailed discussion of the above-noted plurality of Christian interpretations of the Song, the complex history of Jewish interpretation of the Song, nor of the more detailed dynamics of the other religious traditions under discussion.[6] Instead, this essay is a lightly documented probe suggesting some different ways of looking at familiar questions. Rather than starting first with what distinguishes Christian theological interpretations of the Song from the text they interpret, I will start with what distinguishes Christian theological discourse about the Song from some other religious eroticizations of the divine–human relationship. This broader comparative work will highlight five characteristics of Christian discourse about the Song that can then be compared with elements of the Song of Songs itself. After I have discussed these five characteristics, I will conclude by considering how and whether the Song has elements that resonate with each of these aspects of Christian interpretation.

1. The Song of Songs in Broader Religious Context

In previous publications on the Song I have emphasized how both Jewish and Christian theological interpretations of the Song of Songs are part of a

---

4. Renita Weems, "Song of Songs," *NIB* 5:371.

5. See the resources cited in David M. Carr, *The Erotic Word: Sexuality, Spirituality and the Bible* (New York: Oxford University Press, 2003), 202–3 nn. 28–37.

6. See, e.g., excellent discussions of the history of interpretation of the Song in Friedrich Ohly, *Hohelied-Studien: Grundzüge einer Geschichte der Hoheliedauslegung des Abendlandes bis um 1200* (Wiesbaden: Steiner, 1958); E. Ann Matter, *The Voice of My Beloved: The Song of Songs in Western Medieval Christianity* (Middle Ages Series; Philadelphia: University of Pennsylvania Press, 1990); Denys Turner, *Eros and Allegory: Medieval Exegesis of the Song of Songs* (Cistercian Studies; Kalamazoo, Mich.: Cistercian Publications, 1995); Mark W. Elliott, *The Song of Songs and Christology in the Early Church 381–451* (Studien und Texte zu Antike und Christentum 7; Tübingen: Mohr Siebeck, 2000); and Richard A. Norris, *The Song of Songs: Interpreted by Early Christian and Medieval Commentators* (Grand Rapids: Eerdmans, 2003).

broader world-religious phenomenon of eroticization of the divine–human relationship. We see this in the Tibetan tantric tradition, where the individual practitioner finds enlightenment through imagining erotic union with the Green and White Tara consorts of the Bodhisatva of Compassion. We see it as well in the passionate poetry of Sufi mystics, such as the poet Rumi. We also see this eroticization of the divine–human relationship vividly illustrated in the Hindu Bhakti tradition, particularly in traditions surrounding Krishna and the cowherd girls. In a text once called the "Hindu Song of Songs" by its first Victorian translators, the Bengali poet Jayaveda drew on Sanskrit love poetry and Hindu legends about Krishna and his lover, Rhadha, to image the believer's love relationship with God.[7] In all these cases, each one outside the tradition of Judaism and Christianity, we see what I term "crossover" of erotic imagery and passions across the divine–human divide. Each of these religious traditions encourage the individual believer to imagine herself or himself in a passionate, erotic connection with the divine.[8]

So much for analogies. What I will do in the remainder of this essay is to stop focusing on how Christian interpretation of the Song is similar to other traditions. Instead, I will look at how Christian interpretation of the Song is *different*. I will be using cross-religious comparison as a tool for highlighting special aspects of Christian interpretation of the Song. In the following sections, I will start with four characteristics that are partially shared with Jewish interpretation of the Song, before moving to a fifth characteristic that appears to be unique to Christian interpretation of the Song.

---

7. For popular introductions to the above traditions, see the following: for tantra, the book by Philip Rawson, *Tantra: The Indian Cult of Ecstasy* (New York: Avon, 1973), provides a brief introduction and illuminating art (though the focus is on Indian tantra). For Sufism, see the accessible rendering of Rumi's poems in Coleman Barks, *The Essential Rumi* (San Francisco: HarperSanFrancisco, 1995), and also other Sufi mystics, e.g., W. C. Chittick and P. L. Wilson, eds. and trans., *Fakhruddin 'Iraqi: Divine Flashes* (CWS; New York: Paulist, 1982). For the Hindu Bhakti tradition, I use C. Dimmitt and J. A. B. van Buitenen, ed. and trans., *Classical Hindu Mythology: A Reader in the Sanskrit Purānas* (Philadelphia: Temple University Press, 1978), 118–27, for a brief overview of the Puranic tradition about Krishna and Radha. One rendering of the *Gita Govinda* is G. Keyt, ed. and trans., *Gita Govinda: The Loves of Krishna and Rādhā* (Bombay: Kutub-Popular, 1965). For discussion of the Upanishadic tradition, see also Krishna Sivaraman, "The Mysticism of Male-Female Relationships: Some Philosophical and Lyrical Motifs of Hinduism," in *Sexual Archetypes, East and West* (ed. B. Gupta; New York: Paragon House, 1987), 87–105. The following volume appeared too late to be consulted for this essay but may contain very pertinent material and bibliography: C. Manning and P. Zuckerman, eds., *Sex and Religion* (Belmont, Calif.: Wadsworth, 2005).

8. See David M. Carr, "Gender and the Shaping of Desire in the Song of Songs and Its Interpretation," *JBL* 119 (2000): 247 (including n. 49); idem, *Erotic Word*, 145.

2. The Textual-Interpretative Character of the Erotic Divine–Human Relationship in Christian Interpretation of the Song of Songs

The first element relates to the very fact that the Song is the subject of erotic spirituality. Both Jewish and Christian theological readings of the Song of Songs are distinguished from otherwise similar phenomena in other world-religious traditions by their particularly textually oriented character. To be sure, other traditions, such as the Hindu Bhakti tradition with its *Gita Govinda* and similar texts, have at least some textual traditions that treat the divine–human relationship as erotic. Nevertheless, such texts are a relatively minor reflection of a much broader phenomenon of artistic and mystical eroticization of the divine–human relationship. In contrast, the bulk of the erotic imagery of the Jewish and Christian traditions is oriented toward extended exegetical interpretation of the Song of Songs and a handful of other biblical texts. Thus, Jewish and Christian interpretation of the Song—seen in world-religious context—represents a peculiarly exegetical form of divine–human eroticism.

Indeed, initially Christians surpassed Jews in producing a set of early homiletical commentaries that attempt to interpret the Song of Songs according to a single theological schema, verse by verse. Hippolytus started with a series of Easter homilies that worked their way through Song 3:8. Then Origen produced a homiletical commentary that is extant through Song 2:14, and soon there were commentaries from Gregory of Nyssa, Victorinus of Pettau, Reticius of Autun, Hilarius of Poitiers, Gregory of Elvira, Philo of Karpasia, Aponius, Gregory of Nyssa, Gregory the Great, and so forth.[9]

Meanwhile, early Jewish interpreters generally ignored the older biblical metaphor of marriage between God and Israel. Moreover, their interpretations of the Song atomistically drew on the book for isolated fragments of semantic material relevant to broader arguments. For example, in the earliest rabbinic writings, the woman of the Song can be Jerusalem, a righteous group of people, Joshua son of Nun, the fathers and mothers of ancient Israel, or Israel as a whole.[10] Judaism did not develop a systematic commentary approach to the Song until the Targum of the Songs, written around the eighth century, and—as Alon Goshen-Gottstein has pointed out—early Jewish interpreters

---

9. For a useful recent summary of genres and texts, see Elliott, *Song of Songs and Christology*, 15–50.

10. David M. Carr, "The Song of Songs as a Microcosm of the Canonization and Decanonization Process," in *Canonization and Decanonization* (ed. A. van der Kooij and K. van der Toorn; Leiden: Brill, 1998), 175–76.

did not tend to emphasize the idea of divine–human passion.[11] Given the lack of sustained early Jewish interpretation of the Song or well-documented early Jewish interpretations of the Song as focusing on divine–human passion, it appears less probable than it once did that Hippolytus and Origen borrowed their broader approach to the Song from Jewish contemporaries. Although Hippolytus (and occasionally Origen) may have been influenced on individual points by the readings of Jewish contemporaries, it appears that Jewish tradition followed Christianity and did not precede it in the project of providing systematic commentary across the Song.[12]

Thus, although both Jews and Christians approached the Song of Songs as text, it appears to have been Christians who were the most systematic in interpreting the Song as an extended story of God's love relationship with God's people. Jewish interpreters pursued this approach too, both in fragmentary ways around the time of Origen (perhaps in dialogue with him) and more later on, but it was Christians such as Hippolytus and Origen who offered the earliest attempts to master major sections of the Song with their approaches, with some later interpreters producing commentaries on the entire Song.

3. The Sustained Multilayered Quality of Christian Interpretation of the Song

The next distinctive aspect of Christian use of the Song of Songs is related to the first: the way Christian commentators often articulate *multiple* forms of divine–human eroticization through pursuing more than one interpretation of the Song in a sustained way across verses and even chapters.

---

11. See Alon Goshen-Gottstein, "Thinking of/with Scripture: Struggling for the Religious Significance of the Song of Songs," *JSR* 3 (2003): n.p. [cited 2 July 2006]. Online: http://etext.lib.virginia.edu/journals/ssr/issues/volume3/number2/ssr03-02-e03.html.

12. For some plausible examples of Hippolytus's response to Jewish readings, see Gertrud Chappuzeau, "Die Auslegung des Hohenliedes durch Hippolyt von Rom," *JAC* 19 (1976): 49–50. Chappuzeau's reflections, however, do not appear to take account of dating problems in working with rabbinic traditions contained in later collections. For arguments that Jewish scholars may have been responding to Origen, rather than vice versa, see especially R. Kimmelman, "Rabbi Yohanan and Origen on the Song of Songs: A Third-Century Jewish-Christian Disputation," *HTR* 73 (1980): 567–95. His approach balances the model advocated in earlier studies by Baer and Urbach (and assumed in Chappuzeau): Y. Baer, "Israel, the Christian Church, and the Roman Empire, from the Time of Septimus Severus to the Edict of Toleration of A.D. 313," in *Studies in History* (ed. A. Fuks and I. Halpern; ScrHier 7; Jerusalem: Magnes, 1961), 99–106; E. E. Urbach, "The Homiletical Interpretations of the Sages and the Expositions of Origen on Canticles, and the Jewish-Christian Disputation," in *Studies in Aggadah and Folk-Literature* (ed. J. Heinemann and D. Noy; ScrHier 22; Jerusalem: Magnes, 1971), 247–75.

As in the first instance, there is some similarity here to Jewish tradition, which has its own tradition of pluriformity of interpretation. For example, as mentioned above, the earliest datable Jewish interpretations of the Song of Songs in the Mishnah, Tosefta, and two Talmudim interpret the woman of the Song of Songs in a variety of ways: as Moses, as a house of judgment or study, as Diaspora communities, and so forth. These varied Jewish interpretations, however, are generally atomistic links of individual verses to broader arguments, and they are not carried on in a sustained way across multiple verses. Rather, in these earliest datable Jewish traditions (up through the Talmudim) a part of the Song is used one way in a rabbinic discussion here, and the same verse used in another way in a rabbinic discussion somewhere else. The plurality of approaches to the same verse in rabbinic tradition may have provided a precedent for pluriform Christian approaches. Nevertheless, such plurality is episodic and nonsystematic.

Yet already with Origen's homily series one sees Christian interpretation of the Song of Songs on multiple levels. Although he does not treat each level in every case, he begins with and presupposes a framework where the text has a literal level (the drama of Solomon's marriage), an allegorical level (the relation between Christ and the church), and a spiritual level (the relation between the soul and Christ). This method seen in Origen then sets the stage for multilayered interpretation elsewhere. Sometimes both layers are not in the same interpretation, but there is a consciousness in the commentator, say Gregory of Nyssa, that his interpretation of the Song on an individual level presupposes the broader interpretation of the Song on a collective level. Sometimes, as in the famous twelfth-century commentary by Honorarius Augustus, one sees a Christian commentator systematically combine and coordinate multiple levels.[13] In any case, from Origen onward, one can observe a Christian propensity to hold multiple levels in sustained tension in interpretation of the Song.

4. THE GOD-LOVER AS COLLECTIVE IN CHRISTIAN INTERPRETATION OF THE SONG

A third unique element in Christian use of the Song is the way Christianity builds on Jewish precedents in imaging the people *as a whole* as God's erotic partner. Other religious traditions tend to focus more on the individual believer's erotic relationship with God: the tantric practitioner imaging union with the Tara, the Sufi mystic passionate about God, the Hindu devo-

---

13. For an excellent discussion, see Matter, *Voice of My Beloved*, 58–76.

tee of Krishna. Moreover, as Alon Goshen-Gottstein and Michael Satlow in different contexts have noted, early Judaism does not appear to have focused on divine–human marriage or even divine–human "love."[14] Such imagery does emerge in Judaism, particularly in later traditions. Nevertheless, it is not prominent in Jewish texts up through the first few centuries of the Common Era.

To be sure, we do see such imagery in the Hebrew Bible. Already in prophets such as Hosea, Jeremiah, and Ezekiel the people of ancient Israel imagined the people or the city as God's wife, unfaithful in the present or past but (sometimes) reclaimed by God in the future (e.g., Hos 2:2–20 [Eng. 2:4–22]; Jer 3:1–10, 18–22; Ezek 16; 23; see also Isa 5:1–7; 54:4–8; 62:4–5). Still other biblical traditions, particularly in the Deuteronomistic vein, called on the believer to have a wifelike exclusive devotion to God, while God is described with a husbandlike "jealousy" about his people.[15]

In the past, many have presupposed that such biblical texts were the beginning of a continuous Jewish tradition of imagining God and Israel in a marriage relationship. Yet as noted above, Satlow and Goshen-Gottstein point out that early Judaism does not appear to have continued this tradition. Furthermore, their insight can be extended to later biblical traditions. For example, although marriage imagery is explicit in prophets such as Hosea and Jeremiah, the idea of divine–human marriage is merely implicit in Deuteronomic and later pentateuchal traditions. Furthermore, the Song either ignores or reverses such divine–human marriage imagery. For example, the man's descriptions of his female love in the Song often resemble biblical descriptions of the promised land, and she, like the land, is associated with "milk and honey" (Song 4:11). Yet, unlike clearly mystical poetry, such as the Hindu *Gita Govinda*, there is no indicator here that this is a divine–human relationship, even at the latest levels of the editing of the Song.[16] Instead, the male character of the Song uses such epithets for the land to describe the woman he desires. Rather than divine–human "allegory," we may have what might be termed "reverse allegory"—the application to humans of divine–human motifs seen elsewhere.[17]

---

14. See Michael Satlow, *Jewish Marriage in Antiquity* (Princeton: Princeton University Press, 2001), 42–50; Goshen-Gottstein, "Thinking of/with Scripture."

15. I survey this material in David M. Carr, "Passion for God: A Center in Biblical Theology," *HBT* 23 (2001): 5–12.

16. Carr, "Gender and Desire," 246–47.

17. For my earlier treatment, see Carr, *Erotic Word*, 134–36, where I assume a late dating of the Song. At present I am not as sure as I once was that the linguistic basis of this dating is secure, but consideration of this issue must be postponed for another context and time.

All this then highlights the importance of early Christian interpretations such as that of Hippolytus's Easter homilies and Origen's homiletical series on the first chapters of the Song. Hippolytus focused on God's successive relationships with Israel and then the church, while Origen added a focus on the soul and Christ to the allegorical focus on Christ and the church. Such Christian interpretations of the Song built implicitly on a Christian revival of divine–human marriage imagery already seen in Paul, the Apocalypse of John, and other early Christian traditions (1 Cor 11:2–3; Eph 5:23–24, 31–32; Rev 9:7–8, 21; see also Mark 2:19–20//Matt 9:15//Luke 5:34–35; Matt 25:1–13). But they now fleshed out that imagery by way of interpreting the early chapters of the Song of Songs as an encoded account of God's relationship with God's beloved people.

Another characteristic of these early interpretations typifies much later Christian interpretation as well: an anxiety about God's earlier lover. We see this already in Hippolytus's commentary, where Christ's collective lover in the first part of the Song of Songs is first the synagogue, before Christ moves on to the church.[18] This theme of God's erotic bond with the church implying a rejection of God's bond with Israel leads to the next element that characterizes Christian theological use of the Song.

5. Eroticism and Anti-Judaism in Christian Interpretation of the Song

Christian interpretation of the Song of Songs is distinguished from other religious traditions in a fourth way: the extent to which Christian imaging of this God–people erotic relationship involves exclusion of other peoples, particularly Judaism. Other world-religious traditions—Tantrism, Sufism, and the Bhakti tradition of Hinduism—do not feature the same kind of focus on the exclusivity of the divine–human relationship. Perhaps partly because these other traditions focus on individuals, it is presupposed that God might have many lovers. The closest parallel to Christian exclusivism in Song of Songs interpretation is a handful of Jewish traditions about God's exclusive love for Israel, some apparently formed, as we will see, in dialogue with anxious Christian assertions that God now loves the church and has rejected Israel.

As in the case of imaging the people as God's collective lover, the Hebrew Bible provides a precedent for the idea of an exclusive love binding God to God's people. The same traditions that feature a prominent focus on the divine–human marriage—such as Hosea, Jeremiah, Ezekiel, and (implicitly)

---

18. Chappuzeau, "Hippolyt von Rom," 65–67, 78–79.

Deuteronomy—are also the biblical traditions that feature the most prominent calls for the destruction of certain foreign peoples or firm separation
from them and rejection of their ways. Where some other world-religious
traditions imagined multiple believers involved in erotic relationships with
God, these biblical traditions understood Israel to be in an exclusive, binding
marriage relationship with God. And the very biblical texts that emphasized
this theme the most are the very texts that speak most of God's angry jealousy. One text even says that "jealousy" is God's name (Exod 34:14). So on
the explicit level Israel is to love God alone in the same way a wife is to be
faithful to her husband, yet on an implicit level there is the fear of God's relations to other peoples. Other peoples are both potential tempters of Israel
away from faithfulness to God and potential rivals for God's attention. The
same Israel who is depicted in these texts as married to God is also forbidden
to intermarry with foreign peoples. Sexual contact with such foreign peoples is depicted in texts such as the Baal Peor narrative as "infidelity" to God
(Num 25:1–9).

In another context I have argued that these texts illustrate some potential consequences of imaging the divine–human relationship in terms of
erotic partnership. Although groups already tend to reinforce group cohe-
sion through depicting a common enemy, the use of erotic imagery to depict
the relationship of one's group to God adds the dynamic of "jealousy" to this
process. Now the excluded "other" is also a potential rival for that God's attention, and assimilation of one's own group to other groups can be construed
as female "infidelity." It is debated the extent to which such "jealousy" is a
biological or sociological dimension of the human experience of erotic love.
Nevertheless, "jealousy" appears to have been a very real dynamic surrounding marriage in both the Bible and cultures that interpreted it. To be married
to God thus meant being involved with a potentially jealous divine lover.[19]

All this had consequences for the Christian adaptation of the biblical idea of God's marriage to God's people. As suggested above, the biblical
texts featuring this idea—implicitly or explicitly—often express anxiety about
potential rivals for God's love by including calls for separation from and even
destruction of those foreign peoples closest to Israel (both culturally and geographically). Yet this anxiety attending the divine–human marriage metaphor
gained a new dimension when Christianity gradually separated and distinguished itself from Judaism in the early centuries of the Common Era. As is
suggested in Hippolytus's early homilies on the Song, the church now is not
God's first but God's second wife. God has already had another lover, ancient

---

19. Carr, *Erotic Word*, 80–82.

Israel. The church now shares the concerns of many human second spouses. How does the church know that God is really "over" his first spouse? How can those in the church know that the Song is about them and not about God's first love?

These dynamics surface in early Jewish-Christian disputation. One of Origen's homilies interprets Song 1:5–6 to be an address by the church to the Jewish "daughters of Jerusalem." The Hebrew of the verse can be rendered as follows:

> I am black but beautiful,
>> Daughters of Jerusalem,
> Like the tents of Kedar's nomads,
>> Like the tapestries of Solomon.
> Do not stare at my blackness,
>> That the sun has gazed upon me.
> My mother's sons quarreled with me.
>> They set to keep the vineyards.
> But my vineyard I have not kept.[20]

Quoting from Luke 11:31–32 (//Matt 12:42) and working from presuppositions that would be judged by many as racist today, Origen understood the dark woman here to be an Ethiopian "Queen of the South," the church, blackened by sin but loved by God. According to Origen, this black Ethiopian church is addressing herself in Song 1:6 to the "daughters of Jerusalem," the people of Israel. God loves her, not them, she asserts.[21]

Similar details (and presuppositions) appear in a potentially contemporary interpretation attributed to Rabbi Isaac in the late collection *Song of Songs Rabbah*. Rabbi Isaac tells a parable that interprets the verse in an opposing way. The parable concerns an "Ethiopian" maidservant who boasts that her master soon will divorce his wife and marry her. Her companion asks why her master would do such a thing. The maidservant replies that he is going to divorce his wife because he has seen that she has stained her hands. Her companion ridicules the black maidservant, saying, "Listen to what you are saying. Here is his wife whom he loves exceedingly, and you say he is going to divorce her because once he saw her hands stained. How then will he endure

---

20. For discussion of important translation issues here, see Carr, *Erotic Word*, 195–96 (nn. 16 and 17).

21. The relevant passage (from the first homily) is translated in Origen, *The Song of Songs: Commentary and Homilies* (trans. R. P. Lawson; Westminster, Md.: Newman, 1957), 277–78.

you who are stained all over and black from the day of your birth!"[22] What is interesting about this instance is that Rabbi Isaac's interpretation seems focused on proving that the female speaker of Song 1:6 (an "Ethiopian" as in Origen's interpretation) is *not* God's beloved. This is not something typically done by ancient interpreters of the Song, who tended to read themselves into its love story. This probably is an indicator that Rabbi Isaac was responding to and refuting Origen's interpretation rather than the other way around. Where Origen claims that God loves the church despite her blackness, Rabbi Isaac says that the church's claims for God's love are no more plausible than those of the black maid who claimed precedence over the master's wife.[23]

These dynamics of religious exclusivism in Christianity are vividly illustrated by an illustration from a twelfth-century Song of Songs manuscript now in Dijon (fig. 1). In this illustration we see Christ embracing the crowned church with his right hand while he pushes away the synagogue (still crowned!) with his left. Notably, M. Thérel has argued persuasively that this illustration is modeled on another illustration in the same codex, this one from the book of Esther, where Ahasuerus is embracing Esther with his right hand and pushing Vashti away with his left.[24] Throughout varied sources, from Hippolytus's homiletical series to a manuscript illustration such as this one, the Christian God is depicted as involved in a form of serial monogamy, giving up one wife for the other. As argued above, this has added a new tone of anxiety (of the second spouse) to the "jealousy" dynamic already potentially present in such divine–human marriage imagery. As a result, some Christian interpretation of the Song has added intensified religious exclusivism, expressed now as anti-Judaism, to the eroticization of the divine–human relationship seen in other religious traditions.

6. Christian Dynamics Surrounding the Body and Gender in Love of Christ

The fifth unique element in Christianity to be discussed here is a set of complications produced by the fact that Jesus Christ, an embodied human, is seen as the divine love object of the Song. Within ancient systems of gender, at least as present in the Mediterranean world, there was often a juxtaposition

---

22. Translation is from I. Epstein, *Midrash Rabbah: Song of Songs* (London: Soncino, 1939), 58.

23. Note that the case for Jewish influence on Christian interpretation is stronger in Hippolytus's reading of this verse. For discussion, see Chappuzeau, "Hippolyt von Rom," 50.

24. Marie Louise Thérel, "L'origine du thème de la 'Synagogue répudiée,'" *Scriptorium* 25 (1971): 285–90.

Figure 1. Collection Bibliothèque municipale de Dijon, Ms. 14 f. 60,
photographer F. Perrodin.

between maleness and physicality. Whereas "women" were identified more with their bodies, "men" in part were defined by the way they were less subject to their bodies and were more dominated by their minds. According to standard anatomical texts, men and women's bodies were more similar than they were different. What distinguished men and women were more transient characteristics of mind and heart that put individuals at either male or female levels of a broader cosmic hierarchy. At the top was God, who was both nonsexual and yet male in his ultimate nonsexuality. Women were far lower and identified with the body.[25]

25. The primary work up to this point has been in classics and medieval studies, e.g., Thomas Laqueur, *Making Sex: Body and Sex from the Greeks to Freud* (Cambridge: Harvard University Press, 1990); and Joan Cadden, *Meanings of Sex Difference in the Middle Ages: Medicine, Science and Culture* (Cambridge: Cambridge University Press, 1993). Some work, however, has been done in studies of the ancient Near East, such as Julia M. Asher-Greve, "The Essential Body: Mesopotamian Conceptions of the Gendered Body," in *Gender and the Body in the Ancient Mediterranean* (ed. M. Wyke; Oxford: Blackwell, 1988), 8–37; Tikva Frymer-Kensky, *In the Wake of the Goddesses: Women, Culture, and the Biblical Transformation of Pagan Myth* (New York: Free Press, 1992), 118–43 (esp. 140–43) and 262 n. 133; Athalya Brenner, "The

Figure 2. The Disrobing of Christ, David Dancing before the Ark,
Sponsa of the Song of Songs and Achior; "Weigel-Felix" *Biblia Pauperum*;
The Pierpont Morgan Library, New York. MS M. 230 f. 16.

This produced mixed images in Christian interpretation of the Song. The dominant interpretations read the "man" of the Song as Christ in the Song, usually imparting to him associations of rule and dominance that were associated with male gender in that world. Nevertheless, as Susan Smith has shown in a brilliant study, a series of images in exemplars of the *Biblia Pauperum* show that the woman of the Song could also typologically anticipate Christ,

Intercourse of Knowledge: On Gendering Desire and Sexuality in the Hebrew Bible," *BibInt* 5 (1997): 131–51; Dorothea Erbele, "Gender Trouble in the Old Testament: Three Models of the Relation Between Sex and Gender," *SJOT* 13 (1999): 131–41; and Nicole Ruane, "'Male without Blemish': Sacrifice and Gender Ideologies in Priestly Ritual Law" (Ph.D. diss. being revised into a monograph, Union Theological Seminary, 2005).

but only in so far as her stripping and beating (Song 5:7) anticipated the quite physical stripping and beating of the incarnate Christ. In this case her womanly physical gender made the woman of the Song better suited to anticipate Christ than the male. This is illustrated in figure 2, an illustration from the mid-fifteenth century: "Weigel-Felix" *Biblia Pauperum*. The image of Christ being stripped is the focal point, standing in the upper center. Among the various images from the Old Testament taken to anticipate this scene stands an image on the lower right of the "sponsa"/soul of the Song, stripped and being beaten as in Song 5:7.[26]

In this context I should also at least briefly mention gender-bending interpretations of the Song where Christ is imagined with milk-filled breasts to feed the church and/or the individual believer. This was based in part on the Septuagint rendering of the "lovemaking" of the Hebrew (דוד) as "breasts," but it traded on the bodily ambiguity of the ancient world. If men's and women's bodies were more similar than different, it was not so difficult to imagine a male Christ able to nurture Christ's church through his life-giving breasts.

The particular dynamics surrounding Christian interpretation of gender in the Song can be illustrated with one more set of images from the medieval church. These are from what is termed the "John group." Most just show Jesus embracing John, the beloved disciple, but some, such as the image included here (fig. 3 on p. 26), show him leaving his weeping fiancée in order to be embraced by Jesus. Here a male, John, is depicted in an embrace similar to what we saw earlier with the church.[27] This resembles the second-spouse dynamic discussed above, where someone leaves one lover to embrace another.

This image from the John group, combined with the manuscript from Dijon, illustrate some interesting patterns in depiction of successive erotic relationships. Although separated in space and time, they illustrate ancient gender dynamics that often are only visible to us in texts. In both images the gender of the divine partner, Christ, remains constant: male. The gender of the rejected spouse, whether John's wife (Admont) or the synagogue (Dijon),

---

26. Susan L. Smith, "The Bride Stripped Bare: A Rare Type of the Disrobing of Christ," *Gesta* 34 (1995): 126–46.

27. For survey of the John-group images, see Hans Wentzell, "Christus-Johannes-Gruppe," in *Realexikon der Deutschen Kunstgeschichte* (ed. O. Schmitt et al.; 11 vols.; Stuttgart: Metzler, 1937–2004), 3:658–59; Hans Wentzell, *Die Christus-Johannes Gruppen des 14. Jahrhunderts* (2nd ed.; Stuttgart: Reclam, 1960); and, for discussion and linkage to a possible lost beginning to the Acts of John, David Cartlidge, "An Illustration in the Admont 'Anselm' and Its Relevance to a Reconstruction of the Acts of John," *Semeia* 80 (1997): 277–80.

Figure 3. Anselm, *Prayers and Meditations*, Stiftsbibliothek,
ms. lat. 289, fol. 56r, Benedikterstift Admont. Photo courtesy
of David Cartlidge, permission of the Stiftsbibliothek.

remains constant: female. But the gender of the Christ-lover is different: male
in the case of the beloved disciple (Admont) and female in the case of the
church/sponsa (Dijon). In both cases these Christ-lovers stand in between
the rejected (female) spouse and (male) God on the gender continuum. The
point is that through their love of Christ, they move upward toward divinity/
maleness and away from the female/body.

In sum, Christian interpretation of the Song struggles with the ambigui-
ties attendant on having an *embodied* Christ-God as the divine part of the
divine–human erotic relationship. Some interpretations seem to ignore this,
picturing Christ as a male at the top of a gender hierarchy with some sort of
rejected, embodied "woman" at the bottom (as rejected spouse). The believing community (or believer) may be depicted as either male or female on
the way from one to the other, although—given ancient gender understandings—they generally would be understood as having female status vis-à-vis
the ultimate man, God. Christian interpretation of the Song of Songs thus
could build on this male-female dichotomy, generally depicting the male of

the Song as Christ-God while the woman was the communal or individual human lover.

7. SUMMARY AND COMPARISON OF CHRISTIAN INTERPRETATION WITH THE SONG ITSELF

This comparative approach, although done in broad strokes, helps highlight the particular kind of meaning-making involved in Christian interpretation of the Song. Despite my construction of a category "eroticization of the divine–human relationship," there are few religious universals here. Instead, this category has helped highlight the particular ways in which interpretation of the Song has been part of a process of textually articulating an erotic, believing, female "subject" in Judaism and, especially, Christianity. This textually articulated/constructed subject often is collective: building on biblical precedents of the marriage of Israel or Jerusalem to God. Moreover, I have argued that this construction of the community as God's lover has involved both a sense of God's jealousy toward the community having relationships with other peoples and an implicit sense of hostility toward other potential lovers of God. Within Christianity, the latter tendency is manifest in both textual and iconographic interpretations of the Song as a depiction of Christ's love of the church, *not* the synagogue. Thus, this process of interpretative meaning-making interacts with concrete processes of social definition, in this case defining the beloved community vis-à-vis a community who is depicted as once beloved and now rejected.

Finally, several Christian interpretations have illustrated dynamics surrounding the female gender of the collective beloved. On the one hand, the physicality implicit (for these readers) in her femaleness—especially when coupled with being stripped and beaten as in Song 5:7—allows the female figure of the Song (understood as the soul in the *Biblia Pauperum*) to serve as an anticipation of the stripped and beaten, embodied Christ. On the other hand, in other contexts the same physicality distinguishes this female-collective lover from Christ, her divine-male lover. Her love draws her to him, even as other female lovers (whether synagogue or John's betrothed) experience rejection.

By this point it may appear that we have traveled a long way from the Song itself, whatever that expression—"the Song itself"—might mean. Given the above sketch of the distinctive aspects of Christian subject-creation by way of the Song, comments such as those by Marvin Pope above gain added cogency: "The flexibility and adaptability of the allegorical method … the astounding and bewildering results of almost two millennia of application to the Canticle [the Song], have all contributed to its progressive discredit and almost complete desertion."[28] One may ask: What does the Song in the Hebrew Bible have to do with these characteristics of Christian interpretation? Might all of this be merely an alien imposition of later dynamics on an earlier text?

Of course Christian readers were highly influenced by their contexts, and this is particularly evident in the fragments of interpretations relating to religious exclusivism and gender dynamics discussed above. Indeed, because scriptural interpretation plays such an important role in communal and individual identity formation, readers of scripture are particularly prone to read themselves and their beliefs into the text. Nevertheless, I conclude by looking at some ways in which the Song has certain sorts of semantic potential that could be actualized by such Christian readers in their various contexts, thus producing readings that often resemble each other across space and time. I discuss each of the five characteristics in turn.

8. The Textual-Interpretative Character of the Erotic Divine–Human Relationship

Certainly the textual character of the Song plays a role in the way streams of Judaism and Christianity have exegetically articulated an erotic divine–human relationship. Nevertheless, the book itself does not demand that role. In and of itself, it merely represents itself as Solomon's best Song (Song 1:1) and contains poems that purport to do nothing else than typify the feelings and/or interactions of human lovers. Where divine–human love poetry such as the *Gita Govinda* explicitly identifies itself as spiritual discourse through prologue and interjections, there are no such labels in the Song. Where ancient Near Eastern love poetry often has the gods explicitly addressing each other, this does not occur in the Song. Moreover, there are a number of *realia* and other details in the Song, whether descriptions of nature or of human-made items such as the royal wedding litter (Song 3:7–10), that appear to have been originally intended to be part of descriptions related to human interactions. Of course, centuries of interpretation of the Song as divine–human exchange have shown that such elements can be related to a divine–human drama, but they have also demonstrated the ingenuity required to make such leaps.[29]

Upon further consideration, the very difficulty of such leaps—combined with the highly metaphorical character of the Song itself—may have

---

28. Pope, *Song of Songs*, 90.

29. For more discussion, see Carr, *Erotic Word*, 127, 129; for a nice contrast of the Song of Songs with clear allegories, see Tremper Longman III, *The Song of Songs* (NICOT; Grand Rapids: Eerdmans, 2001), 22–24.

contributed to its reinterpretation as divine–human love poetry in scriptural traditions such as Judaism and Christianity. Part of the magic of scriptural interpretation is taking a sometimes obscure text such as the Song and unlocking it with a certain hermeneutical perspective. The metaphorical character of the language of the Song contributed to this, since the rich metaphors and often obscure references of the Song force any interpreter to use imagination in engaging the world evoked by its poems. For example, a reader must make various leaps of interpretative reconstruction when a man in Song 4:12, 16 says "you are a locked garden, my sister, my bride, a secured heap, a sealed well…. wake up, North wind, come in South wind, breathe on my garden, let its spices flow." This became even more true as the sexual mores of Christian communities developed in sex-hostile ways. Most Christian interpreters did not question the scriptural status of the Song, but they did presume—on the basis of their beliefs about problems associated with sexual passion—that the Song could not be celebrating human erotic passion. So the already-obscure, metaphorical language of the Song became an even more intriguing "locked garden" of its own.

This doubled obscurity of the Song—for Christian readers especially—gave interpretations such as Origen's that much more power. It is one thing to take a straightforward text and simply repeat its contents. That is mundane. There is little magic to it. It is quite another to take an obscure, even potentially problematic text such as the Song and to reveal its hidden divine-human erotic power. That is what interpretations such as Origen's did. The issue here, of course, was not that Origen or Bernard of Clairvaux were afraid of and wanted to neutralize the erotic passion of the Song—a common misconception. Rather, their interpretations gained power by the very fact that they took a text that seemed to say one (potentially problematic) thing and revealed that it actually meant, on its deepest level, something quite different. There is not time to argue this point further here, but I would contend that this is a central feature of powerful scriptural interpretation in general: revealing the ultimate significance of a text to be quite different from what it appears—on the surface—to say. This was true for the "allegorical" and other approaches of Origen, and it is true even now with sophisticated historical-critical rereadings of biblical texts. The methods used to unlock and radically reinterpret the texts are different, but the imperative to produce almost magically radical rereadings of archaic (and sometimes problematic) texts remains the same within communities that revere such texts as divine writ.

Be that as it may, it appears that ancient love poetry such as the Song was unusually prone to reinterpretation on a divine–human level (or to a human level), particularly since the Song draws on a tradition of ancient Near Eastern divine–human love poetry in developing its picture of human love. Within

Bengal we see what I elsewhere have termed "crossover," where certain motifs were used by Jayaveda in the *Gita Govinda* for divine–human love and later applied by Vidyapati to human love.[30] Ancient Egyptian love poetry, with which the Song shares many characteristics, is focused on human love but often depicts lovers in semidivine ways.[31] Recently Martti Nissinen has shown ways in which the dialogue structure and other elements of the Song resemble first-millennium texts describing a sacred marriage between Mesopotamian deities.[32] And there are specific elements, such as where the Song's praise of the man's body sounds almost like the praise of a divine statue (Song 5:10–16), that may have been borrowed from ancient dramas of divine–human or divine–divine love. Such reinterpretation or reuse of divine or human love poetry was not at all unusual.

9. The Sustained Multilayered Quality of Christian Interpretation of the Song

My discussion of this second element in relation to the Song can be briefer, because it can build on the one before. On the one hand, it is again clear that the Song itself does not demand a sustained, multilevel interpretation. Several centuries of more atomistic Jewish interpretations attest to the possibility that careful interpreters of the text might choose not to pursue multiple approaches to it across large stretches. On the other hand, the dynamics in the Song (obscure, metaphorical language) and scriptural interpretation (the

---

30. W. G. Archer, *Love Songs of Vidyāpati* (London: Allen & Unwin, 1963), 23–36.

31. The original observations on divine elements in Egyptian love poetry can be found in Franz R. Schröder, "Sakrale Grundlagen der altägyptischen Lyrik," *Deutsche Vierteljahrs-schrift für Literaturwissenschaft und Geistesgeschichte* 25 (1951): 273–93; Philippe Derchain, "Le perruqe et le cristal," *Studien zur altägyptischen Kultur* 2 (1975): 55–74; idem, "Le Lotus, la mandragore et le perséa," *ChrÉg* 50 (1975): 65–86; and idem, "Symbols and Metaphors in Literature and Representations of Private Life," *Royal Anthropological Institute News* 15 (1976): 7–10. See the discussion in Michael V. Fox, *The Song of Songs and Ancient Egyptian Love Songs* (Madison: University of Wisconsin Press, 1985), 235–36; and Carr, *Erotic Word*, 104, along with (for discussion of the problematic distinction of divine and human levels) Lynn Meskell, *Private Life in New Kingdom Egypt* (Princeton: Princeton University Press, 2002), esp. 114–15 and 143.

32. Martti Nissinen, "Love Lyrics of Nabû and Tašmetu: An Assyrian Song of Songs?" in *"Und Mose schrieb dieses Lied Auf": Studien zum Alten Testament und zum Alten Orient* (ed. M. Dietrich and I. Kottsieper; Münster: Ugarit-Verlag, 1998), 585–634; idem, "Akkadian Rituals and Poetry of Divine Love," in *Mythology and Mythologies: Melamu Symposia II* (ed. R. M. Whiting; Helsinki: Neo-Assyrian Text-Corpus Project, 2001), 95–125; and idem, "The Song of Songs as Ancient Near Eastern Love Poetry," in *Sacred Marriages in the Biblical World* (ed. M. Nissinen and R. Uru; Winona Lake, Ind.: Eisenbrauns, forthcoming).

impulse toward revealing hidden meanings in obscure texts [or texts made to be obscure]) discussed above probably also encouraged some Christians to find multiple deeper meanings across larger stretches of the Song. Notably, these meanings often were connected to each other. As mentioned, Origen's interpretation of the Song as depicting love of the soul for God was presented as part of his broader interpretation of the Song as about love of the church for God. At the same time, the pursuit of multiple approaches across large stretches of the Song allowed interpreters such as Origen to harvest even more profoundly the semantic potential of the Song, showing in a tour de force how its obscure elements could be unlocked in not one but multiple directions, and not once but many times. In this way, Christian interpretations such as Origen's (or Honorarius or others) that pursued multiple approaches across many verses were an intensification of the above-discussed scriptural impulse toward unlocking obscure texts.

10. The God-Lover as Collective in Christian Interpretation of the Song

I have already argued that the Song of Songs, in and of itself, does not appear to have originally been a song of love between YHWH and YHWH's people. The Song lacks explicit indicators of such a divine–human dimension that are seen in texts such as the *Gita Govinda*, nor do we see divine direct-addresses such as are found in Mesopotamian divine love poetry. Instead, it appears that much material in the Song relates instead to very human dramas of love of the sort seen in Egyptian love poetry.

Nevertheless, when read as part of the broader Hebrew scriptural corpus, the love language and other elements of the Song of Songs gain new resonances. As mentioned above, the former prophets provide a precedent for seeing YHWH in a love relationship with his people, one that then can be taken as a key for understanding the Song. Further, certain details of the Song, such as its mention of "honey and milk" in Song 4:11, resonate with Deuteronomic descriptions of the land of Israel as a land "of milk and honey" (e.g., Deut 6:3; 11:9; 26:15; 31:20). Such resonances between the Song and its scriptural context are so strong that sensitive contemporary interpreters such as Cohen and Davis have been able to mount a strong argument for reading the Song as originally about the love between God and Israel.[33] Although I and many

---

33. Gershon Cohen, "The Song of Songs and the Jewish Religious Mentality," in *The Samuel Friedland Lectures, 1960–1966* (ed. L. Finkelstein; New York: Jewish Theological Seminary, 1966), 16 (noting that such interpretation followed very soon after compilation); Ellen F. Davis, "Romance of the Land in the Song of Songs," *AThR* 80 (1998): 533–46; idem, *Proverbs,*

others do not find such arguments ultimately persuasive regarding the original function of the Song, these treatments do point to the powerful impact
of reading the Song within the broader context of the Tanak/Old Testament.
Furthermore, these dynamics become even stronger when the Song is read as
part of a Christian scriptural corpus, which includes depictions of marriage
between Christ and the church in Paul, the deutero-Pauline materials, and
the Apocalypse of John.[34]

11. Eroticism and Anti-Judaism in
Christian Interpretation of the Song

The Song of Songs itself gives absolutely no basis for anti-Judaism or other
forms of religious hostility unless it is read in the ways specified above: as a
hidden depiction of love between God and God's people. Once it was read
by Christians as a song of love between Christ and the church, however, it
is not surprising that some streams of Christian interpretation expressed
and even enhanced an anti-Judaism found elsewhere in Christianity as well.
In my discussion of this element above, I alluded to the way the depiction
of love between God and a whole people appeared associated with hostility
toward other peoples, particularly peoples (e.g., Judaism) that could be taken
as having a prior claim on that God's love. We also saw one way in which this
was actualized: Origen's reinterpretation of Song 1:5–6 as the church's proclamation to Judaism of God's superior love for the church. Of course, there are
elements of the Song that would seem to militate against such human jealousy, elements such as the woman's assumption in Song 1:2–4 that her man
is loved by many women. Note, however, other parts of the Song, such as
5:8–6:3, where the woman seems to tease others with the attractiveness of her
man (5:10–16) before claiming her absolute possession of him (6:1–3; see also
2:16). In this sense the Song—although not being a depiction of a wedding or
married love (contra Victorian interpreters)—also is not a depiction of free
love.[35] Instead, the lovers of the Song are attached specifically and particularly

---

Ecclesiastes and the Song of Songs (Louisville: Westminster John Knox, 2000), 231–302; and,
with some additional nuances, idem, "Reading the Song Iconographically," JSR 3 (2003): n.p.
[Cited 2 July 2006]. Online: http://etext.lib.virginia.edu/journals/ssr/issues/volume3/number2/
ssr03-02-e02.html.

34. A survey of this material in the context of Greco-Roman discourse about marriage
and sexuality will appear as David Carr and Colleen Conway, "The Divine-Human Marriage
Matrix and Constructions of Gender and 'Bodies' in the Christian Bible," in Sacred Marriages in
the Biblical World (ed. M. Nissinen and R. Uru; Winona Lake, Ind.: Eisenbrauns, forthcoming).

35. For response to the idea that the Song is focused on marriage, see further Carr, Erotic
Word, 118.

to each other, with human jealousy standing in the wings as the potential flip-side of the deviation of either from this pairing.

12. Christian Dynamics Surrounding the Body and Gender in Love of Christ

Christian dynamics surrounding gender and embodiedness in the Song are so complex that it is difficult to pin down potential links of these dynamics with the Song itself. Nevertheless, at least one thing can be emphasized in discussing this issue: the way gendered interpretations of the Song in Christianity are paralleled by gendered presuppositions in the Song itself. It is important to emphasize this because of the way the Song has been so celebrated within certain streams of feminism, indeed celebrated enough that one might assume that the Song is an egalitarian text lacking any gender presuppositions. On the contrary, recent work on the Song has shown how it depicts the woman and man in quite different ways.[36] The woman of the Song is more enclosed, more observed, and more vulnerable, even to the point of being beaten and stripped in 5:7. Thus it is no coincidence that she becomes one image of bodily vulnerability in depictions such as the *Biblia Pauperum* studied by Susan Smith and touched on above. The man of the Song ranges more freely and has more power than the woman through most of the Song, even if he himself feels powerless before her in his desire (e.g., Song 6:8–10). As Donald Polaski has pointed out, his body is less often depicted than hers is.[37] These characteristics in the Song's own depiction of the male facilitated Christian identification of the "man" in the Song as Christ, and indeed a Christ often standing as a symbol of masculine, nonembodied spiritual power.

---

36. For some representative and illuminating feminist analyses, see, e.g., Daphne Merkin, "The Women in the Balcony: On Rereading the Song of Songs," in *Out of the Garden: Women Writers on the Bible* (ed. C. Buchmann and C. Spiegel; New York: Fawcett Columbine, 1994), 238–51; David Clines, "Why Is There a Song of Songs and What Does It Do to You If You Read It?" in *Interested Parties: The Ideology of Writers and Readers of the Hebrew Bible* (JSOTSup 205; Sheffield: Sheffield Academic Press, 1995), 94–121; Donald C. Polaski, " 'What Will Ye See in the Shulammite?': Women, Power and Panopticism in the Song of Songs," *BibInt* 5 (1997): 64–81; Cheryl Exum, "Ten Things Every Feminist Should Know about the Song of Songs," in *The Feminist Companion to the Song of Songs* (ed. A. Brenner; FCB 1; Sheffield: Sheffield Academic Press, 2000), 24–35; and Fiona Black, *The Artifice of Love: Grotesque Bodies and the Song of Songs* (Edinburgh: T&T Clark, 2006).

37. Polaski, "What Will Ye See?"

13. Concluding Remarks

Moving back over the five characteristics of Christian interpretation of the Song discussed above, it becomes clear that the Song does not demand an interpretation in any of these ways, but the book—read in the context of the broader scriptural corpus—nevertheless has semantic potential that can be actualized in these trends in Christian interpretation. As I have suggested, some of these build on each other. For example, elements of Christian anti-Judaism do not come into play until the Song is reinterpreted as a song of love between Christ and the church. Sometimes the connections are multiple, as in the case of the variety of links between Christian discourses featuring gender and the different depictions of gender in the Song itself. Hopefully, however, this discussion, however general and approximate, has highlighted both the specificity of Christian interpretations of the Song and the way they draw in complex ways on elements of the Song itself, particularly when read as scriptural and within the broader context of the Christian scriptures. Contrary to the way they are often treated, such Christian interpretations are hardly arbitrary, nor are they mere attempts to tame the sexuality of the Song.

Rather, at their best interpretations, such as Origen's show a crucial characteristic of master scripture interpretation: taking an apparently arcane, obscure text and unlocking it for the present audience in completely unexpected ways. Whether that happens through theological exegesis or through historical criticism, this sort of *transformation* of a text lies at the core of powerful scriptural practice. It is an exercise of what John Miles Foley has aptly termed "word power."[38] By this is meant an interpreter-performer's ability to draw fluidly and persuasively on the full range of a culture's authoritative tradition, using agreed-upon hermeneutical techniques to extract new and persuasive meanings from familiar texts. Moreover, Origen and his many heirs (e.g., Gregory of Nyssa, Hadewijch of Brabant, Bernard of Clairvaux) are examples to historical critics of the possibilities that come with seeking *multiple* meanings in such texts.

To be sure, there are also dangers in the exercise of such word power. There are no guarantees of safety in biblical interpretation, any more than there are guarantees in love. In this case, we see how the interpretations of the Song as a song of love between God and God's church also involved an anti-Jewish exclusivism that is one of the most dangerous and problematic parts of the Christian heritage. Such dangers must be guarded against. Per-

---

38. John Miles Foley, *The Singer of Tales in Performance* (Bloomington: Indiana University Press, 1995), 3–28.

haps Christian interpreters who wish to retrieve some of the insights of older approaches could follow the example of other world religious traditions and focus on God–individual relationships rather than God–people relationships. Or perhaps there are other creative possibilities for reading the Song in powerful ways for contemporary communities that fall outside the typical categories of past approaches.

Be that as it may, the deeper one delves into Christian passion for the Song, the more one realizes what a magnificently big and often multifaceted enterprise is the process of scriptural interpretation. It is a project with many possibilities and many dangers. To paraphrase the refrain that echoes throughout the Song (2:7; 3:5; 8:4; see also 5:8):

> I make you swear, O Daughters of Jerusalem,
>> By the gazelles and wild does
> To not awaken or arouse the text,
>> Until you are ready.

Fixity and Potential in Isaiah

C. R. Seitz

1

In the original formulation of the conference that has given rise to these essays, a distinction was made between "literary potential" and "theological fixing." For the purposes of the present volume I accept the distinction but adjust it for heuristic purposes. In so doing a question about literary fixing must first be addressed because, from the side of biblical studies, this is where the challenge lies. How are we to understand the character of the witness before us and what kind of fixity it may be said to set forth?

I also want to approach the matter of potentiality by beginning with fixity, as this sounds like a term that might give us reason to expect something fixed or stable. Readers of Isaiah have approached texts as fixed objects of scrutiny throughout the history of interpretation. The decision of Alt, famously, to read Isa 9:1–7 as referring to Hezekiah operates with a fixed text. I suspect what a term like "literary fixity" might hope to convey is the sense that Isa 9:1–7 is a fixed text within a broader literary context.[1] Its fixity, therefore, would have to do with its rootedness within a stable literary presentation. Recent appeals to canonical shaping and intentionality operate, then, with a higher view of "literary fixity" than approaches that either (1) seek to isolate texts from their context for the purpose of discovering their original historical settings or references (as with Alt) or that (2) focus on the genetics of texts, that is, how texts came to birth and were altered, refocused, and so forth, before settling down into a fixed home in a literary context (which is only an accidental stopping point of literary development).[2]

---

1. Albrecht Alt, "Jesaja 8,23–9,6: Befreiungsnacht und Krönungstag," in *Kleine Schriften zur Geschichte des Volkes Israel* (3 vols.; Munich: Beck, 1959), 2:206–25.
2. On this, see my "Two Testaments and the Failure of One Tradition-History," in idem, *Figured Out: Typology and Providence in Christian Scripture* (Louisville: Westminster John Knox, 2001), 35–47.

I have chosen to look at those texts in the first part of Isaiah that have been classified as royal or messianic texts. These texts are found in chapters 9 and 11 and also involve the mysterious reference to the עלמה and her child Immanuel at Isa 7:14. Here is a classic problem of literary fixity in the manner I am now defining it. One procedure, followed assiduously although not exclusively in the modern period, sought to locate the texts in the history of Israel and, by probing their details, to relate them to kings of Israel, or the progeny of the prophet, and the like. Candidates for this have been Hezekiah and Josiah, for example. In the case of Immanuel, it has been argued that the text refers to the child of the prophet or Hezekiah or a limited number of other contemporaneous figures. The fact that the texts are obscure or that their details are in need of fleshing out is, ironically, the occasion for encouragement in the quest. This quest entails a decision to learn as much as one can about the history of the period and the history of the text in referring to it. The obscurity, on the one hand, is a function of historical distance. It is, on the other hand, a function of the conviction that there is sufficient historical vestige to warrant a search for a meaning that is not ours directly but was that of someone else more contemporaneous with the original composition, delivery, or editorial finalization. Here we might speak of a historical fixity to be recovered through the dark, albeit fixed, lens of the literary witness.

I have chosen these texts as well because interpreters have sensed they have some relationship to one another; the notion of "literary fixity" lies closer to hand than with other examples that might have been chosen. To the degree that they have a relationship with one another, it is difficult merely to isolate them and to focus on only one kind of referentiality. Commentators have long seen the literary shaping in what was first called the Isaiah *Denkschrift*, or memoir (consisting of chapters 6–8), and such a theory reckons with both high or low forms of literary editing and what has come to be called, in its most recent phase, *intertextuality*. Intertextuality of an intentional sort assumes a commitment to something like literary fixity for the historical references of the text. These references, which once existed in pristine form, have come to line up within a literary context at a remove from original historical fixity and relationship.

Finally, I have chosen these texts because they are familiar to readers. Because this familiarity is the function of another context of interpretation and another level of literary fixing (enclosing the New Testament's hearing of the prophet Isaiah), we also can see how literary fixity of different kinds will produce different readings of individual texts. These readings do not necessarily have much to do with prior commitments to a high degree of historicity for such texts. Moreover, two of the more thorough and creative efforts to deal with Isaiah in its final form are represented by Brevard S. Childs and

Marvin A. Sweeney, Christian and Jewish interpreters respectively, whose post–Old Testament context of literary fixity is different.[3] Childs has written a commending tribute to Sweeney on the back of his recent FOTL volume (*Isaiah 1–39*), so while they may reach different conclusions, it is clear they are reading kindred secondary materials and plying forms of interpretation reasonably familiar to one another.

2

Sweeney's conclusion about Immanuel can be isolated from his very detailed analysis: "Because the identity of the *'alma* is never made clear, it is impossible to identify Immanuel with any certainty."[4] Childs's conclusion sounds similar:

> One of the most significant features of this verse is the mysterious, even vague and indeterminate, tone that pervades the entire passage. The reader is simply not given information regarding the identity of the maiden.… It is therefore idle to speculate on these matters; rather, the reader can determine if there are other avenues of understanding opened up by the larger context. Specifically, what is the significance of learning how the sign of Immanuel was interpreted from within the subsequent tradition in chapter 8?[5]

Childs goes beyond Sweeney in appealing to the editorial reuse of "Immanuel" in chapter 8 to help one know how, or how not, to proceed with the interpretation of 7:14. But they are also not in agreement about the nature of the obscurity in 7:14. Childs seems to believe it is a built-in feature of the text, at least as this has been passed on to us by editors. Hence Childs appeals to their alleged work in chapter 8 as a good guide to interpretation.[6] Sweeney engages in a very painstaking evaluation of the efforts to declare a reference for Immanuel and simply admits that, while Hezekiah looks like the best candidate, chronological problems stand in the way of an identification with him.

---

3. Brevard S. Childs, *Isaiah* (OTL; Louisville: Westminster John Knox, 2001); Marvin A. Sweeney, *Isaiah 1–39: With an Introduction to Prophetic Literature* (FOTL 16; Grand Rapids: Eerdmans, 1996).

4. Sweeney, *Isaiah 1–39*, 162.

5. Childs, *Isaiah*, 66.

6. Ibid., 73: "the addition of the name Immanuel to a prophetic threat is striking evidence that the transmitters of the tradition of chapter 7 have continued to reflect on the theological significance of the mysterious child of promise. The reference in 8:4 also shows that Immanuel has remained not just a sign name, but now receives a definite profile and is addressed as the Lord of the land of Judah."

In my Isaiah commentary, I concluded that the chronological problems were a problem of their own making in the context of rival Old Testament reports and so held to a Hezekiah identification in the face of apparent, and greater, confusion on the chronological front.[7] My appeal, furthermore, was in a context of literary fixity made famous by Clements and Ackroyd and well-known to Sweeney, that is, the editorially contrasting accounts of Hezekiah and Ahaz found in chapters 6–9 and 36–39 in the final form of Isaiah.[8] Childs resists seeing anything much of importance in this literary fixity, perhaps because it is so far afield (literarily) from the serial reading of a chapter-by-chapter character, such as he is pursuing. In such a reading, proximate literary context may be more important (though even that judgment is belied by his handling of Isa 9's royal text; more below).

Was there any historical referent for the Immanuel figure? This question cannot be answered by Sweeney. It is not the right question, according to Childs. It is Hezekiah on the basis of Isa 9 and 36–39 for both Seitz and Clements. Clements, however, argues for this referent on the basis of the juxtaposition of chapter 9 with chapters 7–8 that created such a reading where once there was another: Immanuel was originally the prophet's son. I also see the linkage to Immanuel as an editorially intended matter, from 7:14 to 8:5 and 8:10, but view the link as focusing on Hezekiah, who is referred to in similar terms in 9:5 and also 2 Kgs 18:17. Herewith my appeal to a form of literary fixing:

> Whatever one may think of the Immanuel child in chapters 7–8 … one's reading of the Immanuel passages is now affected by the larger context, specifically the royal oracle in 9:2–7. Isaiah 7:14 spoke of a child to be born; 9:6 states, as if in response: "For to us a child is born." Isaiah 7:16 speaks of the Syro-Ephraimite threat coming to an end; 9:5 tells of the broken rod of the oppressor. The child would be called "God with us"; and he is named "Wonderful Counselor, Mighty God." (9:6) It is virtually impossible to read the Immanuel passages in the light of 9:2–7 and not catch the clear connections that exist as a consequence of the present organization of the material.[9]

7. Christopher R. Seitz, *Isaiah 1–39* (IBC; Louisville: Knox, 1993).

8. R. E. Clements, *Isaiah 1–39* (Grand Rapids: Eerdmans, 1980); idem, "The Immanuel Prophecy of Isaiah 7:17–17 and Its Messianic Interpretation," in *Old Testament Prophecy: From Oracles to Canon* (Louisville: Westminster John Knox, 1996), 65–77; P. R. Ackroyd, "Isaiah 36–39: Structure and Function," in *Von Kanaan bis Kerala: FS J. P. M. van der Ploeg* (ed. W. C. Delsman et al.; AOAT 211; Kevelaer: Butzon & Bercker; Neukirchen-Vluyn: Neukirchener, 1982), 3–21.

9. Seitz, *Isaiah 1–39*, 74.

Here is a place where I might view a higher degree of linkage in the "literary fixity" than does Childs, who focuses instead on the obscurity of the Immanuel reference across chapters 7 and 8 only.

When it comes to Sweeney's interpretation of the royal oracle of chapter 9, we read first, "There is no indication, however, that this psalm was written for any specific king, much less Hezekiah."[10] But the reader needs to be alert, as Sweeney is distinguishing between original composition and original application. So, in a sentence or two he follows up: "it (the royal oracle) now appears in the context of literature that was written in conjunction with the Syro-Ephraimite War and the years that followed. Consequently, the new king presupposed in the present context must be Hezekiah."[11] The royal psalm was not composed for Hezekiah but has been applied to him, as Sweeney sees it, and clearly so.

Childs rehearses the famous theory associated with Alt, whereby stock ancient Near Eastern language of hyperbolic accession has been associated with Hezekiah.

> Alt argued that the form and style revealed an authentic Isaianic succession oracle for the crowning of Hezekiah as king.... Yet at this juncture it is crucial to distinguish between the conventional language of the oracle and its biblical function within the book of Isaiah. To suggest that this oracle is simply hyperbolic, oriental language used to celebrate the accession of a new Israelite king is to historicize the biblical text and to overlook its role within the larger literary context.[12]

Childs objects to a kind of historical fixing that cannot tolerate secondary fixing within a literary form, which for him is the mature wine of preferred tasting.

Childs concludes by asserting a messianic referent as clearly presented in the fixed literary form.

> The description of his reign makes it absolutely clear that his role is messianic. There is no end to his rule upon the throne of David, and he will reign with justice and righteousness forever. Moreover, it is the ardor of the Lord of hosts who will bring this eschatological purpose to fulfillment. The language is not just of a wishful thinking for a better time, but the confession of Israel's belief in a divine ruler who will replace once and for all the unfaithful reign of kings like Ahaz.[13]

---

10. Sweeney, Isaiah 1–39, 182.
11. Ibid.
12. Childs, Isaiah, 80.
13. Ibid., 81.

What Alt sought to secure in the realm of historical fixity, Childs interprets as eschatological and an intentional outstripping of contemporaneous exemplars.

Finally, we come to the royal oracle of chapter 11. Here Sweeney manifests his commitment to what is the clearest form of literary fixing for him: the Josianic editing of chapter 11 within the stable literary form of chapters 1–12. The referent of chapter 11, unlike 7:14, is as clear as clear can be. The match between historical fixing and literary fixing is almost perfect. After stating that "a number of factors indicate the Josianic background of 11:1–12:6,"[14] Sweeney goes on to describe five of these: (1) the shoot from a stump imagery indicates "a tree that has nearly been destroyed but is still capable of rejuvenating itself," that is, commensurate with the Josianic recovery in the seventh century; (2) the small boy leading them "suggests an allusion to the boy-king Josiah, one of the youngest ruling monarchs of the Davidic dynasty"; (3) "the new king's justice and mercy" is linked to his view that "one should note that one of the major features of Josiah's reform was the establishment of a newly found book of the law as its basis"; (4) "Isaiah 11:11–16 emphasizes the cessation of enmity between Ephraim and Judah," and "this scenario corresponds precisely to Josiah's attempt to rebuild the Davidic empire"; and (5) "the interest in exodus traditions apparent in both 11:11–16 and 12:1–6 is particularly noteworthy" because "the celebration of Passover served as the festival basis for Josiah's reform."[15]

In contrast, Childs sees the same level of eschatological fixing—if that is the proper term—in chapter 11's royal oracle as in chapter 9. We are speaking here of a messianic depiction. Let us move slowly to his conclusion through a quote that shows the importance of taking the fixed literary context seriously. On this latter point, he and Sweeney and my own Isaiah commentary are in agreement, yet the fixity is of such a character, apparently, that it admits of a variety of interpretations. This has to do with the degree of intended historical roots detected, the character of the editing, and the kinds of literary contexts called upon to bear significance for our final-form reading. Now we can see where *fixing* has given way, instead, to *potential.*

First, Childs on chapter 11 within the stable literary form:

> Chapter 11 has been editorially positioned to form the culmination of a theological direction that commenced at chapter 6, moved through the promise of a coming messianic ruler in chapter 7, and emerged in chapter 9 with the portrayal of a righteous messianic king upon the throne of David. Chapter 11 offers both a correction and an exposition of the coming reign.

---

14. Sweeney, *Isaiah 1–39,* 204.
15. Ibid., 204–5.

Lest one suppose an unbroken continuity between the house of David and the coming king—the encounter with Ahaz in chapter 7 had destroyed this possibility—chapter 11 begins with the end of the old.[16]

Then Childs on the character of the process of editing:

by careful attention to the function of intertextuality through its lengthy editorial process, one can discern a very strong force emerging that sought to unify the prophetic proclamations into a coherent composition. Quite clearly, different literary restraints were at work in this canonical process from those in the modern world. Certainly no heavy-handed systematization of the prophetic oracles was attempted, but guidelines were carefully established that signalled points of resonance for the whole.[17]

My commentary agrees with the narrower conclusion regarding chapter 11's royal oracle, that is, that it speaks of an eschatological figure. In that sense, as well, I also hold to a notion of what Childs calls "the culmination of a theological direction" at work within the final literary form. Sweeney can also speak of a culmination, but it would be of a different historical order. For him, Josiah is the referent of chapter 11, and thus the entire collection of 1–12 comes to be what it is as a consequence of his reform and his exalted status. The text's final horizon, its theological direction, points to a figure in past history.

The direction that my commentary plots begins with the historical counterpart to Ahaz, that is, Hezekiah. My claim is reinforced by the proximity of chapters 7–8 to 9, on the one hand, and the contrast between Ahaz and Hezekiah, on the other hand. The latter is reinforced by the two narrative sequences of 36–39, where Hezekiah establishes what Ahaz disestablished, and chapters 7–8, where the Immanuel child is promised as a sign of weal and woe (on this, see n. 19 below). Hezekiah remains but a type of the kind of exalted rule Isa 11 speaks of, and here the trajectory moves in an eschatological direction, as suggested by Childs.

Childs presents himself with a special kind of challenge by arguing for *two* messianic oracles in close literary proximity. Both are fairly exalted, indeed theologically emphatic, announcements of coming messianic rule. Why two, then? Sweeney does not have this challenge because the first refers to Hezekiah and the second to Josiah—the two kings given exalted status in the evaluation of the Deuteronomistic Historian. Childs must entertain, therefore, the notion of correction. In order to avoid the notion of simple rep-

---

16. Childs, *Isaiah*, 102.
17. Ibid., 106.

etition, Isa 11 must, on Childs's reading, be doing something over and above the plain sense of chapter 9. So, he concludes, it emphasizes that the old order is over. It remains unclear to me why, by his reading, chapter 9 cannot already be doing that on its own.

Regarding final literary fixity, I conclude in my commentary: "The larger context of Isaiah 1–12 has affected our interpretation of the core material in 7:1–9:6. Just as it is impossible to read the Immanuel texts in isolation from the royal oracle at 9:2–7, so too the royal oracle at 11:1–9 tends to affect our comprehensive vision of kingship as found in chapters 1–12."[18] With this quote one can see that there is no disagreement among the three interpreters regarding the significance of final literary fixing. Where there is disagreement is over how to assess the final literary form, not just of chapters 1–12, but of 1–12 over against 36–39, and within the context of both Isaiah the former and Isaiah the latter, that is, the final literary presentation of Isaiah as a whole.

We do not have time here to speak of the effect of Isa 32 on the theological direction of former Isaiah. More significantly, the absence of royal oracles in latter Isaiah, and the "sure promises to David" enclosing the servants in chapter 55 will likewise affect our interpretation of what it means to speak of Isaiah's final messianic horizon.[19]

---

18. Seitz, *Isaiah 1–39*, 75.

19. The following quote shows the fine interplay between literary potential and theological fixing in the book of Isaiah as a whole: "the prediction of the Immanuel child in 7:13–17 appears to be fulfilled initially in chapter 8 with the birth of the prophet's son (note the repetition of vocabulary and concepts in 8:3–10, 18). However, 9:1–7 reveals that this one, who is to deliver Jerusalem from the Assyrians, is to be a royal child (cf. 11:1ff.; 16:5; 32:1–9), so the reader must set aside Maher-Shalal-Hash-Baz as an option. This person remains nameless apparently until chapters 36–39, as Hezekiah seems to fulfill this hope (again through a series of echoes of chapter 7; note, e.g., the place, 36:1–2; a sign, 37:30; 38:7, 22; the need to trust in Yahweh's help, 37:1–20). Yet, his failure in chapter 39 disqualifies him as well. Isaiah 40–66 presents the Servant, one of whose tasks is to establish justice in Israel and among the nations. This and other characteristics (e.g., the Spirit, light) link him to the royal hope of chapters 1–39. The person that the people of God must wait for, then, is a composite figure, whose ultimate identity keeps pushing the reader forward through a series of historical eras yet without final closure. In addition, the many lexical and thematic connections between the Servant and the people in chapters 40ff. yield an even more complex picture, which is full of theological and ethical implications. Of course, a Christian reader would identify Jesus as the final fulfillment of this literary movement. Nevertheless, our concern at this juncture is to demonstrate the flow and power of the eschatological hopes within the Old Testament itself" (M. Daniel Carroll R., "The Power of the Future in the Present: Eschatology and Ethics in O'Donovan and Beyond," in *A Royal Priesthood? The Use of the Bible Ethically and Politically: A Dialogue with Oliver O'Donovan* [ed. C. Bartholomew et al.; Scripture and Hermeneutics 3; Carlisle, U.K.: Paternoster; Grand Rapids: Zondervan, 2002], 132 n. 57).

I conclude my treatment of the royal oracles of former Isaiah with a suggestion about their potential and subsequent theological fixing, taken from my 1993 commentary. My concern there was to honor the plain-sense witness of Isaiah, as a sovereign word spoken by God to his elect people, and yet to appreciate the potential such a word had for later theological confession. It is this dialectic—historical word and theological reapplication—that Childs has sought to underscore, and it belongs decisively to the heart of careful historical-theological exegesis.

> the messianic role that Jesus fulfils is not an eternal "type" with no earthly referent. The church confesses that out of the messiness of earthly government, specifically rooted in the house of David, God prepares a place for his son to rule as King. That Jesus explodes all mundane aspects of kingship is itself not unprecedented. Israel's own vision of kingship, and from time to time its own historical kings, prepared the church to see in Jesus a king like no other, yet like what Israel longed for and at times experienced a foretaste of in kings like Hezekiah.[20]

There is a literary potential in Isaiah's presentation of hopes for David and his line. But this potential is fixed within a reasonable limit, as close exegesis shows, and it never cuts itself loose from concrete historical realities within God's ways with Israel. By the same token, a clear horizon of potential arises from theological reflection on those given historical realities, and the result is, within Israel and within a particular line of the reception history of Isaiah, theological agreement and a degree of subsequent fixity. It belongs to the task of exegesis to handle this relationship with care and close reading, for the sake of Israel and the church's confession of Jesus as Christ. What would require further treatment is the church's coordination of first- and second-advent perspectives in the light of a single Isaiah witness. I have tried to explore this tentatively in other contexts and can only refer to that in passing here.[21]

---

20. Seitz, *Isaiah 1–39*, 75.

21. Christopher R. Seitz, "Isaiah in New Testament, Lectionary, Pulpit," in *Word without End: The Old Testament as Abiding Theological Witness* (Grand Rapids: Eerdmans, 1998), 213–28; idem, " 'Of Mortal Appearance'—Earthly Jesus and Isaiah as a Type of Christian Scripture," in *Figured Out*, 103–16.

The Term "Sacrifice" and the Problem of Theological Abstraction: A Study of the Reception History of Genesis 22:1–19

Christian A. Eberhart

This essay examines the problem of theological-conceptual abstraction through a case study of the famous story of Abraham's sacrifice, also known as Aqedah (Gen 22:1–19). The discipline of theology necessarily engages in processes of abstraction because "the biblical texts are theologically underdetermined,"[1] and, as a result, the text always invites further analysis. Yet theological interpretation continually faces the question of its relationship to debates over the original meanings conveyed in the biblical text. I will show that Gen 22, with a particular focus on the category of sacrifice, illustrates this tension well. Many see the story of the Aqedah as the paradigmatic example of the biblical concept of sacrifice, but the meaning of this concept has undergone serious modifications. In Christian contexts many contend that Gen 22 functions as a prototype for the sacrificial death of Jesus. It is in light of these common views that Robert J. Daly notes: "That the Akedah does not indeed play a greater role than it does in N[ew] T[estament] soteriology is something of a puzzle."[2]

In the following essay I attempt to solve this puzzle by following two trajectories. First I investigate the term sacrifice and show that its meaning is ambiguous. According to a secularized metaphorical meaning, the term

---

I presented an original version of this essay at the International Meeting of the Society of Biblical Literature in Cambridge, U.K., on 23 July 2003 for the Biblical Theology Group. I thank Christine Helmer for inviting me to speak on this occasion. I offer this essay in honor of Klaus Berger, on the occasion of his sixty-fifth birthday.

1. Christine Helmer, "Introduction: Multivalence in Biblical Theology," 3, in this volume.

2. Robert J. Daly, *Christian Sacrifice: The Judaeo-Christian Background before Origen* (Studies in Christian Antiquity 18; Washington, D.C.: Catholic University of America Press, 1978), 181.

implies loss and destruction. When sacrifice is empirically anchored in the priestly traditions of the Hebrew Bible/Old Testament, a different meaning emerges. I show that for the priestly traditions a cultic sacrifice is a dynamic process of consecrating profane material to God through the practice of the burning rite. This type of cultic sacrifice occurs in Gen 22:1–19, but I argue that it is only of marginal relevance to the overall meaning of the story. Instead, Gen 22 emphasizes Abraham's obedience and the impending loss of Isaac's life. This reflects an understanding of sacrifice that diverges from the original meaning of cultic performance and coincides with the secularized metaphorical meaning in which the central aspect of sacrifice is lost.

Second, I offer an outline of the reception history of Gen 22 in Judaism and early Christianity. The Judean reception of Gen 22 typically centers the story on the concepts of "testing faith" and "obedience" against the backdrop of the imminent loss of Isaac's life. It thus focuses on aspects of the story that are characteristic of the secularized metaphorical meaning of sacrifice. I show that the story's New Testament reception continues to pursue these themes and that explicitly christological contexts do not reference Gen 22 as an example of cultic sacrifice. Both the ambivalent terminology of Gen 22 and its reception history suggest that the central meaning of this biblical text is not cultic sacrifice but the secularized metaphorical understanding of sacrifice.

I presuppose in my analysis the shift in meaning that the term *sacrifice* undergoes from its biblical origins to its modern connotation. Generally speaking, this term denotes a religious act of giving (consecrating) to God that is motivated by an anticipation of reciprocal receiving. The original biblical meaning of the term should be derived from actual sacrificial rituals represented in the priestly traditions of the Hebrew Bible/Old Testament. The meaning of these rituals is captured by the Hebrew term for cultic sacrifice, קרבן ליהוה ("that which is brought near to Yhwh"). The sense that sacrifice is an act of bringing to God underscores the possibility of successful communication with God. The texts from the priestly tradition show that the ritual performance of burning sacrificial materials constitutes this communication. But in the modern usage of the term sacrifice, its original biblical meaning has gradually been forgotten. Instead, sacrifice is a term that has been adopted as a metaphor devoid of any specific notion of the addressee to whom the sacrificial act of giving is directed. It has been secularized. The remaining connotation of sacrifice is negative, reduced to material loss.

1. The Secularized Metaphorical Interpretation of Sacrifice

In the story of Gen 22, Abraham is instructed to sacrifice his son Isaac—to be precise, Abraham is told to offer Isaac as a burnt offering (עלה). Considering recurrent claims that this story is a prototype for the biblical understanding of sacrifice,[3] it is important to carefully reflect on two different meanings conveyed by this term: on the one hand, its meaning as a secularized metaphor, and, on the other hand, the purpose of actual cultic sacrifices as described in biblical texts.

In both everyday English and French speech, the term *sacrifice* usually applies to an individual who consciously agrees to suffer a loss, typically for a particular cause or for the sake of a greater good. According to Royden K. Yerkes, the meaning of this term "is constituted by renouncing or giving *up* the valuable thing."[4] An underlying dimension of destruction and loss dominates this sense of sacrifice. A typical example is the way in which the Latin expression *sacrificium intellectus* currently denotes the willingness to surrender one's intellect or critical thinking.[5] Yerkes notes that, according to this secularized understanding, a "sacrifice is *by* somebody, *of* something, and *for* something, but never *to* anybody."[6] Generally this particular understanding informs the usage of the term sacrifice in the process of theological abstraction.

Examples of sacrifice in this metaphorical sense can be found in biblical texts. When Abram agrees to leave Haran (Gen 12), he gives up his home and family of origin. After a process of deliberation, he is willing to suffer loss; one could say that he is ready to sacrifice family ties for an unknown future. Another example is the story of David, who falls victim to the anger and envy of King Saul (1 Sam 18–26). David agrees to stay at the royal court

---

3. See, e.g., Robert J. Daly, *The Origins of the Christian Doctrine of Sacrifice* (Philadelphia: Fortress, 1978), 47: "the Akedah … of Isaac is in many ways the great 'founding' sacrifice of the Old Testament"; see also Geza Vermes, *Scripture and Tradition in Judaism: Haggadic Studies* (StPB 4; Leiden: Brill, 1983), 206, 208–11; Gordon J. Wenham, "The Akedah: A Paradigm of Sacrifice," in *Pomegranates and Golden Bells: Studies in Biblical, Jewish, and Near Eastern Ritual, Law, and Literature in Honor of Jacob Milgrom* (ed. D. N. Freedman et al.; Winona Lake, Ind.: Eisenbrauns, 1995), 93–102.

4. Royden K. Yerkes, *Sacrifice in Greek and Roman Religions and Early Judaism* (New York: Scribner's, 1952), 2. See also William J. Bamberger, "ויקרא Leviticus," in תורה *The Torah: A Modern Commentary* (ed. W. G. Plaut; New York: Union of American Hebrew Congregations, 1981), 750. Hubert Seiwert defines the secular term "sacrifice" as nonritual actions characterized by an element of denial or self-abandonment ("nichtritualisierte Handlungen…, denen ein Element des Verzichts oder der Selbstaufgabe eigen ist"; Hubert Seiwert, "Opfer," *HRWG* 4:271); see further Horst Seebaß, "Opfer II: Altes Testament," *TRE* 25:259.

5. A similar pejorative sense prevails in the modern secular usage of the German term *Opfer*. The saying "jede Wahl enthält ein Opfer" ("every choice comprises a sacrifice") shows that "sacrifice" stands for exclusively negative and unavoidable consequences that are part and parcel of deliberative processes.

6. Yerkes, *Sacrifice*, 2 (emphasis original).

despite Saul's repeated assaults on his life. David is thus willing to sacrifice his personal safety for the well-being of both his king and Israel, his nation. In contemporary scholarship, René Girard has analyzed biblical myths depicting violent human relationships such as Cain's murder of Abel (Gen 4) and Jacob's betrayal of Esau (Gen 27), stories that he understands to be examples of biblical sacrifice.[7] The crucial distinction to be made, however, is that the term *sacrifice* in the sense of loss and destruction may be applied to biblical texts, but it never actually occurs there. Girard derives his understanding of sacrifice from biblical texts that do not mention the term. These texts recount stories of loss and misfortune, undertaken willingly or not, but the loss is recounted exclusively in the narrative genre and is never captured by a single expression equivalent to a theological interpretation such as sacrifice.

This important observation leads to the questions as to where sacrifice occurs as a term in the Hebrew Bible/Old Testament and what the term means in these contexts. In the following section I study sacrificial rituals as they appear in the Hebrew Bible/Old Testament. I refer to them as "cultic sacrifices" in order to distinguish them from the secularized metaphorical interpretation of sacrifice.

2. Cultic Sacrifice in the Hebrew Bible/Old Testament

In this section I study the meaning of sacrifice as it emerges from the priestly texts of the Hebrew Bible/Old Testament. In these texts the term refers exclusively to expressions of human worship of God, particularly as consecration rituals. I argue that this sense of cultic practice differs significantly from the secularized metaphorical sense that appears in theological abstraction. For example, cultic sacrifices can be effective without animal slaughter, in essence without a victim. Animal slaughter does not constitute the culmination of sacrifice but is a preliminary action for the ritual. I show in this section that the actual consecration of the sacrificial material takes place during the burning rite on the central holy altar. At this moment material is transformed and transported to God through fire and smoke. The essence of this ritual dynamic is captured by the Hebrew term for sacrifice, קרבן ליהוה ("that which is brought near to Yhwh"). This giving occurs in anticipation

---

7. See René Girard, *La Violence et le Sacré* (Paris: Grasset, 1972), 14–15, 469–71; see also the interview with Girard conducted by Brian McDonald in which Girard defines sacrifice by referring to the attitude of the harlot in 1 Kgs 3:16–28, who "is willing to sacrifice a child to the needs of rivalry" ("Violence and the Lamb Slain," *Touchstone: A Journal of Mere Christianity* [2003], n.p. [cited 4 November 2005]. Online: http://www.touchstonemag.com/archives/article. php?id=16-10-040-i).

of receiving blessing from God. The status of victim or loss is therefore less significant to the priestly tradition's understanding of sacrifice than it is to the secularized metaphorical understanding. At the end of the section I show that a metaphorical use of the term *sacrifice* also appears in the Hebrew Bible/Old Testament. Sacrifice in this sense typically qualifies righteous human behavior and prayer dedicated to God as an element of human worship.

What is the meaning of cultic sacrifice as part of temple worship in the Hebrew Bible/Old Testament? Today few are familiar with this fundamental dimension of Israelite worship. The relative ignorance of Israelite cultic practices may be attributed to the fact that actual cultic sacrifices belong to a distant past and are no longer practiced in modern religions or cultures.[8] Hence historical care and respect must be exercised when investigating the topic.[9] Another reason for the ignorance of the topic especially among Christians may be attributed to the fact that the Hebrew Bible/Old Testament laws on sacrificial rituals appear in Leviticus, a book traditionally overlooked by the Christian church and Christian scholarship.[10]

According to the sacrificial laws of Lev 1–7, cultic sacrifices are solemn events that require the assistance of priests. The sacrifices are carried out in the forecourt of the temple and on the "altar of burnt offering." They follow specific regulations pertaining primarily to the correct performance of ritual steps, but what the modern scholar does not find is an explanation of how biblical writers understood the function of various sacrificial rituals or a clear description of the ritual step that might be considered the key element of the rite.[11] For biblical writers, sacrifices were part of everyday life and did not require any explicit explanation. Given this situation, the historical meaning of cultic sacrifices continues to be the topic of much scholarly debate, and consensus has been achieved only with regard to its basic function. During cultic sacrifices something is sanctified; a cultic sacrifice is an act of consecration.[12] The literal

---

8. In the context of the Eucharist/Last Supper, sacrificial *metaphors* are employed, but an actual sacrifice is not performed.

9. See Rolf Rendtorff, "Das Opfer im Alten Testament," in *Das Opfer: Religionsgeschichtliche, theologische und politische Aspekte* (ed. D. Neuhaus; Arnoldshainer Texte 102; Frankfurt: Haag + Herchen, 1998), 36.

10. See Erhard S. Gerstenberger, *Das dritte Buch Mose: Leviticus* (ATD 6; Göttingen: Vandenhoeck & Ruprecht, 1993), 1–2, 13–15; Samuel E. Balentine, *The Torah's Vision of Worship* (OBT; Minneapolis: Fortress, 1999), 148–49.

11. See Alfred Marx, "The Theology of the Sacrifice According to Leviticus 1–7," in *The Book of Leviticus: Composition and Reception* (ed. R. A. Kugler and R. Rendtorff; VTSup 93; Leiden: Brill, 2003), 103–4.

12. This is a definition of sacrifice already proposed by Henri Hubert and Marcel Mauss, "Essai sur la Nature et la Fonction du Sacrifice," *Année sociologique* 2 (1899): 36–41. Yerkes

meaning is illustrated by the Latin *sacrificium*: "to make holy" and "to dedi-
cate" but also "to perform holy actions."[13] A cultic sacrifice is a consecration
ritual of giving to God carried out at a sacred location.

This definition still invites further clarification as to which ritual element effects the consecration. I have dealt with this question in several recent
publications[14] and will summarize the relevant findings here. According to
widely shared opinion, the ritual element of animal slaughter consecrates the
sacrifice and is therefore considered its moment of culmination.[15] This cor-
relates with the notion that animal sacrifices constitute a distinct and special
category in the Israelite cult.[16] I have challenged this scholarly opinion on
several grounds.

---

makes the important observation that, contrary to the secularized meaning of the term, a cultic
sacrifice is always offered *to* God or a deity (Yerkes, *Sacrifice*, 4–5); see also Marx, "The Theology of the Sacrifice," 106.

13. Yerkes, *Sacrifice*, 6–7; Bamberger, "ויקרא Leviticus," 750; Seiwert, "Opfer," 270. For
the translation of the Latin *sacro*, see, e.g., *Langenscheidts Grosswörterbuch Lateinisch*, part 1
(20th ed.; Berlin: Langenscheidt, 1978), 670; *Pons Globalwörterbuch Lateinisch-Deutsch* (2nd
ed.; Stuttgart: Klett, 1986), 918.

14. Christian Eberhart, *Studien zur Bedeutung der Opfer im Alten Testament: Die Signifi-
kanz von Blut- und Verbrennungsriten im kultischen Rahmen* (WMANT 94; Neukirchen-Vluyn:
Neukirchener, 2002), 289–330; idem, "Die Prüfung Abrahams—oder: Wo aber ist das Opfer im
Neuen Testament? Exegese von 1. Mose 22 aus christlicher Sicht," in *Wo aber ist das Opferlamm?
Opfer und Opferkritik in den drei abrahamitischen Religionen* (ed. U. Dehn; EZW-Texte 168;
Berlin: Evangelische Zentralstelle für Weltanschauungsfragen, 2003), 28–49; idem, "A Neglected
Feature of Sacrifice in the Hebrew Bible: Remarks on the Burning Rite on the Altar," *HTR* 97
(2004): 485–93. It should be mentioned that my study focuses on common features of Hebrew
Bible/Old Testament sacrifices. For a detailed profile of, and individual differences between the
five types of sacrifice, see Eberhart, *Studien zur Bedeutung der Opfer*, 16–176.

15. See Girard, *Violence*; Walter Burkert, *Homo Necans: Interpretationen Altgriechischer
Opferriten und Mythen* (RVV 32; Berlin: de Gruyter, 1972); Hartmut Gese, "Die Sühne," in
Zur biblischen Theologie: Alttestamentliche Vorträge (2nd ed.; Tübingen: Mohr Siebeck, 1983),
85–106.

16. At the beginning of his study on atonement in Israel's sacrificial cult, Hartmut Gese
claims that sacrifices involving the shedding of blood have a special status ("Unter den Opfern
haben die blutigen Opfer besonderen Rang" [Gese, "Die Sühne," 93]). In a similar fashion,
Marcel Detienne limits his study of Greek sacrifice to those practices associated with blood-
shedding ("sacrifice sanglant"; see Marcel Detienne, "Pratiques Culinaires et Esprit de Sacrifice,"
in *La Cuisine du Sacrifice en Pays Grec* [ed. M. Detienne and J-P. Vernant; Paris: Gallimard,
1979], 7). The assumption that animal sacrifice constitutes a separate category among cultic
sacrifices is conveyed by the modern English and French definitions of (cult) offering: "any
act of presenting something to a supernatural being." A cult sacrifice, on the other hand, is
understood as "an offering accompanied by the ritual killing of the object of the offering" (J.
van Baal, "Offering, Sacrifice and Gift," *Numen* 23 [1976]: 161; for a similar definition, see, e.g.,
T. H. Gaster, "Sacrifices and Offerings, OT," *IDB* 4:147). As a preliminary criticism of such a
distinction between sacrifice and offering, Hubert and Mauss reject the idea of animal sacrifice

First, I have suggested that animal slaughter cannot be considered the moment of consecration in sacrificial rituals in the Hebrew Bible/Old Testament because slaughter appears as a preliminary action to the rite, not its culmination. Animal slaughter is never performed on the most holy altar but only in areas of lesser sanctity (Lev 1:11; Ezek 40:39–41) or outside the sanctuary (Lev 17:3–4 LXX). It is usually to be carried out by the lay person, not by a priest (Lev 1:5, 11). In Ezek 44:9–16 the task is assigned to Levites as punishment for their lack of obedience toward God.[17] Second, animal slaughter does not occur in all of the sacrificial rituals described in Lev 1–7. The cereal offering (מנחה, Lev 2 and 6:7–16[18]) consisting of wheat, oil, and frankincense is a fully valid sacrifice (קרבן) that can, according to Lev 5:11–13, be substituted for a sin offering (חטאת). The Judean sacrificial cult celebrated at the Elephantine temple was performed solely with cereal offerings and frankincense; animals were not offered. Sacrifice functions in these instances without animal slaughter and without a victim.[19] The absence of animal slaughter suggests that this element cannot constitute the central moment of sacrificial rituals. The question regarding the key aspect of sacrifice must be reassessed.

I have examined this question by turning to the act of burning sacrificial material on the main altar. I discovered that this ritual element rather than the element of slaughter is common to all five types of sacrifice listed in Lev 1–7, including the cereal offering. In most cases, the biblical descriptions of sacrificial burning are accompanied by two interpretative terms. The first term, "fire offering" (אשה), is used to describe the crucial moment when the material offering changes its consistency and is transformed into a new, ethereal essence. The second term, "pleasing odor" (ריח ניחוח), alludes to the sacrificial smoke that ascends from the earthly to the heavenly sphere where God perceives it.[20] This suggests that the main purpose of the sacrifice is not primarily the annihilation of human goods. Such interpretative focus on the loss for human beings or on destruction is purely materialistic and fails to

---

as a distinct category, calling the restriction of sacrifice to those kinds of sacrifices involving the shedding of blood "arbitrary" (Hubert and Mauss, "Essai sur la Nature," 39).

17. See Eberhart, *Studien zur Bedeutung der Opfer*, 179–83, 203–18; see also Yerkes, *Sacrifice*, 4–5; Bruno W. Dombrowski, "Killing in Sacrifice: The Most Profound Experience of God?" *Numen* 23 (1976): 136–44.

18. Verse references follow the MT; to be noted is that Lev 6:7–16 MT corresponds to 6:14–23 in English Bible editions.

19. Eberhart, *Studien zur Bedeutung der Opfer*, 77–88, 207–8; idem, "Prüfung Abrahams," 30–31.

20. Eberhart, *Studien zur Bedeutung der Opfer*, 289–331, 361–81; idem, "Neglected Feature," 489–93. See also Alfred Marx, *Les Systèmes Sacrificiels de l'Ancien Testament: Formes et Fonctions du Culte Sacrificiel à Yhwh* (VTSup 105; Leiden: Brill, 2005), 138–39.

recognize the theological, God-directed dimension of this ritual step. Instead, I have argued that the culmination of a cultic sacrifice is the burning rite. It is the moment of consecration at which the sacrificial material taken from the profane realm is brought into the realm of the holy.[21] The Hebrew term for sacrifice, קרבן ליהוה, meaning "that which is brought near to Yнwн," conveys the ritual's dynamic.

In cultic contexts, the act of giving to God is sometimes motivated by anticipation of divine blessing. The Latin formula *do ut des* ("I give so that you may give") accurately captures the underlying reciprocity of the sacrificial process in these cases. The individual or community offering cultic sacrifices expects blessings of various kinds; they may also expect deliverance from distress or oppression. Cultic sacrifices are offered at other times as signs of gratitude for divine blessing. Such signs presuppose that the blessing has temporally preceded the sacrifice. The formula *do quia dedisti* ("I give because you have given") accurately describes this second motivation for offering cultic sacrifices.[22] The following table illustrates these two processes:

Sacrifice
(קרבן ליהוה—"that which is brought near to Yнwн")

Action:
Giving to God (*do*—"I give")
by means of burning rite

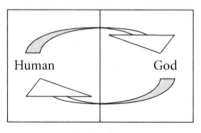

Human   God

Motivation:
Anticipation of divine blessing (… *ut des*—"so that you may give")
or
Gratitude for previous divine blessing (… *quia dedisti*—
"because you have given")

---

21. See Seebaß, "Opfer," 259.
22. Eberhart, *Studien zur Bedeutung der Opfer,* 336–39; idem, "Neglected Feature," 492.

To summarize: I suggest that the central feature of the temple cult is not animal slaughter but the burning rite. This rite represents the sacrificial ritual as a whole. The sacrificial smoke ascending to heaven is a visual manifestation of Israel's devotion and worship.

It is important to note here that the connection between cultic sacrifice and devotion actually facilitates the change that the term sacrifice eventually undergoes from its cultic connotation to the secularized metaphorical meaning. A metaphorical use of the term sacrifice already occurs, for example, in the Psalms and Sirach; righteous human behavior and prayer are labeled "sacrifice" or represent the sacrificial ritual (see, e.g., Pss 50:14; 51:19; 119:108; Sir 35:1–3). Like the actual sacrifices offered in front of the temple, these expressions of devotion occur in the context of human worship. Acts of righteousness and prayer share aspects of sacrificial rituals in that they are directed toward and dedicated to God and consequently are understood to acquire a special quality. They have been consecrated, that is, "made sacred."

In concluding I want to reflect again on the difference between cultic sacrifices and the secularized metaphorical understanding of sacrifice as well as on the fact that today the latter understanding prevails and is commonly used in the process of abstracting meaning from biblical texts. I have shown in section 1 that the modern secularized understanding of the term tends to connote loss and destruction. On the contrary, the Hebrew term קרבן ליהוה means "that which is brought near to Yʜᴡʜ," and the etymology of the Latin derivate for sacrifice implies consecration. Both the Hebrew and Latin terms convey dynamics toward the holy that are missing from the secularized meaning of the term sacrifice. It should therefore be acknowledged that the secularized understanding is inappropriate if applied to cultic contexts.[23]

3. Is the Story of Abraham's Sacrifice about Cultic Sacrifice?

I now reflect on the story of Gen 22 to consider how sacrifice in this text tends toward a secularized metaphorical interpretation. Clearly the burnt offering that Abraham is asked to perform is an example of cultic sacrifice. I show that cultic sacrifice is nevertheless only marginally relevant to the narrative account. Instead, the threat to Isaac's life is the crucial feature of the story. This threat constitutes the story's moral challenge. Genesis 22 is not a typical

---

23. Hans-Josef Klauck has, for example, questioned the understanding of cultic sacrifice as an offering to God precisely because he understands the burning rite to signify the "total destruction" of human goods and their "painful renunciation" (Hans-Josef Klauck, *Stadt- und Hausreligion, Mysterienkulte, Volksglaube* [vol. 1 of *Die Religiöse Umwelt des Urchristentums*; Kohlhammer-Studienbücher Theologie 9; Stuttgart: Kohlhammer, 1995], 46).

example of the biblical understanding of cultic sacrifice; instead, it should be seen as a prototype of the secularized metaphorical understanding.

In Gen 22 God requests that Abraham sacrifice his only son as a burnt offering (עלה, 22:2), yet this request to perform a cultic sacrifice is not necessarily central to the text. Instead, the story culminates at the moment when God's angel intercedes and delivers the message to Abraham that he need not carry through with God's request. The burnt offering is still carried out using a ram as a substitute (22:13), implying that God does receive the allotted portion through the cultic burning rite. But the performance of the ritual with the ram is a detail of minor importance. The fact that Isaac is in danger of becoming a victim—and hence of being sacrificed according to the secularized meaning of the term—is the climax of the story. Traditional and modern interpretations contending that Isaac could have been killed (and not sacrificed) substantiate this claim.[24]

It is frequently noted that Abraham's sacrifice was aborted. This is the main reason why the title "Abraham's Sacrifice" is often deemed inappropriate for this story.[25] Yet Abraham's cultic sacrifice is not aborted after the divine intervention; it is only temporarily interrupted and eventually completed (22:13). Hence the title "Abraham's Sacrifice" could be considered appropriate. This debate concerning the title's suitability suggests that something other than cultic sacrifice according to the priestly tradition is at stake in Gen 22. This understanding of sacrifice with its emphasis on what is offered to God does not serve as the story's culmination but as its context. A shift to a secularized interpretation of the term sacrifice with its emphasis on victim and loss points to the crucial feature of the story. This crucial feature is the threat that God's demand poses to the life of Isaac.

An important difference can be highlighted between the story in Gen 22 and other narrative texts addressing specific cultic sacrifices. In the biblical story of the competition between the prophets of Baal and Elijah in 1 Kgs 18:21–40, for example, both parties sacrifice a bull as a burnt offering (עלה). Its preparation is described in great detail. Yet the slaughter of the bull is never mentioned, even though it must have happened. The neglect in describing

---

24. See, e.g., the reference to Gen 22 in 4 Macc 13:12, which employs the term σφαγιασθῆναι (to slay); see also Jonathan Magonet, "Die Fesselung Isaaks" (trans. U. Dehn), in Dehn, *Wo aber ist das Opferlamm,* 19.

25. Cf. Magonet, "Fesselung Isaaks," 19. In the rabbinic tradition, the title עקדה (binding) or עקדת יצחק (binding of Isaac) has become the customary title for the story in Gen 22 since the third century c.e. (see Joseph A. Fitzmyer, "The Sacrifice of Isaac in Qumran Literature," *Bib* 83 [2002]: 212). This historical evidence suggests that Gen 22 is not primarily about cultic sacrifice.

this ritual element is characteristic of other narrative texts mentioning cultic sacrifices. The contrary is, however, the case in Gen 22.[26] This story is atypical in its emphasis on the moment of imminent slaughter. It is the only narrative in the entire Bible that mentions the tool used for ritual slaughter: the knife (22:6 and 10)—even the detailed laws on cultic sacrifice in Lev 1-7 avoid this detail. In addition, the succinct style characterizing the beginning of the story is carried through the text. The account becomes increasingly detailed from Gen 22:6 until the moment when Abraham reaches out his hand to slay his son (22:10). The attempted slaughter appears as the climax of the story. In this regard, Gen 22 is the biblical exception to narratives dealing with cultic sacrifice.

In spite of the fact that no human is put to death, the distinctive climax of Gen 22 accounts for the enduring recognition of its moral challenge and cruelty. A father is requested to slay his only son.[27] When Abraham and Isaac finally approach "the place," the son asks his father, "Where is the lamb for a burnt offering?" (ואיה השה לעלה, Gen 22:7). While the internal emotions

---

26. See Marx, *Systèmes Sacrificiels*, 92. In contrast, Daly (*Christian Sacrifice*, 41) compares Abraham's sacrifice with that of Elijah on Mount Carmel and assumes that both accounts agree "closely."

27. Some commentators try to show that the moral challenge of Gen 22 is lessened if its linguistic aspects are carefully analyzed. Jonathan Magonet, for example, refers to an observation already made in the Talmud tract *Sanhedrin* 89b that the authoritative character of God's initial request (Gen 22:2) is weakened because the particle נא־, which indicates a plea or petition, is appended to the first imperative קח ("take...!"). Abraham thus shares some of the burden for subsequent events (Magonet, "Fesselung Isaaks," 20–21). Midrashic interpretation, followed by some modern commentators, even adds that God never asked Abraham to sacrifice Isaac as a burnt offering. The Hebrew Hiphil stem of עלה can have the meaning of "to sacrifice" in cultic contexts, but it can mean "to bring up" in other contexts. If the latter is the case, Gen 22:2 would mean that God asks Abraham to merely guide his son up a hill in order to perform a burnt offering. Abraham misunderstands this request by binding Isaac and placing him on the altar. The initial divine request is, therefore, not cruel at all (cf. W. G. Plaut, "בראשית Genesis," in תורה *The Torah: A Modern Commentary* [ed. W. G. Plaut; New York: Union of American Hebrew Congregations, 1981], 150); Louis A. Berman, *The Akedah: The Binding of Isaac* (Jerusalem: Jason Aronson, 1997), 14; Frédéric Manns, "Presentation," in *The Sacrifice of Isaac in the Three Monotheistic Religions: Proceedings of a Symposium on the Interpretation of the Scriptures Held in Jerusalem, March 16-17, 1995* (ed. F. Manns; Studium Biblicum Franciscanum Analecta 41; Jerusalem: Franciscan Printing Press, 1995), 6; see also Christa Schäfer-Lichtenberger, "Abraham zwischen Gott und Isaak (Gen 22,1-19)," *WuD* 26 (2001): 50–51. The former interpretation, however, only divides the responsibility of the morally ambiguous events between Abraham and God but does not eliminate it. The second interpretation is questionable in light of the intervention of God's angel, who praises Abraham's fear of God precisely because he did not spare his son (Gen 22:12). It furthermore fails to answer the question concerning the nature of Abraham's test.

of the characters are not explicitly mentioned, Isaac's question implies that he is aware of the imminent doom and fears for his life. A further aspect to the moral challenge of the story is the specific circumstance that it is God who requests the slaying of Isaac. The fact that this request is eventually revoked does not downplay the seriousness of the story's ethical implications. There are traces in the earliest redactions of Genesis of how the audience perceived this specific aspect of the story. The unique title "Fear of Isaac" (פחד יצחק) is attributed in Gen 31:42 and 31:53 to God.[28]

Genesis 22 has been criticized throughout the history of interpretation because it endorses blind obedience instead of respect for life. Two centuries ago philosopher Immanuel Kant commented, "it is certainly true that I am not supposed to kill my dear son; but I am not certain and can never be certain that you, who have appeared to me, *are God*, even if it (the voice) would come down from heaven."[29] Today a similar criticism has been voiced by anthropologist Carol Delaney, who poses the legitimate question as to Abraham's willingness to kill a child at God's request.[30] Why would God not demand the child's protection?

Moral sense might be made of Gen 22 by interpreting it in historical perspective. Even if the threat to Isaac's life is considered central to the story, its Judean audience was aware that this threat would not be actualized in the narrative. Given their self-understanding as descendants of Abraham and Isaac, the Judeans' very existence was proof that the divine promise had not ceased regardless of how seriously their ancestors were tested. It is clear from the outset that Isaac must have survived despite the apparent paradox that God was responsible for the ultimate challenge conveyed in Gen 22.[31] The initial information about the test has a different purpose: it places Abraham at the center of attention and provides the matrix for theologically understanding the story as conveying God's ultimate faithfulness to Israel.

Given these parameters, however, Gen 22 is not a typical example of the biblical understanding of cultic sacrifice. Taking place within the more or less coincidental context of a cultic sacrifice, the story deals with the impending loss of a father's only son. It deals with what the secularized metaphorical

28. See Catherina Wenzel, "Abraham—Ibrahim: Ähnlichkeit statt Verwandtschaft," *EvTh* 62 (2002): 380–81.

29. Immanuel Kant, *Der Streit der Fakultäten (1798)* (ed. W. Weischedel; Werke 6; Darmstadt: Wissenschaftliche Buchgesellschaft, 1966), 333 (translation mine).

30. Carol Delaney, "Abraham and the Seeds of Patriarchy," in *A Feminist Companion to Genesis* (ed. A. Brenner; FCB 2; Sheffield: Sheffield Academic Press, 1998), 149.

31. I am grateful to Erhard Blum of the University of Tübingen for having shared with me this insightful interpretation.

interpretation of sacrifice usually conveys. To highlight this difference, let us replace the divine command to sacrifice Isaac as a burnt offering with a command to stone or drown him. According to the secularized metaphorical interpretation, it would still be appropriate to say that Abraham was willing to sacrifice his only son in order to demonstrate his obedience. Thus the term sacrifice commonly used in theological abstraction is not at all limited to, or exclusively compatible with, the performance of cultic sacrifices. In the Hebrew Bible/Old Testament, sacrifice is not applicable to random methods of killing but is limited to the performance of a cultic rite and can also, because of its emphasis on consecration, metaphorically designate human acts of worship.

4. Abraham's Sacrifice in Traditions of Early Judaism

The reception history of Gen 22 in early Judaism is rich and creative. This should come as no surprise. Many have noted that the meaning of Gen 22 is neither clear nor precise; its open-endedness has fascinated audiences for centuries. In this section I focus on how the early Judean reception history modifies and intensifies dominant aspects of Gen 22 such as "testing of faith," "obedience," and the threat to Isaac's life. All these aspects are crucial to the secularized metaphorical understanding of sacrifice.

One example of the reception of Gen 22 in early Judaism is the book of *Jubilees*, where the testing of Abraham's faith receives particular attention. While Gen 22:1 briefly notes that the test is solely God's initiative (והאלהים נסה את־אברהם), *Jub.* 17:16–18 features a much more elaborate scene. It introduces Mastemah, who challenges God to test Abraham, thus describing a situation analogous to the scene in the book of Job in which Satan initiates the trial of the righteous (1:6–12). The strictly monotheistic background of Gen 22 is thus compromised in favor of a dualistic setting. Finally, the subsequent sacrifice in *Jub.* 19:8 appears as the last of a total of ten trials, while another tradition recognizes Abraham's faith only after he has passed them all (1 Macc 2:52).[32]

There is another key difference between the Genesis text and its reception in early Judaism. While the *Vorlage* in Gen 22:1 limits the actual test to Abraham alone, early Judean tradition gradually attributes responsibility

---

32. For a discussion of the early Judean tradition of Abraham's ten trials, see Jo Milgrom, *The Binding of Isaac: The Akedah—A Primary Symbol in Jewish Thought and Art* (Berkeley, Calif.: Bibal, 1988), 31–62. Milgrom nevertheless recognizes the interpretative development within this tradition when pointing out that a "trial" is explicitly mentioned only in the context of Gen 22 (*Binding of Isaac*, 34).

to Isaac. This tradition elaborates in detail Isaac's awareness of the imminent threat to his life and his readiness to obey the divine command. In the book of *Pseudo-Jubilees* (4QPsJubª, or 4Q225 2:4), in the Targumim *Pseudo-Jonathan* and *Neofiti I*, and in *Gen. Rab.* 56:8, for example, Isaac explicitly requests that his father bind him before the sacrifice. *Sifra Deuteronomy* 32 goes even further in relating that Isaac binds himself on the altar. The logical consequence for taking on this responsibility is, according to 4QPsJubª and Sir 44:22–23 (Greek text), that Isaac also receives God's blessing.[33]

The heavenly scene of the story is transformed in the reception tradition of early Judaism in order to depict more graphically the horror of the impending loss of Isaac's life. In Gen 22, God addresses Abraham directly (22:2) or communicates through an angel (22:11–12, 15–18); the narrative does not yield any details as to how Abraham feels about the imminent tragedy. The book of *Jubilees*, however, makes the emotional response explicit. It describes good angels who weep at the prospect of Isaac's death, while Mastemah and his angels openly rejoice in this event (*Jub.* 17:15–18:16; see also 4QPsJubª). Furthermore, heaven is depicted as a law court in which Mastemah has an important function as Israel's adversary and accuser.[34] But Mastemah is bound as a consequence of Isaac's fear of God. These events become the precondition for Israel's later salvation in which Isaac appears as the savior of his people. The expansion in this interpretative tradition shows Isaac as the central figure of the story.

Philo of Alexandria (ca. 20 B.C.E.–45 C.E.) builds on this weighty tradition of Judean reflection on Abraham's sacrifice. In some of his writings he even goes further than this tradition and thereby heightens the tragedy of the story. Alluding to Gen 22:2, Philo writes that Abraham brings to God "the loved, the only trueborn offspring of the soul" (τὸ ἀγαπητὸν καὶ μόνον τῆς ψυχῆς ἔγγονον γνήσιον, *Deus* 1.4). Philo interprets Isaac's miraculous conception as narrated in Gen 21:1–2 allegorically. Isaac is the

---

33. The tendency to highlight Isaac's participation continues in later midrashic writings. A thirteenth-century midrash, for example, states in a somewhat redundant fashion that "the two of them came to the place, and the two of them brought the stones, and the two of them brought the fire, and the two of them brought the wood." Isaac then instructs his father to proceed quickly and to burn him (*Yalkut Shim'oni* 101; the text is printed in Seth Daniel Kunin, "The Death of Isaac: Structural Analysis of Genesis 22," in Manns, *Sacrifice of Isaac in the Three Monotheistic Religions*, 55). The depiction of how Isaac willingly cooperates contrasts sharply with Gen 31:42, 53, where God is called "Fear of Isaac" (see section 3).

34. See also Joseph Fitzmyer's remarks on the meaning of the name "Mastemah": "The name denotes 'opposition' of a legal or judicial nature, and the verb שׂטם is used in the juridical sense of lodging a complaint with a higher authority or in a court of law" (Fitzmyer, "Sacrifice," 218).

son of God who is identical with the Logos; he is the epitome of wisdom (e.g., *Cher.* 13.45; *Fug.* 30.167–168). Philo also recounts two different endings for the story. According to some of his writings Isaac survives (*Fug.* 24.132; *Somn.* 1.34.194–195; *Abr.* 33.177), while other writings relate that Isaac is sacrificed (*Leg.* 3.209; *Migr.* 140).[35] The biblical support for the latter interpretation is the implicit suggestion in verse 19 that Isaac is sacrificed. In this verse Abraham, after receiving the divine blessing, returns to the two young men who had accompanied him and Isaac to the land of Moriah. The surprising absence of Isaac in verse 19 has led some interpreters—perhaps including Philo—to conclude that Abraham left the place where his test had culminated by himself. The threatened loss of Isaac's life is interpreted at its extreme tragic consequence.

Such interpretative developments inspired later traditions concerning the "ashes of Isaac" or the "blood of Isaac."[36] Isaac thereby came to be regarded as a prototypical Judean martyr. An example is the story of Eleazar's steadfastness in 4 Maccabees.[37] While being tortured, Eleazar expresses the hope that his blood may be a means of purification and his life a ransom for his people (καθάρσιον αὐτῶν ποίησον τὸ ἐμὸν αἷμα καὶ ἀντίψυχον αὐτῶν λαβὲ τὴν ἐμὴν ψυχήν, 4 Macc 6:29). While being martyred, Eleazar remembers Isaac's obedience (13:12). Similarly, Eleazar's mother remembers not only "Abel slain by Cain" but also "Isaac, who was offered as a burnt offering" (18:11). By placing the profane murder of Gen 4 next to the cultic sacrifice of Gen 22, this text demonstrates how stories from the tradition about the tragic loss of life serve as examples for martyrs in later times. People who "sacrificed" their lives for their faith could follow in Abel's and Isaac's footsteps.

Early Judean commentators, as I have shown, often expanded upon themes in Gen 22, such as Abraham's serious test and steadfast faith. They further developed the theme of obedience by including Isaac, sometimes intensifying his imminent death to the extreme of martyrdom. By their reception, the connections were tightened between the story's elements of sacrifice,

---

35. See also Lukas Kundert, *Gen 22,1–19 im Alten Testament, im Frühjudentum und im Neuen Testament* (vol. 1 of *Die Opferung/Bindung Isaaks*; WMANT 78. Neukirchen-Vluyn: Neukirchener, 1998), 130–33.

36. E.g., *L.A.B.* 18:5; *Sifra*. For further rabbinical references, see Vermes, *Scripture and Tradition in Judaism*, 205–6; Michael Brocke, "Isaak III: Judentum," *TRE* 16:300; Kunin, "Death of Isaac," 51–54.

37. It should be noted that 4 Maccabees cannot be dated with certainty. Proposed dates range from 50 B.C.E. to 100 C.E. See Klaus-Dieter Schlunck, "Makkabäer/Makkabäerbücher," *TRE* 21:742; Hans-Josef Klauck, *4. Makkabäerbuch* (*JSHRZ* 3.6; Gütersloh: Mohn, 1989), 668–69. As a result, 4 Maccabees can be considered to represent early Judean or rabbinic traditions.

loss, and a willing victim—connections incongruous with the tradition of cultic sacrifice.

5. Abraham's Sacrifice in the New Testament

I now turn to the New Testament's reception of Abraham's sacrifice. I argue in this section that some New Testament texts (Heb 11:17–19; Jas 2:21–23) appropriate the early Judean theme of the testing of faith rather than use the Hebrew Bible/Old Testament version (Gen 22:1–19) as their basis. Yet the New Testament reception focuses on Abraham as the main character rather than on Isaac. I also show how some brief allusions to Gen 22 in the New Testament are contextualized christologically and argue that these christological references lack the crucial aspect of cultic sacrifice—a religious act of giving to God that is motivated by the anticipation of reciprocal receiving.

A general survey of New Testament reception history suggests that the story of Abraham's sacrifice does not play an important role in the formation of New Testament Christology or soteriology. Neither the Epistle to the Hebrews nor any other New Testament writing refers to Abraham's sacrifice as an example of the (cultic) sacrifice of Jesus. These observations implicitly corroborate the thesis that cultic sacrifice is not the central aspect of Gen 22 and help to answer the initial question why the Aqedah does not play a greater role in New Testament soteriology.[38]

In early Christianity, the story of Abraham's sacrifice is appropriated on the basis of traditions developed in early Judaism. Compared with early Judean reception history, early Christian reception of the story displays a stronger tendency toward abstraction, thus reducing the original textual potential of its *Vorlage* to concise summaries. A preferred theme is the testing and confirmation of faith. Unlike the Judean commentators, early Christian interpreters disregarded Isaac's responsibility, focusing on Abraham as the principal actor. For example, Heb 11:17 alludes to Gen 22 as an example of Abraham's faith that requires testing through actual events: "By faith Abraham, when put to the test, offered/brought Isaac. He who had received the promises was ready to offer/bring the firstborn" (Πίστει προσενήνοχεν

---

38. Parallels between Abraham's sacrifice and Christ's passion occur frequently in paintings. These images generally date from later periods and are based on interpretations by Irenaeus, Tertullian, and Origen, for example. A survey of the reception in art of Abraham's sacrifice is presented in Milgrom, *Binding of Isaac*, 160–311; Alex Stock, "Abraham und Isaak: Zur Bildgeschichte von Gen 22," in *Mythische Provokationen in Philosophie, Theologie, Kunst und Politik* (ed. C. Bussmann and F. A. Uehlein; Pommersfeldener Beiträge 9; Würzburg: Königshausen & Neumann, 1999), 204–30.

Ἀβραὰμ τὸν Ἰσαὰκ πειραζόμενος καὶ τὸν μονογενῆ προσέφερεν). The participle πειραζόμενος refers to a central aspect of the narrative (Gen 22:1) that has received significant attention in the early Judean tradition. In the Epistle to the Hebrews, the early Judean emphasis of testing Abraham's faith is taken up and appears as an important feature of Christ's priestly office (see 2:18; 4:15). In the comprehensive list of Heb 11:1, Abraham appears among the Old Testament protagonists whose faith has been confirmed through works.

Another New Testament passage, Jas 2:21, focuses on Abraham's obedience "when he brought up/offered his son Isaac on the altar" (ἀνενέγκας Ἰσαὰκ τὸν υἱὸν αὐτοῦ ἐπὶ τὸ θυσιαστήριον). This passage understands Abraham's obedience in terms of his faith that would be "dead" (2:17) without works. Scholars have debated whether James assumes that Abraham's sacrifice was executed or not. The Greek term ἀναφέρω in Jas 2:21 is ambiguous; it means "to offer" in cultic contexts but "to bring up" in other contexts. The Greek word is equivalent to the Hebrew Hiphil stem of עלה, which has these same meanings (see section 3). It is nevertheless possible that ἀναφέρω in Jas 2:21 has a cultic term meaning—"to offer"—which would have a different nuance than simply "to bring up." It would reflect the one stream of the Judean tradition that interprets the story according to the secularized metaphorical meaning of sacrifice, which is that Isaac did lose his life.

Given that the meaning of προσφέρω is as ambiguous as that of ἀναφέρω, the question is whether Isaac was sacrificed according to Heb 11:17. The issue is nuanced by verse 19, in which Abraham hopes that his son could be raised from the dead (λογισάμενος ὅτι καὶ ἐκ νεκρῶν ἐγείρειν δυνατὸς ὁ θεός, ὅθεν αὐτὸν καὶ ἐν παραβολῇ ἐκομίσατο). In this verse προσφέρω refers to more than just the circumstance of "bringing" Isaac.[39] It is used as a cultic term in the sense of "offering," emphasizing Isaac's death as an essential part of the story. Abraham's hope, however, contradicts the logic of cultic sacrifice according to which the actual object offered to God is not expected back. Hebrews 11:17 therefore closely follows Gen 22 by interpreting sacrifice according to its secularized metaphorical meaning, that loss and destruction take place in the context of cultic sacrifice.

The only New Testament text that features a christological concept explicitly based on sacrificial metaphors is Heb 7–10. Yet even when these chapters refer to cultic Old Testament traditions, they never mention Gen 22. This omission can be understood to provide (implicit) support for my argument that the story of Abraham's sacrifice should not be interpreted as the pro-

39. Harold W. Attridge notes that the resurrection from the dead is a concept already found in Judean traditions; see his *The Epistle to the Hebrews: A Commentary on the Epistle to the Hebrews* (Hermeneia; Philadelphia: Fortress, 1989), 335.

totypical example of cultic sacrifice in the Hebrew Bible/Old Testament and therefore that it is not the interpretative framework in which Christ's death is understood in the New Testament.

James 2:21 and Heb 11:17–19, on the other hand, explicitly refer to Gen 22, but these references do not occur in christological contexts. In other New Testament passages, however, brief allusions to Gen 22 occur in christological contexts. In the emotionally charged passage of Rom 8:31–39, for example, Paul declares that God is on the side of humans once and for all. He cites Gen 22:12 (see also 22:16), the intervention of God's angel: God "did not spare his own son" (τοῦ ἰδίου υἱοῦ οὐκ ἐφείσατο). The setting of Rom 8:31–34 is an eschatological law court.[40] While missing in Gen 22, a law-court setting links Rom 8 with the story of Abraham and Isaac through its early Judean reception tradition in the book of *Jubilees* and 4QPsJub[a], as I have shown in section 4. Romans 8 alludes to a law court by assuming a judicial authority that brings charges against humans (8:33) and condemns them (8:34). The rhetorical question in the text, "If God is for us, who is against us?" (εἰ ὁ θεὸς ὑπὲρ ἡμῶν, τίς καθ᾽ ἡμῶν, 8:31), leaves no doubt that the highest authority in this scene is on the side of humans. This assertion of confidence is underlined twice: God justifies (8:33), and after the necessary prerequisite of death and ascension to heaven, Christ, who is in charge of the defense, renders any accusation against humans ineffective (8:34). This vision provides humans with the strength to endure any physical hardship (8:35–36).[41] In this way Paul illustrates both God's justification and the soteriological significance of Christ's death and resurrection as the core of the gospel. Paul makes this central theological claim by drawing on a divine court setting that had been developed by early Judean interpretations of Gen 22.

---

40. See Klaus Berger, *Theologiegeschichte des Urchristentums: Theologie des Neuen Testaments* (2nd ed.; Tübingen; Francke, 1995), 244; Kundert, *Gen 22,1–19 im Alten Testament*, 189; Joseph A. Fitzmyer, *Romans: A New Translation with Introduction and Commentary* (AB 33; New York: Doubleday, 1993), 529, 532–33.

41. The physical suffering detailed in Rom 8:35–36 hints at a particular situation in Paul's life. Acts 7:54–8:1 relates the stoning of Stephen as an example of "persecution," "hardship," and "distress," as well as—in a metaphorical sense—of "sword." According to Acts 7:55–56, Stephen saw Christ standing at the right hand of God, an image that occurs in Rom 8:34. According to Acts 7:60, Stephen prayed that God would not condemn those who kill him, echoing the very message Paul conveys in this chapter of Romans. Paul is said to have assisted in the stoning of Stephen and to have approved it (Acts 8:1). If any historical credibility can be attributed to this passage in Acts, then the emotionally charged tone of Rom 8 may be explained by the memory of these events for which Paul was at least partially responsible. In this case, Paul himself was among those who experienced the divine forgiveness that Stephen had asked God to grant.

In another parallel between Rom 8:31–34 and Gen 22, Isaac and Christ appear as sons but are not spared by their respective fathers. Both Abraham and God willingly contend with imminent loss and subject the innocent to suffering. In the context of theological abstraction, it is appropriate to say God and Abraham were willing to sacrifice their sons, where sacrifice has a secularized metaphorical meaning. A carefully nuanced reading of Rom 8 must, however, stress that there is no term occurring in this chapter that captures the secularized metaphorical meaning in a single expression. Consonant with the reception history of Gen 22 that I have been tracing, Rom 8 is devoid of any cultic connotation of sacrifice.

Allusions to Gen 22 also occur in the pericopes of Jesus' baptism (Mark 1:9–11 par.) and transfiguration (Mark 9:2–8 par.). Both passages feature the father-son relationship in which the son is called "beloved" (ἀγαπητός), a characteristic attribute of Gen 22:2, 12, 16 (LXX), where this term is translated from the Hebrew word יחיד ("only").[42] The heavenly voice in these texts parallels that of the angel in Gen 22:11–12. Another key aspect of Gen 22 is picked up in the pericope of Jesus' temptation (Mark 1:12–13), which immediately follows the story of his baptism. This latter passage alludes to the Gen 22 theme that God's chosen people must undergo testing.

The allusions to Abraham's sacrifice in the Gospel according to Mark remain quite vague when compared to the clarity of such allusions in Philo's writings.[43] Philo describes Isaac as the son of God and the epitome of wisdom. In the New Testament, these attributes are applied exclusively to Jesus. The Judean tradition with its expansion of Isaac's role thus links New Testament christological concepts with Gen 22. The two passages of Jesus' baptism and transfiguration, however, lack any explicit references to the key aspects of Gen 22, either the threat imposed on the son's life or his sacrifice. Further references to the Aqedah do not occur in any of the New Testament passion narratives.

---

42. See Nahum M. Sarna, *Genesis* בראשית: *The Traditional Hebrew Text with New JPS Translation* (ed. N. M. Sarna; JPS Torah Commentary; Philadelphia: Jewish Publication Society, 1989–96), 151 ("your favored one"); Kundert, *Gen 22,1–19 im Alten Testament*, 35, 50–63.

43. Mark 1:11 is understood as an allusion to Gen 22 by, e.g., Vermes, *Scripture and Tradition in Judaism*, 222–23; Robert J. Daly, "The Soteriological Significance of the Sacrifice of Isaac," *CBQ* 39 (1977): 45–75; C. S. Mann, *Mark: A New Translation with Introduction and Commentary* (AB 27; New York: Doubleday, 1986), 199. Considerations for other Old Testament references include Ps 2:7 ("You are my son; today I have begotten you") and Isa 42:1 ("Here is my servant, whom I uphold, my chosen one in whom I delight; I will put my Spirit on him").

6. Epilogue: The Sacrifice of Jesus

This essay has examined Gen 22 and its reception history in early Judaism and Christianity as a case study to explore two different meanings of the term *sacrifice* and to show why the famous Aqedah plays only a marginal role in New Testament christological and soteriological concepts. At this point one might consider questions concerning the soteriological concept of Jesus' sacrifice. In the limited frame of this essay I can only hint at possible answers. The concept of Jesus' sacrifice is admittedly a well-established christological concept in the realm of theological abstraction. Its exegetical basis is, however, rather modestly attested. Jesus is compared to a cultic sacrifice (as defined above in section 2) only in Eph 5:2 and in Heb 7–10. In addition, the cultic image that humans can be purified and consecrated through contact with blood is found in the eucharistic passages as well as in Heb 12:24 and 1 Pet 1:2. Among these passages, Eph 5:2 is unique in that Jesus is said to have "given himself for us as an offering and sacrifice to God as a pleasing odor." I have shown elsewhere that the author of Ephesians uses priestly cult terminology to refer to the special quality of Jesus' ministry that is understood to please God like sacrifices offered to God.[44] The terms are not limited to Jesus' death but connote his entire life, including the moment of his death. Also, the author of Hebrews compares Jesus to a cultic sacrifice but attempts to focus on the significance of Jesus' death. In Heb 9:11–22, for example, the blood of Jesus purifies in a way analogous to various Hebrew Bible/Old Testament atonement rituals.[45]

With these exceptions, most New Testament passages used as warrants for atonement theories are not derived from Hebrew Bible/Old Testament cultic images. They emerge from a range of other (noncultic) backgrounds that, each from its individual perspective, illustrate the salvific death of Jesus. Hence each can be subsumed under the term *sacrifice,* which, as a secularized metaphorical interpretation, can signify the loss of life.[46]

---

44. Eberhart, *Studien zur Bedeutung der Opfer*, 394–98; idem, "Prüfung Abrahams," 42–44.

45. See Christian Eberhart, "Characteristics of Sacrificial Metaphors in Hebrews," in *Hebrews: Contemporary Methods—New Insights* (ed. G. Gelardini; BibInt 75; Leiden: Brill, 2005), 37–64.

46. I am grateful to Mark Kleiner for his assistance with the proofreading of this essay.

"Consider the Lilies of the Field...": A Sociorhetorical Analysis of Matthew 6:25–34

Lincoln E. Galloway

In Matt 6:25–34 we find one of Jesus' most famous speeches, where he seems to rebuke those listeners who are overwhelmed with concerns of daily living. Interpreters have generally claimed that this passage portrays faith as a complete reliance on the providential care of God that requires no concern for the necessities of life.[1] Such readings have led to scholarly incredulity that such a perspective could form the basis for Christian living. Some skeptical interpreters of the passage suggest that the speech reflects naïve economics, while others downplay its theological importance by highlighting the gap between the first-century world of the text and that of contemporary communities of faith.[2] In this latter case, the speech is dismissed as pertinent only to the first-century community and interpreted as providing eschatological instructions to live in the context of the imminent end of the age.[3]

This essay demonstrates that for an adequate theological interpretation the teachings of this text can neither be dismissed as historicist nor naïvely appropriated. The speech in Matt 6:25–34 is not a static reference point to be simply decoded but is a complex matrix of textures that can be read in historically responsible and theologically rich ways. I argue that a sociorhetorical

---

1. For a review of various perspectives and arguments, see Ulrich Luz, *Matthew 1–7: A Continental Commentary* (trans. W. C. Linss; Minneapolis: Fortress, 1992), 402–3, 409–12; Douglas R. A. Hare, *Matthew* (IBC; Louisville: Knox, 1993), 74.

2. Carlston evaluates the passage: "Nor are things much better if one probes what is really being said about money. One does not have to be an ideologue to consider what is said here about economics naïve: Can we not take money seriously as an economic issue without falling into self-satisfaction?" (Charles E. Carlston, "Matthew 6:24–34," *Int* 41 [1987]: 179).

3. Betz approaches the speech as an address to all humanity. See Hans D. Betz, *The Sermon on the Mount* (Hermeneia; Minneapolis: Fortress, 1995), 462. Jeremias sees the speech as addressed to the disciples exhorting them not to waste their time (cf. Mark 6:8). See Joachim Jeremias, *The Sermon on the Mount* (trans. N. Perrin; Philadelphia: Fortress, 1963).

analysis accesses the multiple layers of meaning and negotiates the tensions arising from the process of theological reflection upon the text.

Sociorhetorical criticism approaches a text as though it were a thickly textured tapestry that must be examined from different perspectives. This method allows the interpreter to bring the multiple textures of the text in view.[4] The three sections of this essay explore (1) the inner texture, (2) the intertexture, and (3) the ideological texture of the text.[5] I show that the layers converge around a radical theological challenge to a lifestyle characterized by acquisitiveness.

1. Inner Texture

Matthew 6:25–34 presents a distinct rhetorical unit within the context of Jesus' teachings in Matt 5–7. But its appeal to proper orientation toward God is already evident in the negative imperative of verse 19: "Do not store up for yourselves treasures on earth."[6] The text also shares the broader theme of Matthew's Gospel with its emphasis on creating a community that produces the fruit of the kingdom, in this case, righteousness.[7] In this section, I explore the inner texture of the passage. Vernon Robbins defines "inner texture" as follows: "Inner texture concerns relationships among word-phrase and narrational patterns that produce argumentative and aesthetic patterns in texts. These intermingling patterns are the context for the 'networks of significa- tion' in a text."[8] I describe the rhetorical unit in terms of (1) its repetitive and progressive patterns and (2) its aesthetic devices. The analysis in this section explores the language of the text, the speech's inner texture, by examining the patterns that provide the text with its unique capacity to communicate.

---

4. See Vernon K. Robbins, *The Tapestry of Early Christian Discourse: Rhetoric, Society and Ideology* (New York: Routledge, 1996), 18–20.

5. Sociorhetorical criticism looks at the text in terms of its inner texture, intertexture, social and cultural texture, ideological texture, and sacred texture. The approach to sociorhe- torical interpretation and the categories that are used in this essay are drawn from the work of Vernon K. Robbins, *Exploring the Texture of Texts: A Guide to Socio-rhetorical Interpretation* (Valley Forge, Pa.: Trinity Press International, 1996).

6. This reference and subsequent references to the Bible are taken from the NRSV.

7. Donald A. Hagner, "The *Sitz-im-Leben* of the Gospel of Matthew," in *Treasures New and Old: Contributions to Matthean Studies* (ed. D. R. Bauer and M. A. Powell; SBLSymS 1; Atlanta: Scholars Press, 1996), 31.

8. Robbins, *Tapestry of Early Christian Discourse*, 46.

1.1. Repetitive and Progressive Patterns

The speech's inner texture can be analyzed in terms of its repetitive and progressive patterns. In the columns below, I display words that occur several times in the passage. These multiple occurrences produce repetitive texture that in turn provides glimpses into the overall rhetorical movement and emphases of the passage.

Repetitive Patterns in Matthew 6:25–34

25	μεριμνᾶτε	μή	καί	τί
		μηδέ,		[τί]
		οὐχί		τί
26		οὖ	καί	
		οὐδέ		
		οὐδέ		
		οὐχ		
27	μεριμνῶν			
28	μεριμνᾶτε	οὖ	καί	τί
		οὐδέ		
29		οὐδέ		
30		οὖ	καί	
31	μεριμνήσητε	μή		τί
				τί
				τί
33			καί	
			καί	
34	μεριμνήσητε	μή		
	μεριμνήσει			

The table above highlights only four major groups of repeated terms. However, that is sufficient to reveal repetition as one of the most striking linguistic features of Matt 6:25–34. A distinct repetition is found with the term μέριμνα ("worry") that delineates the outer boundaries of the unit (Matt 6:25, 34). A repetitive pattern makes the concept of worrying the recurring theme of the passage. The passage underlines this theme with a relentless and overwhelming use of negatives (μή, μηδέ, οὖ, οὐδέ, οὐχ, οὐχί). Moreover, the negatives are combined with imperatives ("Do not worry..." Matt 6:25, 31, 34) that produce the effect of insisting on the futility of worrying.

Particles such as καὶ combine elements and move the speech forward. The presence of τί ("what/why") indicates the presence of questions, a rhetorical feature that I will examine in the next section. Apart from those mentioned above, the speech progresses through a repetition of a combination of expressions, topics, and conjunctions. For example, the expression λέγω ὑμῖν is combined with an imperative (6:25) and with a declarative (6:29), and the effect is a movement in the speech from things of minimum concern to those of ultimate value.[9] In the same way, negative conjunctions (μηδέ, οὐδέ) are used in lists that create contrasts to denounce particular strivings. For example, the phrases "they neither sow *nor* reap *nor* gather into barns" (6:26) and "they neither toil *nor* spin" (6:28) highlight current preoccupations within the Matthean community that are contrasted with God's activity. The use of "but" (δὲ) functions to guide these contrasts to a new awareness of God's providential care as the speech moves toward a conclusion: "*But* if God so clothes the grass of the field..." (6:30) and then finally to a radical alternative, "*But* strive first for the kingdom of God..." (6:33).

These contrasts move the hearer to a theological injunction. The speech moves from a mention of Solomon's clothing (6:29) to God's activity of clothing (6:30). In each case, through the use of πλεῖόν, μᾶλλον, and πολλῷ μᾶλλον, the speech suggests a hierarchy of values: "Is *not* life *more* than food...?" (6:25); in terms of the birds of the air: "Are you *not* of *more* value than they?" (6:26); and, finally, God's care is emphasized: "Will [God] *not much more* clothe you...?" (6:30). In each contrast, God's activity is highlighted by the text as the ultimate activity.

These contrasting images are deepened when the speech moves the hearer to understand that there are areas of human experience over which one has no control. No one can "add" to one's stature or lifespan; God is the only one who "adds" to the wonder of human life. The terms προσθεῖναι (6:27) and προστεθήσεται (6:33) nicely capture this theological insight. The speech's progression moves from the rhetorical question, "Who of you by worrying can add a single hour to his life?" to the response that all these things will be added to one as well. The question implicit in verse 27, "Who is able to add or who can add?" is answered by the strong declarative statement of verse 33: God is able, and God will add.

In addition to repetition and contrasts, the concluding part of the speech contains what may loosely be termed an exhortation. This concluding exhortation has its own boundaries marked by opening and closing imperatives:

---

9. Matthew uses the expression λέγω ὑμῖν to contrast a rejected practice with an alternative attitude. See Warren Carter, " 'Solomon in All His Glory': Intertextuality and Matthew 6:29," *JSNT* 65 (1997): 8.

μὴ οὖν μεριμνήσητε (6:31, 34). The exhortation is built on three assertions. The first claims that it is "the nations" (τὰ ἔθνη) who strive for these things; the second declares that "your heavenly Father knows that you need all these things"; and the third posits that "tomorrow will worry about itself." This final exhortation, with its three assertions, moves the hearer of the speech to contrast human dispositions and actions with those dispositions and actions aligned to God and righteousness. The speech's inner texture shows how the language moves toward this didactic goal and begins to gesture toward possibilities for theological meaning.

Not only in this final exhortation but also throughout the speech there are larger sequencing patterns that are made visible by inner textual analysis. For example, the broader narrational patterns are arranged with imperative, interrogative, and declarative statements. Although the speech is driven by imperatives, it moves rhythmically and revolves around a series of questions. This very strong emphasis and progression through the use of questions reflects George Kennedy's observation that questions function in ancient rhetoric to maintain audience contact.[10] In the case of Matt 6:25–34, the questions connect speaker to audience as they reveal the common sets of values assumed by the world of the text. The rhetorical questions in verses 26 and 30 are negatively formulated, suggesting that a positive answer is expected. "Are you not of more value than they?" (6:26). "Will [God] not much more clothe you...?" (6:30). These questions appeal to the collective wisdom and values of the hearers, affirming what they know and believe to be true and reliable. Life is understood to be of greater value than all other categories including food and clothing. One is invited to accept that God alone gives life, adds to life, or sustains life. The values associated with God's activity are therefore of much greater importance than food or clothing. Since changes to *the greater*, the more valuable (life or body), are not achieved by human effort (worrying), why should one entrust oneself to the values associated with *the lesser* enterprise or economic activity of procuring food or clothing?

Closely aligned with these questions that highlight commonly accepted values are three negatively formulated imperatives in verses 25, 31, and 34. Each imperative presents worrying as an undesirable state, something to be discouraged, effectively stating in each instance, "Do not worry." While the questions affirm and bring to light what is already accepted in the community, the imperatives emphasize this point further by drawing attention to

---

10. George A. Kennedy, *New Testament Interpretation through Rhetorical Criticism* (Chapel Hill: University of North Carolina Press), 29, 57.

the right rearrangement of priorities: "Look at the birds of the air..." (6:26); "Consider the lilies of the field..." (6:28); and "strive first for the kingdom of God..." (6:33). The interplay between the speech's interrogatives, imperatives, and declaratives allows the audience to recall its collective wisdom, to be reminded of its proper dispositions and behaviors, and finally to adopt values and practices consistent with striving for the kingdom of God.

We have seen how the speech as a unit progresses toward its didactic purpose through repetitions and the placement of imperatives, questions, and declaratives and how this structure moves the hearer to reflect critically on the theme of worrying and material acquisitiveness. The speech progresses through both linguistic elements and a number of themes, examples, and aphorisms. The theme of worrying frames the entire speech, first as a negative imperative in the introduction in verse 25, "Do not worry about your life, what you shall eat, what you shall drink, nor for your body," and in the conclusion in verse 34: Therefore do not worry; God knows what you need. This framing of the speech brings into sharp focus the central issue of the community's strivings. The authoritative voice that says, "Therefore, I tell you," is the voice that points the community to an alternative vision, in this case, the conviction that God is able to sustain the created order. The community is challenged to recognize that God who orders and sustains creation can add infinitely more to its life. The transition from birds to lilies is achieved by asking the critical question about the human capacity to add (προσθεῖναι), and this theological inquiry finds ultimate expression in the final exhortation: "Do not worry" (καὶ ταῦτα πάντα προστεθήσεται ὑμῖν).

Matthew offers a concise example in the middle of the speech that serves to contrast the clothing that God provides with the end product of human toiling and spinning. The example draws from the paradigm that represents for the hearers the best of human achieving, namely, the wisdom of Solomon. Solomon asked God for wisdom and understanding and as a consequence had glory and wealth "added" to him. Verse 33 contains the allusion: "all these things will be added [προστεθήσεται] to you." The reference to Solomon evokes positive images of wealth and notions of wisdom. Wealth or economic resources underlie the capacity to sustain life or to provide food and clothing, and wisdom is referenced by one's capacity to assign proper valuation to the place of human and divine activity in the realm of the created order.

The paradox, however, is that Solomon is used in this speech as a negative example.[11] Solomon is portrayed as the prototype because his glory (δόξα) is the *telos* that shapes the striving of those who worry about wealth

---

11. For a similar argument, see Carter, "Solomon in All His Glory," 3–25.

and achievement. This speech in Matthew's Gospel portrays such striving as a confusion of priorities. A corrective is necessary and is provided in the exhortation: "But strive first for the kingdom of God, and its righteousness, and all these things will be added [προστεθήσεται] to you" (6:33). Even Solomon's glory is ephemeral when compared to the one who gives glory to the lilies of the field. Once again, the theological challenge is highlighted by the text. Solomon is linked to ideals of human striving, namely, wealth and glory, to demonstrate the futility of anxiety and the striving for goods that have no permanence.

The allusions to collective wisdom as the speech moves from birds and lilies to the glory of Solomon are also evident in the use of the terms "today" and "tomorrow." These two terms are juxtaposed in verse 34 to capture the span of a single day. The phrase that the grass is "alive today and tomorrow is thrown into the oven" establishes an argument *a minori ad maius* with its own structuring and valuation of the created order that seeks affirmation in the response to the question: "Will [God] not much more clothe you, O you of little faith?" The declaration in verse 34, "tomorrow will worry about itself," is the final word of wisdom that again captures the theme of worrying and snatches it out of the realm of human striving.

1.2. AESTHETIC PATTERNS

The yield of a sociorhetorical analysis of Matthew is the way in which the language's inner texture moves the speech along and highlights specific theological themes. I now turn to the aesthetic patterns in the text and argue that the speech derives a certain aesthetic quality from the rhythm and balance that is achieved by the careful juxtaposition of certain questions, imperatives, and declaratives. A look at verse 25 reveals a particular organizational structure. The questions in the text are posed to complement each other. For example, "What you will eat…" is complemented by "what you will drink…." Similarly, "Is not life more than food…?" is balanced by "and the body more than clothing?"[12] So also the imperatives, "Look at the birds of the heaven," from the perspective of sowing, reaping, and gathering, and, "Consider the lilies of the field," from the perspective of growing, toiling, and spinning, provide an aurally pleasing rhythmic balance.

Aesthetic features of the speech evoke particular sensory responses or appeal to specific parts of the body. Bruce Malina's work integrating cultural

---

12. For a similar explanation of the organizational patterns of biblical text, see Bernard Brandon Scott and Margaret E. Dean, "A Sound Map of the Sermon on the Mount," in Bauer and Powell, *Treasures New and Old*, 345.

anthropology with New Testament studies is a provocative way to consider the text's affective capacity. In *The New Testament World: Insights from Cultural Anthropology* Malina proposes three zones of interaction: emotion-fused thought, self-expressive speech, and purposeful action.[13] An application of Malina's theory to Matt 6:25–34 can show that the appeals to the mouth by the questions, "What shall we eat, drink, or wear?" can be interpreted in terms of the zone of expressive speech. The speech also goads purposeful action through its use of terms such as "strive" (6:33). However, the overwhelming appeal is to the zone of emotion-fused thought. The hearer is directed to look at the birds, to consider the lilies, and told repeatedly not to worry. The appeal embodied in the speech is to the intellect, to right judgment, to wisdom, and to a right disposition. The aesthetic dimension of the speech thereby links bodily zones of interaction to ways of being-in-the-world: disposition, thinking, and action. The aesthetic dimension also reinforces the theological themes underlined by the speech's inner texture. Once again, the speech guides the hearers through its appeal to the will, mind, and heart to accept the collective wisdom and then to engage in purposeful action derived from a proper disposition toward righteousness.

2. Intertexture

The above exploration of the passage's inner texture focused on rhetorical-linguistic and aesthetics aspects in order to show how they function to enable the speech to challenge the disposition toward material acquisitiveness. I showed how an analysis of the inner texture tracks the movement of the speech to its theological focal point, in this case, a disposition toward God who sustains, adds, and orients all things to wisdom and practice of righteousness. I now introduce the category of "intertexture" as a way of exploring this passage's relationship to broader textual, cultural, and social contexts. This exploration of intertexture deepens the possibilities for highlighting and exhibiting the speech's theological meanings.

An analysis of the oral-scribal intertexture reveals how other texts are used in the passage through recitation, recontextualization, reconfiguration,

---

13. The zone of emotion-fused thought is concerned with words such as *eyes* or *heart* and related activities of these organs: to see, know, understand, love, and all the areas associated with intellect, mind, and wisdom. The zone of self-expressive speech deals with mouth and ears, the activities of speaking, instructing, questioning, or listening, and the areas of speech and communication. The zone of purposeful action deals with the feet, hands, or fingers, the actions of doing, acting or touching, and general areas of human behavior. See Bruce J. Malina, *The New Testament World: Insights from Cultural Anthropology* (rev. ed.; Atlanta: Knox, 1993), 60–64.

amplification, or elaboration.[14] In Matt 6:25–34 there are at first glance no explicit citations of other biblical texts. A reconstruction, however, indicates that a significant portion of the speech (with seemingly close recitation in 6:27, 29–30) originates in the Q material. A parallel teaching of wisdom and exhortation is found in Luke 12:22–32.[15] A comparative analysis between Matthew and Luke's use of the Q material highlights Matthew's literary artistry. Matthew's text, in my opinion, has greater aesthetic beauty and rhythm than Luke's text, and this is accomplished primarily through the use of poetic parallelism and other literary features. For example, only Matthew writes "or what you will drink" (ἢ τί πίητε) in the opening line (6:25).[16] This line anticipates and balances the triple expression, "What shall we eat?" or "What shall we drink?" or "What shall we wear?" (6:31). Luke mentions a specific bird, the raven, and refers to God as "your father," whereas Matthew reflects an intentional juxtaposition of more elaborated expressions: "the birds of the heavens" with "your heavenly father" (Matt 6:32) or a harmonizing of phrases "the lilies of the field" (cf. Luke 12:27: "the lilies") with "the grass of the field" (Matt 6:30).

While Matthew may be the more rhetorically elaborate text, the material in both Matthew and Luke reinforce the claim that this speech is meant as a direct challenge to a lifestyle marked by strivings. Both writers set this speech in the context of warnings against a particular orientation to wealth. Luke's passage follows the parable of the rich fool that ends with the indictment of those who "store up treasures for themselves but are not rich toward God" (Luke 12:21). Matthew's speech follows the injunction not to store up treasures on earth for oneself (Matt 6:19). There is no doubt that the challenge to the striving (Luke 12:29–30) that is endemic to the community is a key dimension of this speech in both contexts. Matthew elaborates on this theme by holding up an alternative striving that is marked by righteousness. He thereby gives the speech theological significance not only in worldly condemnations but in the demonstration of a viable theological alternative.

In terms of the speech's relation to biblical passages outside the New Testament canon, it is notable that the speech in Matthew shares certain affinities to wisdom literature. The most compelling affinity is found in the speech's conclusion. The concluding maxim echoes Prov 27:1: "Do not boast about tomorrow, for you do not know what a day may bring forth." The concluding imperative in Matthew's speech is articulated in similar terms: "Do not worry

---

14. Robbins, *Exploring the Texture of Texts*, 40.

15. John S. Kloppenborg, *Q Parallels: Synopsis, Critical Notes and Concordance* (Sonoma, Calif.: Polebridge, 1988).

16. ἢ τί πίητε is omitted from some of the ancient manuscripts.

about tomorrow, for tomorrow will worry about itself. Each day has enough trouble of its own" (Matt 6:34). Both maxims are formulated as negative injunctions against a certain preoccupation with tomorrow, and both embody a certain resolve to deal with tomorrow on its own terms.

Perhaps more subtly, an analysis of the speech's intertexture allows us to recognize the connections to the broader cultural background. Cultural intertexture appears in a text either through reference or allusion and echo.[17] For example, in verse 29 the speech gestures toward certain traditions about Solomon. Intertextuality cross-references Solomonic wisdom with Matthew's speech by the way in which Matthew associates Solomon with "all his glory." As indicated above, the traditions concerning Solomon generally assume the primacy of Solomon's wisdom followed by his wealth and glory.[18]

Matthew also appeals to wisdom tradition expressed in Ps 104. The reference to the "birds of the air" alludes to this psalm in order to underline the speech's portrayal of God as creator who cares for the created order. In the psalm, it is God who clothes the earth, provides for the birds of the air (104:12), and causes the grass to grow (104:14). All this lavished attention culminates in the ultimate declaration: "These all look to you, to give them their food in due season. When you give to them, they gather it up; when you open your hand, they are filled with good things" (104:27). Read against the backdrop of Ps 104, Matthew's references to birds of the air, lilies, and grass of the field proclaim the conviction that God has created and will sustain all living creatures.

Implicit images from the Hebrew Bible emerge elsewhere in Matthew's speech. For example, the phrase "grass of the field" draws on a broader cultural understanding that evokes images of transience and ephemerality. Persons who embody the temporal values of the culture "will soon fade like the grass," the psalmist writes (Ps 37:2). All of human life is "like grass ... in the morning it flourishes ... in the evening it fades and withers" (Ps 90:5). The same imagery is evoked in the speech of the prophet Isaiah: "All people are grass; their constancy is like the flower of the field. The grass withers, the flower fades, when the breath of the Lord blows upon it; surely the people are grass. The grass withers, the flower fades; but the word of our God will stand forever" (Isa 40:6–8).

The speech also seems to echo a particular cultural tradition that is marked by a negative perception of any preoccupation with a life of eating

---

17. Robbins, *Exploring the Texture of Texts*, 58.
18. For textual traditions concerning Solomon's wisdom, see 1 Kgs 4:29–30, 34. Solomon's wealth is mentioned to a lesser extent (1 Kgs 10:23), and his wealth is linked to glory. His request to God for wisdom is met with this response: "I give you also what you have not asked, both wealth and glory" (1 Kgs 3:13).

and drinking, characterized by the slogan: "Let us eat and drink, for tomorrow we die" (Isa 22:13). This opposition to inappropriate and negative behavior is reflected in the call to righteousness rather than by the preoccupation with such concerns as "What shall we eat?" or "What shall we drink" or "What shall we wear?"(Matt 6:31). The cultural values that are reinforced reflect a high valuation of both the uniqueness of human life in the created order and the permanence of divine activity and righteousness as compared to the ephemeral nature of human striving, glory, and achievement.

So far in this section I have analyzed the oral-scribal and cultural inter-texture of this speech and demonstrated the role of sociorhetorical analysis in unfolding different layers of a text that reveal how the text gestures toward theological meaning. A further step in my analysis is to look at the cultural world and social realities that are reflected in the text. The cultural world of Matt 6:25–34 represents an agriculturally based economic enterprise that is marked by activities such as sowing, reaping, and gathering into barns (6:26). Even the indoor tasks are suggestive of an agrarian society, and the reference to those who spin (6:28) indicates the production of fabric and the manu-facturing of clothing. The "storing in barns" also suggests an enterprise on a large scale, one that moves beyond household requirements to activity within the wider market of goods and services.

The social intertexture can provide insights into the social roles, institu-tions, codes, and relationships that characterize the community. The roles of both father and king in view of the human household are reflected in the speech, and they would have resonated with the hearers. The primary role that emerges in this text for God is that of (heavenly) father whose household is the created order. The social role of king is evoked by the reference to Solo-mon, who is also a sage (man of wisdom) and a man of wealth and glory. The image of a king, in this case the reign of God, provides the background for understanding "the kingdom of God," which unlike any human institution is characterized by righteousness and is God's to give.

Matthew's text does not reflect a social world organized around patron-client relationships in which benefits accrue from one party to the other. Instead, we observe familial language ("your heavenly father") blended with notions of creator and king to call forth trust and loyalty. Jerome Neyrey introduces another social dimension by exploring how the text reflects spe-cific aspects of the honor-shame world of antiquity.[19] Neyrey approaches Matt 6:25–34 from the perspective of an exhortation that thematizes the

---

19. Jerome H. Neyrey, *Honor and Shame in the Gospel of Matthew* (Louisville: Westmin-ster John Knox, 1998), 176–77.

loss of wealth among peasants. He assumes that the peasants in Matthew are dealing with a loss of honor. I see in Matthew, however, a community striving for economic wealth and glory whose members struggle with the fear of loss of honor if their economic enterprise does not flourish and bring them glory. I argue that this speech is to be interpreted in light of the social, economic, and cultural dimensions reflected in the world of the text. A view of the social world of the text restrains us from resignation to theological interpretations that are expressed in terms of generalized anxiety over the human condition.

3. Ideological Texture

My final category of sociorhetorical analysis addresses the ideological texture of the speech and pays attention to the commonly held values and interests of particular groups in the text as well as those who interpret the text. In terms of the ideal community described in Matt 6:25–34, we see that the vision for the community is a universal one; all ideals are expressed in light of the fatherhood of God, who exercises governance, care, and oversight over all creation. Even the nations (τὰ ἔθνη) who do not strive for the kingdom and who do not attain its righteousness are not excluded from the fatherhood of God. This theological claim is consistent with other passages in Matthew in which universalism is maintained: "But I say to you, love your enemies and pray for those who persecute you, so that you may be children of your Father in heaven; for he makes his sun rise on the evil and on the good, and sends rain on the righteous and on the unrighteous" (Matt 5:44–45). Such a span of care can only bring into view the fatherhood of God over an inclusive and universal community.

Sjef van Tilborg has observed that some scholars have too readily assumed that the mention of basic needs of food, drink, and clothing in this community indicate a concern with survival. While he accepts that the Sermon on the Mount may have given a voice to persons who would have otherwise remained unheard, he points out that this Matthean community is not economically marginalized.[20] Instead, as I argued earlier, the community is marked by agrarian economic activity that includes trade and ownership of fields. Here I agree with van Tilborg that a community is evoked in this text that generates surplus and gathers into barns, strives for the glory of Solomon,

---

20. Sjef van Tilborg, *The Sermon on the Mount as an Ideological Intervention* (Assen: Van Gorcum, 1986), 5.

and embodies the ruling ideology that places value on striving for wealth and glory rather than on righteousness or justice.

The ideological objective in this speech is to shift the allegiance of the community away from the folly and futility of human striving to values of the kingdom of God and its righteousness. Through its didactic features and its appeal to collective wisdom, and social and cultural norms, the speech points to what is of ultimate value. The community's preoccupation with "adding" to their lives ignores the traditions that recall Solomon as one who *first* sought wisdom and understanding from God and subsequently had wealth and glory "added." Matthew's community needs to be reminded that the kind of glory for which it strives is transient and cannot be compared with the glory that God gives. Rather than striving for fleeting glory, the community is instructed to strive *first* for God's kingdom; then all these things will be "added." The message is to give glory to God, who alone can "add" to human life in every aspect or dimension. This is the axis on which the ideological shift is to take place.

In terms of contemporary communities of interpretation, an examination of ideology recognizes that each interpreter is located within an intellectual discourse that is shaped by one's own symbolic universe, social location, and worldview. In this case, interpreters who have particular audiences in view may seek to respond to audience concerns or discomforts about the teaching of this passage. Are interpreters and their audiences challenged by the theological claims they ascribe to this text? Do readers in a capitalist society need to be assured that the text does not demean or dismiss hard work, energy, and inventiveness? Should the text be bypassed as having no relevance for contemporary readers because it has an eschatological emphasis that calls people to live as if the end were pending?[21] Such interpretative moves may demonstrate discomfort on the part of the reader with the message of this text, leading to a domestication of its theological power. Tensions raised in questions such as these highlight the need for theological interpretation that is informed by the multiple layers of a text and derived from an exploration of the rich textures of a biblical text.

Duncan M. Derrett, for example, reviews different approaches to this passage. Two broad negative concerns are evident.[22] In the first instance, there are those who interpret the injunctions in this speech from an eschatological perspective that enjoins the community to leave behind all material or economic enterprises and to rely exclusively on God's providential care. A second line

---

21. Cf. 1 Cor 7:25–35, esp. v. 32a: "I want you to be free from worry."

22. Duncan M. Derrett, "Birds of the Air and Lilies of the Field," in *The Sea-Change of the Old Testament in the New* (vol. 5 of idem, *Studies in the New Testament*; Leiden: Brill, 1989), 24–35.

of interpretation is developed along economic lines to suggest how impractical or naïve it would be to interpret the passage as a call away from economic activity. The assumption underlying both approaches is that there is a utopian response embedded in the text that cannot be translated into real life. Such an interpretation seeks to subvert the text and produce a new understanding that has some chance of being accepted as closer to reality, more measurable in its pragmatism, and therefore more achievable as a response. These concerns regarding pragmatism or human survival find expression in the work of Andreij Kodjak:

> Thus, humanity appears to be meant to live in what would normally be called poverty with only the basic sustenance as "the birds of the air" and "the lilies of the field" have. On the other hand, one can assume that the Speaker regards affluence as an abnormality or disease, and therefore, as frightening as poverty is usually perceived to be. Thus, in the Speaker's *Weltanschauung* we can discern a total reversal of commonly accepted economics.[23]

Kodjak's work is preoccupied with the challenge to economic survival and misses the call to justice. He misunderstands the striving that the text warns against and consequently lends his theological voice to provide solace to the ideology of the contemporary status quo that wants affluence to be affirmed. This approach heightens the gap between the *Weltanschauung* of the text and that of contemporary theological interpretation in a way that diminishes the ethical and theological power of the text.

These interpretative postures seem to be derived from ideological standpoints that posit a conflict between the text and contemporary realities. Both those who posit an eschatological framework that is no longer pervasive and those who see a naïve economic mandate that has to be countered with good sense and pragmatism find the text to be somewhat unsettling and lacking in application to modern times. Their response to the speech in their respective interpretations represents ideological subversion. Such responses are possible because interpreters avoid the multiple engagements that are necessary to appreciate cultural and social aspects of the community behind the text and the theological warrants that become evident in attending to the linguistic patterns.

In the sociorhetorical approach to this text its countercultural or utopian aspects cannot be stripped away and its challenge cannot be historicized. The

---

23. Andreij Kodjak, *A Structural Analysis of the Sermon on the Mount* (Religion and Reason 34; Berlin: de Gruyter, 1986), 134.

speech (with its authoritative voice: "therefore, I say to you") challenges all communities both historical and contemporary whose values are not primarily driven by a striving for righteousness. It speaks to all communities that are marked by acquisitiveness and all who strive for glory and achievement in the human realm. In exploring the inner texture and the embedded cultural and social dimensions, it becomes evident that the text through its multiple layers resists theological interpretation that is derived from surface readings that lead to its marginalization and subversion.

4. Conclusion

I have shown in this essay that theological approaches to biblical texts must resist dismissive historicism, on the one hand, and naïve translation into the contemporary theological worlds, on the other. To do theology from biblical texts is to immerse oneself in complex debates at the linguistic, cultural, and historical levels. An engagement with biblical texts requires one to pay attention to their complexity and to resist any attempt theologically to smooth the difficulties away. In the case of Matt 6:25–34, a sociorhetorical approach can move beyond a description of multiplicity and gesture toward responsible theological prescription.

Multiple engagements with the layers of a text and its world can give rise to theological theory. I have attempted to illustrate this point by showing how the speech according to an analysis of its inner texture presents the theme of human striving and preoccupation juxtaposed with a disposition rightly ordered toward God and righteousness. I also explored the intertextual level, hearing echoes of other biblical texts in the passage in order to attend to the images or themes that are used. In this regard, the echoes of the wisdom traditions of the Hebrew Bible serve to highlight common understandings of the ephemeral nature of human striving and witness to God's universal providence over the created order. Furthermore, I drew attention to other textual layers for a cultural and social reading. The speech does not diminish concerns for daily living but urges hearers to realign their priorities from a human-centered disposition characterized by acquisitiveness and glory to a God-centered disposition that bears fruits in actions of righteousness.

Finally, I argued that a biblical analysis must also engage the reader at the ideological level. In terms of the world of the text, the speech directs the hearers to affirm particular values and to recognize certain cherished aspirations in order to challenge the community to shift its allegiances to the values of their heavenly father and the righteousness associated with the kingdom of God. The text should not be domesticated by contemporary theological interpretation but should be read as a challenge to change loyalty and behavior and to strive for God's righteousness. By using many rhetorical and didactic strategies, Matthew's speech directs its hearers, past and present, to focus on the God who alone sustains the universe and adds meaningfully to human life.

Luke-Acts and Negotiation of Authority and Identity in the Roman World

Gary Gilbert

1. Introduction

In the film *The Life of Brian*, Reg, leader of the People's Front of Judea, gathers together a small band of commandos to plot the kidnapping of Pilate's wife, whom they will hold as ransom against their demands, namely, "to dismantle the entire apparatus of the Roman imperialist state" and to "rid this country of the Romans once and for all." He inspires his fellow revolutionaries by recounting the oppression they have suffered at the hands of the Romans, "They've bled us white, the bastards. They've taken everything we had, not just from us, from our fathers and from our fathers' fathers." Rome's venality is compounded by its failure to contribute anything of value to the well-being of Judea. "And what," he asks, "have they ever given us in return?" To the question, which Reg assuredly believes has no affirmative answer, one member of the group meekly responds, "the aqueduct." Reg begrudgingly acknowledges this singular example. Instead of the exception, however, mention of the technological advance prompts other commandos to unleash a litany of Roman benefaction: sanitation, roads, irrigation, medicine, education, health, wine, baths, public order, and peace.[1]

Monty Python developed this comedic bit as a piece of social commentary. John Cleese, who was responsible for most of the dialogue, described the scene as a commentary on self-aggrandizing political parties, which were quite prominent in Britain during the 1970s, the misguided idealism and dogmatic bureaucracy, and the incessant and paralyzing bickering that goes on at group meetings. For the peoples living in the time, however, Roman domination was no joke. The creation of the *imperium Romanum*, exhibited through

---

1. Graham Chapman et al., *Monty Python's The Life of Brian (of Nazareth)* (London: Eyre Methuen, 1979), 20–21.

its political and judicial authority and military power, could not be ignored. Like the fictional commandos of Monty Python, the actual residents of the new Roman provinces and client kingdoms expressed their own opinions of Rome and its claims to rule them, their lands, and the whole world. Some developed a genuine appreciation for Rome and its leaders. Others, however, despaired of Rome's presence and in extreme instances sought to restore their liberty through armed revolt. Whatever the attitude, Rome's claim to be ruler of the inhabited world could not be ignored, and invited and in some instances demanded a response.

2. MULTIVALENCE AND CHRISTIAN VIEWS ON ROMAN AUTHORITY AND CHRISTIAN IDENTITY

Like other subordinate groups of the time, early Christians confronted both the rhetoric and reality of Rome and, like their contemporaries, responded in different ways. The diversity of Christian reactions to Rome became inscribed into the New Testament itself. Here one finds not only differing but competing voices. In his Letter to the Romans, Paul instructs his readers that every person should be subject to the governing authorities (Rom 13:1). While the Greek word *exousia*, here translated as "governing authorities," has sometimes been understood as a reference to angelic powers, Paul almost certainly has in mind human authorities in the form of imperial and civic officials.[2] Paul enjoins his readers to accept the existence of Roman authority because Rome's authority has been given to it by God. "Therefore whoever resists authority resists what God has appointed, and those who resist will incur judgment" (Rom 13:2).[3] Paul shares a generally recognized political philosophy of the day based on divine right; earthly rulers derive their power and authority from divine beings. A very different appreciation of Rome comes from the book of Revelation. In these visions, Rome, represented through a dense network of mythological images, holds authority over the entire world and makes war on the saints (Rev 13:6–7), whose blood the Whore of Babylon drinks with great abandon (17:6). The call from the author is for endurance against evil rather than acceptance (13:10; 14:12). Resistance, even unto death as a martyr, is only appropriate since the source of Rome's power is not God, but the devil.

Nowhere in the New Testament does Rome figure more prominently than in the Gospel of Luke and Acts of the Apostles. Luke-Acts presents not

---

2. Joseph A. Fitzmyer, *Romans* (AB 33; New York: Doubleday, 1992), 662–64.

3. Translations of biblical texts are taken from the NRSV; translations of Josephus, Philo, and classical Greek and Latin texts are from the respective Loeb editions.

only the New Testament's most extended presentation of Rome but even within itself a multifaceted reflection on Roman power and its implications for Christian identity. Read within the context of the New Testament, Luke-Acts presents a story about God and God's actions in history through the characters of Jesus and the apostles. From one perspective, the text's view of Rome can be epitomized by the Roman citizenship enjoyed by Paul. As the exemplar apostle and Christian, Paul neither seeks to disturb the *pax Romana* nor sees his identity as a Roman in conflict with his mission as an apostle and life within the community of other Christians. When placed within the larger literary and political context, however, we hear a very different voice. At the same time, Luke-Acts offers the careful reader another view of Rome and Christian identity. When the text is read alongside and over against the contemporary competing discourses of power, one can hear a more critical, even subversive tone in the narratorial voice. It is this second voice that I wish to explore in this essay.

References to Rome and its agents are woven throughout the narrative, from the mentions of the emperors Augustus and Tiberius in the early chapters of the Gospel (Luke 2:1; 3:1), Cornelius, the Roman centurion converted by Peter (Acts 10), the proconsuls Sergius Paulus (Acts 13) and Gallio (Acts 18), procurators of Judea Felix and Festus (Acts 24–26), to the conclusion of the work set in the city of Rome itself (Acts 28). Critical scholarship has long tried to account for the frequent appearances of Roman figures. An early perspective held that Luke-Acts was written to cement a positive relation between Christians and the Roman Empire. Luke's particular rendering of Jesus' life and his account of the activities of the early apostles served as an *apologia pro ecclesia*, a defense of Christianity against charges brought by Roman officials and an attempt to present Christians and Christianity as harmless and supportive of or at least neutral toward imperial rule.[4] Luke-Acts, in this view, was addressed to a Roman audience, portraying Christians as law-abiding and loyal in contrast to the rabble-rousing Jews, and attempted to "achieve a permanent settlement" between the church and the state.[5] Recent scholarship has largely rejected this position.[6] C. K. Barrett offered perhaps the most

---

4. One version of this position understands Luke-Acts as advocating that Christianity be considered a *religio licita*, a legally sanctioned religious community. For the literature on both sides of the argument, see Robert Maddox, *The Purpose of Luke-Acts* (Studies in the New Testament World; Edinburgh: T&T Clark, 1982), 91–93; Philip F. Esler, *Community and Gospel in Luke-Acts* (SNTSMS 57; Cambridge: Cambridge University Press, 1987), 205–7, 211–14.

5. Hans Conzelmann, *The Theology of St. Luke* (trans. G. Buswell; Philadelphia: Fortress, 1961), 138–49; the quotation appears on 138.

6. Richard J. Cassidy, *Jesus, Politics, and Society* (Maryknoll, N.Y.: Orbis, 1978), 128–30.

powerful and succinct rejoinder in noting that "no Roman official would ever have filtered out so much of what to him would be theological and ecclesiastical rubbish in order to reach so tiny a grain of relevant apology."[7]

Unable to refute Barrett's trenchant observation, scholars have largely abandoned any understanding that posits Luke-Acts speaking to Romans out of a desire to secure their favor. Nonetheless, most new approaches have retained the basic understanding that Luke-Acts presents Christians and Christianity in a way that is essentially compatible with Roman rule. Robert Maddox, for instance, concludes that Luke possesses "an optimistic view of the imperial government.... The proper business of Christians is to live at peace with the sovereign power, so far as possible, and not to play the hero."[8] Paul Walaskay reverses the apologetic gaze in suggesting that Luke-Acts was written as an *apologia pro imperio,* addressed to Christians in order to defend the Roman government and its attitudes and actions toward Christianity.[9] Luke-Acts emphasizes "the positive aspects of Roman involvement in the history of the church."[10] In so doing Luke hoped that his work would help "the Christian community live effectively with the social, political, and religious realities of the present situation until the advent of God's reign."[11] Philip Esler, while preferring the terminology of legitimation to apology, also proposes that Luke-Acts presents Christianity as being "no threat to Rome nor to the order and stability so prized by the Romans."[12]

The revised position has much to recommend it. Luke-Acts, in contrast to Revelation, does not envision the destruction of Rome, nor does it present Christianity as a threat to Roman society. It does not necessarily follow, however, that a generally harmonious depiction of relations between Christians and Romans implies approval of Rome's imperial claims. Recent analysis of the relations between dominant and subordinate cultures has shown that the absence of active resistance, physical or verbal, on the part of a subordinate group does not thereby convey acceptance or acquiescence to a dominant power. Rather, subordinate groups often develop arts of resistance that are

---

7. C. K. Barrett, *Luke the Historian in Recent Research* (London: Epworth, 1961), 63. For a more detailed refutation of the theory, see Paul Walaskay, *"And So We Came to Rome": The Political Perspectives of St. Luke* (SNTSMS 49; Cambridge: Cambridge University Press, 1983), 15–37.

8. Maddox, *Purpose of Luke-Acts,* 97.

9. Walaskay, *"And So We Came to Rome,"* 64–67.

10. Ibid., 64.

11. Ibid., 67.

12. Esler, *Community and Gospel in Luke-Acts,* 218.

more subtle and nuanced but no less real.[13] This modern understanding of power and resistance can help us to recognize the highly critical attitude toward Rome articulated through Luke-Acts. Luke's experience of Roman imperial power was refracted through the prism of his understanding of Jesus' life, death, and resurrection. From Luke's perspective, these events gave evidence for the existence of a new reality that calls into question the legitimacy of Rome and its claims to imperial authority. By contesting Rome's claims, transposing Roman expressions of authority to Jesus and the early church, and offering alternative models of world rule, Luke-Acts creates a counter-discourse that responds to and resists Roman imperial authority and, in so doing, seeks to constitute an understanding of being a Christian in the Roman world. In the next section I turn to contemporary Greek literature to show how Luke-Acts engages in the process of political contestation and identity formation by rewriting and restructuring a prior ideological subtext, the *imperium Romanum*.

3. The Voice of Roman Power

Whether by design or fortuitous circumstance, Rome's power spread quickly through the eastern Mediterranean basin.[14] Military victories against Macedonian and Seleucid rulers in the first half of the second century B.C.E. elevated Rome in the eyes of many to the position of undisputed master of the world. The recognition became mutual among ruler and ruled alike. During the second and first centuries B.C.E. the concept of *imperium* grew from the limited authority vested in an individual magistrate to the general authority of the state. By the late Republic, the Roman historian Sallust could speak of the *imperium Romanum* (*Bell. Cat.* 10.1). Not only had the nature of Roman power changed, but also its geographic scope. Roman *imperium* came to be understood as universal, encompassing all peoples and stretching as far as the ends of the earth. The first-century B.C.E. rhetorical treatise *Rhetorica ad Herennium* speaks of Rome and its "rule of the world, the rule to which all nations kings and peoples have consented, partly compelled by force and partly of their own will, having been overcome by the arms of the Roman people or by its liberality" (4.13). Cicero, once thought to have been the author of the preceding text, speaks of the *imperium* of the Roman people

---

13. James Scott, *Domination and the Arts of Resistance* (New Haven: Yale University Press, 1990).

14. William Harris, *War and Imperialism in Republican Rome: 327–70 BC* (Oxford: Oxford University Press, 1979); Erich Gruen, *The Hellenistic World and the Coming of Rome* (Berkeley and Los Angeles: University of California Press, 1984).

extending throughout the entire *orbis terrarum* (*Sest.* 67, 129; *Balb.* 9, 16; *Dom.* 110; *Pis.* 16).[15] Pompey's military victories in Syria and elsewhere made real this perspective (Pliny the Elder, *Nat.* 37.13; Plutarch, *Pomp.* 45; Appianus, *Mith.* 116–117). He extended the frontiers of Roman authority to the end of the earth and validated Rome's status as the true masters of all the peoples and all the nations on earth and sea (Cicero, *Leg. man.* 56; cf. Diodorus Siculus 40.4; Pliny the Elder, *Nat.* 7.97).

Affirmations and displays of Rome's supremacy intensified with the inception of the empire. Augustan literature, particularly its poetry, played a large role in shaping and articulating the claim of universal domination as Rome's inherent destiny. Vergil's *Aeneid*, the "national epic of Augustan Rome,"[16] represents a *locus classicus* for this perspective. Near the opening Jupiter utters his famous prophecy that Rome will possess an empire without end (*imperium sine fine*).[17] Later in the poem Aeneas travels to the underworld, where his guide, his recently deceased father Anchises, describes the numerous territories that Augustus will acquire. So vast is the space that Hercules himself had never crossed it (*Aen.* 6.791–803). Universal *imperium* was not only a political or military achievement but a cultural one as well, akin to the artistic grandeur of Greece (*Aen.* 6.851–852). Horace, another favorite of Augustus, frequently celebrates the achievements of the *princeps* and lauds him as "father of the human race" (*Carm.* 1.12.49–52; 4.15). Even Ovid, whose own attitude toward the emperor is at best elusive and quite possibly critical of many Augustan policies, could speak of Rome as having placed the entire world under its foot (*Fast.* 4.857–858; also 1.85–86) and could extol Augustus as "father of the world" (*Fast.* 2.130).[18] Writers of prose also celebrated Rome as universal ruler. Livy claims it was Rome's destiny to be head of the world (1.16.7). Vitruvius begins his architectural study by praising Augustus's vic-

---

15. On the term *imperium* itself, see J. S. Richardson, "*Imperium Romanum*: Empire and the Language of Power," *JRS* 81 (1991): 1–9.

16. Francis Cairns, *Virgil's Augustan Epic* (Cambridge: Cambridge University Press, 1989), 105. Cairns goes on to describe the poem as "embodying the aspirations, the pride and the self-image of the rulers of the world."

17. Vergil, *Aen.* 1.278–279. Jupiter is responding to Venus's reminder that he had promised that Aeneas's descendants would come to rule the sea and all the land (*Aen.* 1.234–237). The prophecy is repeated in 4.229–231 and again by Anchises when Aeneas journeys to the underworld (*Aen.* 6.782, 792–797, 851), both to and by Latinus (*Aen.* 7.99–101; 7.258), and through *ekphrasis* in the description of Aeneas's shield (*Aen.* 8.626–728).

18. For more on Ovid's political leanings, see S. G. Nugent, "*Tristia* 2: Ovid and Augustus," in *Between Republic and Empire* (ed. K. Raaflaub and M. Toher; Berkeley and Los Angeles: University of California Press, 1990), 239–57.

tory at Actium and by declaring that he has acquired control over the *orbis terrarum* (*De arch.* 1, preface 1).

The people who became subordinated to Roman rule often echoed Rome's claims and, at least in the late Republic and early empire, expressed favor and support for the newest and most powerful imperial claimant. The earliest sustained treatment of Rome by a Greek comes in Polybius's histories. Polybius was born in Megalopolis in Arcadia (Greece) and served as leader of the Achaean League. The League became embroiled in Roman conflicts with Macedonia, and, in 167 B.C.E., following Rome's victory over the Macedonian king Perseus at the battle of Pydna, Polybius was taken off to Rome, where he lived for almost two decades under the patronage of leading Romans. In light of Rome's subsequent dismantling of the League and the end of Achaean independence in 146 B.C.E., Polybius acknowledged Rome's unrivaled power and its status as ruler of the world, *oikoumene* (1.1.5; 3.1.4–5; 3.4.2; 6.2.3).[19] Over a century later, toward the end of the reign of Augustus, Strabo, historian and geographer from Pontus in Asia Minor, expressed great admiration for Rome and for the peace, security, and prosperity that Roman rule had accomplished (1.1.16; 6.4.2). He gives an "account of the whole world known to the Romans," that both reflected and contributed toward the voice of Roman imperialism.[20]

Around the same time a third Greek author, Dionysius of Harlicarnassus, a Greek city also in western Asia Minor, offered unequivocal recognition of Rome as destined for uncontested rule (1.2.1; 1.3.3–5). In contrast to empires of earlier eras, Assyria, Athens, Macedonia among them, Rome far surpasses them all (1.3.2–3). In focusing his writing on the early history of Rome, Dionysius wishes to correct a common "misunderstanding" among Greeks and to show that Rome was founded as a Greek colony and therefore is essentially a Greek and not a barbarian city. Dionysius's unique treatment of Rome can be understood in different ways. He may be attempting to demonstrate the solidarity of Greek and Roman society and to offer his fellow Greeks a perspective of Rome that will allow them to accept Roman supremacy not as a foreign power but as an essentially Greek one. Alternatively, he may be attempting to lessen any anxiety among his Greek readers despondent over their loss of autonomy by suggesting that, despite appearances, Greeks remain in power, albeit in the form of Rome, the best of the Greeks (20.6). In either case, Dionysius shows how Greek writers confronted

19. J. S. Richardson, "Polybius' View of the Roman Empire," *Papers of the British School at Rome* 47 (1979): 1–2; P. S. Derow, "Polybius, Rome, and the East," *JRS* 69 (1979): 1–15.

20. Katherine Clarke, *Between Geography and History: Hellenistic Constructions of the Roman World* (Oxford: Oxford University Press, 2000), 344.

the reality of Roman *imperium* and devoted their literary work to an exploration of the relation between Roman authority and the Greek world. Not all Greeks shared Dionysius's generally favorable assessment of Rome. In the next section I focus on a well-known cadre of Greeks who negotiated their relation with Rome largely through the heritage of the Greek past. This strategy allowed Greek writers, and here I will include the author of Luke-Acts, to expose and in some instances to contest Rome's hegemonic discourse and, although conscious of being in a position of political subordination, to project for themselves an authentic identity independent of Rome and its networks of domination.

4. Luke-Acts and the Second Sophistic

By the time of the writing of Luke-Acts, a new intellectual and literary movement had emerged among Greek elites who shared similarities in language, cultural outlook, and, most important for this study, an interest in Rome. These Greek-speaking intellectuals, mostly from the eastern Mediterranean regions, often used their literary efforts to reflect on Roman power and its significance for understanding Greek identity. Many of these figures, such as Plutarch, Dio Chrysostom, and Pausanias, developed similar linguistic, rhetorical, and cultural patterns commonly referred to in modern scholarship as the Second Sophistic, which emerged toward the end of the first century and continued well into the third.[21] Those who traveled in these circles were generally elite, well-educated men who wrote in Greek, hailed from Greece, western Asia Minor, and other regions of the eastern Mediterranean, traveled widely, and experienced Roman power firsthand. Their professional lives were marked by a variety of civic and professional functions, including priest, civic magistrate, imperial official, orator, philosopher, and physician. Luke, the author of Luke-Acts, shares some of these same characteristics with those of

---

21. Glen Bowersock, *Greek Sophists in the Roman Empire* (Oxford: Oxford University Press, 1969); E. L. Bowie, *Greeks and Their Past in Second Sophistic: Studies in Ancient Society* (ed. M. I. Finley; Past and Present Series; London: Routledge & Kegan Paul, 1974), 166–209; Graham Anderson, *The Second Sophistic: A Cultural Phenomenon in the Roman Empire* (London: Routledge, 1993); Maud Gleason, *Making Men: Sophists and Self-Perception in Ancient Rome* (Princeton: Princeton University Press, 1995); Simon Swain, *Hellenism and Empire: Language, Classicism, and Power in the Greek World, AD 50–250* (Oxford: Oxford University Press, 1996); Tim Whitmarsh, *Greek Literature and the Roman Empire: The Politics of Imitation* (Oxford: Oxford University Press, 2001); Simon Goldhill, ed., *Being Greek under Rome: Cultural Identity, the Second Sophistic and the Development of Empire* (Cambridge: Cambridge University Press, 2001).

the Second Sophistic.[22] Like them, Luke was a well-educated Greek speaker, most likely from a city in the eastern Mediterranean, who wrote at the end of the first or beginning of the second centuries, a time by which the Second Sophistic has become well developed. The writings of the Second Sophistic as well as Luke-Acts frequently speak of Rome and address the relation between Roman *imperium*, here understood as the power exercised by or on behalf of the Roman emperor, and the subordinate cultures of Greece or Christianity, respectively. I wish to argue that the similarities between Luke-Acts and the Second Sophistic, however, go much deeper. Like much of the literature of the Second Sophistic, Luke-Acts contains within it a voice that is critical of the presence of Rome and contests its claim to be ruler of the world. This voice is embedded in the language used to characterize Jesus and the church and exists alongside another voice that speaks in more conciliatory tones. Only by listening to both voices can we gain a full appreciation for what Luke-Acts wishes to say about the relations between dominant Rome and the subordinate community of those now called Christians (cf. Acts 11:26).

Before I turn to the relevant literature, I want to be clear what it is I am not claiming in making this argument. First, I am not claiming Luke-Acts should be thought of as representative of Second Sophistic literature. The differences in language alone foreclose this identification.[23] Second, this analysis is not dependent upon and makes no claim upon the complex and unsettled question over the genre of the Gospel and Acts. Rather than trying to squeeze Luke-Acts into a particular literary box, I am more interested in placing it within the broader intellectual milieu of the time. One final methodological issue requires mention. Because my interest rests with reflections and repre-

---

22. On comparisons between the Second Sophistic and other early Christian writings, see Timothy D. Barnes, *Tertullian: A Historical and Literary Study* (Oxford: Oxford University Press, 1971); Timothy Horner, *Listening to Trypho: Justin Martyr's Dialogue Reconsidered* (Contributions to Biblical Exegesis and Theology 28; Leuven: Peeters, 2001), 73–84; Laura Nasrallah, "Mapping the World: Justin, Tatian, Lucian, and the Second Sophistic," *HTR* 98 (2005): 293–98. Recent studies have made productive comparisons between Luke-Acts and Plutarch, although not specifically within the context of the Second Sophistic; see Vernon K. Robbins, "Writing as a Rhetorical Act in Plutarch and the Gospels," in *Persuasive Artistry: Studies in New Testament Rhetoric in Honor of George A. Kennedy* (ed. D. F. Watson; JSNTSup 50; Sheffield: Sheffield Academic Press, 1991), 142–68; David L. Balch, "ΜΕΤΑΒΟΛΗ ΠΟΛΙΤΕΙΩΝ: Jesus as Founder of the Church in Luke-Acts: Form and Function," in *Contextualizing Acts: Lukan Narrative and Greco-Roman Discourse* (ed. T. Penner and C. Vander Stichele; SBLSymS 20; Atlanta: Society of Biblical Literature, 2004), 139–88.

23. The Second Sophistic often retained Greek names for regions now converted into Roman provinces and used old Greek rather than contemporary Latin names of cities. Luke's reference to the Italian city of Puteoli (Acts 28:13), rather than Dicaercheia, the preferred designation, shows Luke's distance from the Second Sophistic.

sentations of empire in a literary text, namely, Luke-Acts, I have restricted my analysis to other literary texts. In so doing, I have excluded two other important types of response to Roman power, visual and martial. Greeks in the imperial period employed a variety of material media, in addition to literature, in articulating their relations with Rome and constructing their civic and ethnic identities in the presence of Roman domination. A complete treatment of Greek responses to Roman power would have to include imperial temples, statuary, Greek imperial coinage, and the like. Similarly, subordinate peoples could and sometimes did respond to Rome with armed violence. The two Jewish revolts stand out as prime examples, although rebellions arose in numerous parts of the empire, including Britain, Spain, Gaul, Germany, Pannonia, Greece, and North Africa.[24] I am, however, interested in how these ideas are constructed within the framework of a literary text, and it is to these sources that I restrict myself.

The term Second Sophistic was coined by Philostratus in his biographical sketches of Sophists beginning with Nicetas of Smyrna, who lived in second half of the first century C.E., down to his own day in the third century. According to Philostratus, the Second Sophistic traced its origins to the Sophists of classical Athens, particularly Aeschines. Whereas the First Sophistic movement concerned itself with philosophical themes, those in the Second Sophistic were known for their rhetorical skills and ability to speak on a variety of subjects (Philostratus, *Vit. soph.* 479; 486). Representatives of the Second Sophistic came from throughout the Roman world and wrote in a variety of genres. Of particular significance are the biographer and moralist Plutarch, the orator Dio Chrysostom, historians Arrian and Appian, rhetorician Aelius Aristides, satirist Lucian, novelist Longus, geographer Pausanias, and physician Galen. Most of these men were connected, through birth or domicile, to the important cities of the eastern regions of the Roman Empire; many also spent considerable time living and teaching in Rome.[25] It should hardly be surprising that, given the great diversity of voices, the term Second Sophistic is not without its problems.[26] The exact criteria for being a Sophist and its distinction from related activities such as philosophy and rhetoric are inexact. Moreover, the beginning of the Second Sophistic, while commonly

---

24. Martin Goodman, "Opponents of Rome: Jews and Others," in *Images of Empire* (ed. L. Alexander; JSOTSup 122; Sheffield: Sheffield Academic Press, 1991), 222–38.

25. Plutarch was born in Chaeronea (Greece), Dio in Prusa (Asia Minor), Arrian in Nicomedia (Asia Minor), Appian in Alexandria (Egypt), Aristides in Hadrdianotherae (Asia Minor), Lucian in Samosata (Syria), Pausanias in Magnesia (Asia Minor), and Galen in Pergamum (Asia Minor). Those who taught in Rome include Plutarch, Dio, Appian, and Galen.

26. Simon Goldhill, "Introduction," in Goldhill, *Being Greek under Rome*, 14.

set in the middle of the first century C.E., cannot be dated with any certainty. Dionysius of Halicarnassus, for instance, already in the late first century B.C.E. shows some of the same tendencies toward Atticism that become commonplace a century later.[27] In addition, some of the individuals commonly associated with the Second Sophistic rejected the title Sophist or had no explicit conception of participation in a larger intellectual circle. The second-century physician Galen, for instance, usually understood as a central figure in this cultural world, dismisses the attribution of Sophist for himself. Despite the problems with the term, it has become accepted that the orators and writers named by Philostratus along with several others who share similar linguistic and cultural proclivities were part of a "vast and complex cultural fabric" of the Greek-speaking world in the Roman period.[28]

As authors, and apart from their public roles as teachers, orators, and civic leaders, those connected to the Second Sophistic shared a passion for the vocabulary, syntax, and grammar of Attic Greek and disdain for the Koine (common dialect) Greek that developed in the Hellenistic period and had become standard in their own day.[29] The linguistic archaizing was part of a larger cultural agenda in which an idealized language of Plato, Thucydides, and Demosthenes was coupled with an idealization of the glories of classical Greece. The past glory of Greece, however, stood out in stark contrast to the present glory of Rome. It is within this contrast that the literary enterprise broadly construed as the Second Sophistic functioned as a response to the reality of Roman *imperium* and the rhetoric of Rome's position as ruler of the world. These authors not only dwelled on the past but often expressed a longing for the Greece that, whether they admitted it or not, no longer existed. In breathing life into the language, personalities, historical events, and religious monuments of the past, the writers were not simply expressing nostalgia for the good old days but were forming a cultural identity as a subordinate group, Greeks, in a world dominated by Rome. In his study of the Second Sophistic Tim Whitmarsh notes that "cultural activity—and in particular writing literature—was a fundamental means of constructing a Greek identity discrete from Rome."[30] I have selected two examples, Plutarch and Dio Chrysostom, whose work demonstrates the connections between literary artistry, resis-

---

27. Graham Anderson, "Sophists and Their Outlook in the Early Empire," *ANRW* 2.33.1:85–87.

28. Glen W. Bowersock, "Philosophy in the Second Sophistic," in *Philosophy and Power in the Graeco-Roman World* (ed. G. Clark and T. Rajak; Oxford: Oxford University Press, 2002), 160.

29. Swain, *Hellenism and Empire*, 21.

30. Whitmarsh, *Greek Literature*, 20.

tance to Roman authority, and identity formation. I have chosen these two representatives of the Second Sophistic in part because they exhibit many of the basic personal experiences and literary qualities that come to characterize the culture among Roman Greek writers, but also because they wrote at a time that saw the composition of Luke-Acts.

Plutarch was born in the Boeotian city of Chaeroneia sometime in the 40s of the first century. He died during the reign of Hadrian, sometime after 120. He was active in civic politics and served as a priest of Apollo at the oracular shrine in Delphi, one of the most important sacred precincts in the Greek world. Plutarch is best known for two extensive corpora: the parallel lives of Greek and Roman leaders and numerous works of moral philosophy, religious questions and topics, literary criticism, political essays, and conversations collected under the title of *Moralia*. Plutarch's own attitude toward Rome is complex. He wrote as a Roman citizen, although nothing in his writings betrays this information, taught in Rome for a period, and held imperial offices, including procurator of Achaea. His experiences left him with a rather sympathetic disposition toward Rome. He valued Rome's achievement in putting an end to civil wars and piracy and for its effectiveness in silencing the incessant disputes among Greek cities (*Mor.* 784–785). Like Josephus, Plutarch engaged the proposition that Roman power spread in the Greek world with the aid of divine support (*Phil.* 17.2; *Flam.* 12.10).

Despite his overall approval, Plutarch could be critical of Rome and Romans. He was offended by their fascination with ostentatious luxury and their all-too-frequent boorish behavior.[31] More to the point of our examination, his writings reflect discomfort with Greece's decline.[32] The last Greek to receive biographical coverage in the parallel lives is Philopoemen, statesman and general of the Achaean confederacy in the early second century B.C.E. and known as the "the last of the Greeks." This period marks for Plutarch and others in the Second Sophistic the turning point in political dominance of the Mediterranean from Greece to Rome. Plutarch comes to accept and even approves of Rome's *imperium*, but only if understood for what it is (e.g., bringer of peace) and what it is not (e.g., competent administrator in local matters). His discomfort with Roman hegemony affords him the opportunity to reflect on what it means to be Greek. Plutarch presents the opinion, shared by many of the Second Sophistic, that Greeks enjoy a unique position in the Roman world. While Greece may be subjugated politically, it remains Rome's cultural and intellectual superior. Rome might have the power, but

---

31. C. P. Jones, *Plutarch and Rome* (Oxford: Oxford University Press, 1971), 122.
32. Ibid., 126.

Greece has the wisdom and has much to teach Rome.[33] Lurking within the writings of Plutarch lies the suspicion that "Romans lacked proper, Greek culture, which was the only path to philosophical happiness."[34] Through his writings Plutarch offers his Greek readers a sense of who they are, or at least could be. For Plutarch, "to be Greek means to think, and (crucially) to act, in an ethical way."[35]

Dio Chrysostom, a contemporary of Plutarch, came from the city of Prusa in northwest Asia Minor. He spent much of his early career as a rhetorician in Rome, where he became acquainted with and a proponent of Stoic philosophy. Some reason—Dio is not clear—caused the emperor Domitian to banish Dio from Rome and his native Bithynia.[36] He spent the next several years wandering around Greece, the Balkans, and Asia Minor in the guise of an itinerant philosopher. His fortunes changed dramatically when Nerva recalled him from exile and then again when, according to his own account, he became a valued advisor to Trajan.[37] Like Plutarch, Dio is critical of Roman indulgence in luxury and immorality and in the malfeasance of its provincial administrators. He, too, has a strong distaste for Roman involvement in civic matters.[38] Dio, however, develops his response to Roman *imperium* in a more critical direction. In contrast to Plutarch, "he does not really eulogize Rome or enthuse about the benefits of Roman world rule. In some cases he is clearly hostile and irritated by the impuissance of the Greek cities and the Greek world in the face of Rome and … is severely critical of some of her provincial governors."[39] Rome might be considered great and powerful, but its greatness is insecure and arouses distrust (*Or.* 13.34). The absence of Greek wisdom acquired through education, *paideia,* according to Dio, calls into question the value of Roman *imperium*'s authenticity. Dio's orations often "explore the role of the Greek *pepaideumenos* [properly educated male] in relation to Roman power, seeking to establish the critical role of [Greek] *paideia* in the positive or negative evaluation of the [Roman] monarch in question."[40]

The literature of the Second Sophistic offers diverse assessments of Rome and employs various methods to respond to the dominant imperial ideology. Plutarch and Dio cannot represent the entirety of the Second Sophistic, but

---

33. Swain, *Hellenism and Empire,* 140.
34. Ibid., 186.
35. Whitmarsh, *Greek Literature,* 117.
36. The cause and extent of Dio's exile is unclear; see ibid., 157.
37. On the trustworthiness of this account, see ibid., 156–67.
38. Swain, *Hellenism and Empire,* 239.
39. Ibid., 191.
40. Whitmarsh, *Greek Literature,* 245.

they do express some of its important features and themes. Through its self-conscious decision to speak and write in Attic Greek and the fascination with the personalities and events of Greece at its political, military, and cultural zenith, the Second Sophistic engaged in an ongoing effort to make sense of the political decline in the Greek world and loss of local autonomy and to understand its place in a world now dominated by Rome. The Greek elites used their writings to explore the complex relations between past and present and between themselves, as Greeks, and Romans.[41] Plutarch is not alone in developing a largely positive appraisal of Roman society. Later in the second century the rhetorician Aelius Aristides expresses almost unqualified support of Rome and its position in the world.[42] Even Rome's mastery over Greek cities fails to concern him. His famous Roman oration functions as a highly polished mirror, reflecting and in some instances magnifying Roman ideology back onto his Roman audience. He speaks of Rome having established a peaceful, prosperous, and harmonious rule over the whole world (30; 92–106). The gods confirm the empire (105), and all persons should be grateful to the gods and thankful to the emperor to be living in a world governed by Rome (287). By contrast, Dio's more critical comments are shared by Lucian and Pausanias after him. In the dialogue *Nigrinus*, Lucian contrasts Rome unfavorably with an idealized Athens.[43] Elsewhere he even denies Rome's claim to superiority in armed combat, a position widely conceded in light of Rome's overwhelming military power.[44] For his part, Pausanias engages Rome largely through silence. His catalogue of the Greek religious sanctuaries, monuments, statues, and the like includes almost no item later than the third century B.C.E. By avoiding the recent past Pausanias can depict a pristine Greece, absent of any Roman presence. The narrative strategy "reflects a restructuring of memory, leading to a more profound, nuanced resistance to Rome by dwelling on other times when the boundaries of Greece, and Greek, identity had been preserved."[45]

The value of the Second Sophistic for understanding Luke-Acts can be summarized in three observations. First, Greek writers in the Roman period

41. Rebecca Preston, "Roman Questions, Greek Answers: Plutarch and the Construction of Identity," in Goldhill, *Being Greek under Rome*, 91.

42. The genuineness of Aristides' declarations has been questioned; see Swain, *Hellenism and Empire*, 260–80.

43. Ibid., 314.

44. *Hippias, or the Bath* 1.

45. Susan E. Alcock, "Landscapes of Memory and the Authority of Pausanias," in *Pausanias Historien: Huit Exposés Suivis de Discussions: Vandœuvres–Genève, 15–19 août 1994* (ed. J. Bingen; Entretiens sur l'Antiquité classique 41; Geneva: Fondation Hardt, 1994), 241–67; John Elsner, "Pausanias: A Greek Pilgrim in the Roman World," *Past and Present* 135 (1992): 3–29.

experienced forms of Roman domination, particularly through its propaganda and provincial administrators, and were fully conversant with Rome's claims to universal authority throughout the world. Second, Greek literature of this period often serves to affirm, modify, or reject these claims. Finally, Greek writers turned to the Greek past, its language, personalities, and monuments, as a way to fashion a cultural identity that was distinct from and in some instances superior to Rome. Ramsay MacMullen once commented that "the so-called Second Sophistic [was] perfectly harmless on the surface but anti-Roman in its implications, since its intent was the reassertion of Hellenism."[46] MacMullen's conclusion may have been stated more broadly and boldly than the evidence warrants. Not many of the Second Sophistic, for instance, would have approved of the Cynic Peregrinus's call upon Greece to rise up against Rome (Lucian, *Peregr.* 19). He nonetheless points to a significant feature of the writings of the Second Sophistic, namely, the desire on the part of Greek elites to fashion a response to the presence of Roman *imperium* and through their writings to construct an understanding of what it means to be Greek in a world dominated by Rome. Literature, in other words, often functioned as a tool in contesting Roman hegemony. Reading the literature of the Second Sophistic reveals a world in which Greek-speaking intellectuals were keen to evaluate Rome's claims of *imperium* and to use the relation between the dominant power of Rome and the subordinate status of Greece as a way to understand their identity in a world largely not of their own making.[47]

Luke also could converse in the language of this time. To cite but one example, Luke shows familiarity with texts that are important to Greek writers of the time. In Paul's most "Sophistic" moment, his speech delivered on the Areopagus, he cites without attribution the writings of the seventh-century B.C.E. holy man Epimenides and the third-century B.C.E. Stoic philosopher Aratus (Acts 17:28). Both authors were well known and often quoted by Greek writers of Luke's time, including those of the Second Sophistic such as Plutarch (see *Mor.* 157d on Epimenides) and Lucian (see *Nigr.* 16 on Aratus).[48] Although Luke-Acts does not qualify as an example of Second Sophistic literature, sharing neither the linguistic pretensions to Atticism nor the cultural attachment to classical Greece, the Second Sophistic and Luke-Acts share at

---

46. Ramsay MacMullen, *Enemies of the Roman Order* (Cambridge: Harvard University Press, 1966), 244.

47. The precise location for the writing of Luke-Acts does not affect this argument. While most of the Second Sophistic came from the traditionally Greek-speaking regions (e.g., Greece and Asia Minor), Favorinus came from Arles and Lucian from Syria.

48. Aratus, *Phaenomena* (ed. and trans. D. Kidd; Cambridge Classical Texts and Commentaries; Cambridge: Cambridge University Press, 1997), 165.

least two common interests: rhetoric and Rome. Acts concludes with a report
of Paul's time in Rome while "proclaiming the kingdom of God and teaching
about the Lord Jesus Christ with all boldness and without hindrance" (Acts
28:30). This last detail has particular resonance with the Second Sophistic.
It not only brings Paul, like Dio, Favorinus, Aristides, and other Sophists, to
the heart of the Roman world, but also connects Luke-Acts with the Second
Sophistic through a shared passion for rhetoric. The Greek word *parresia,*
here translated "boldness," was often used by orators of the Second Sophistic,
particularly Dio, who championed his ability to speak openly in the face of
power even when, like Paul, the circumstances threatened him with death.[49]
Not only at the end but throughout Acts Paul's activity as an apostle follows a
pattern familiar among rhetoricians of the Second Sophistic. Sophists would
typically deliver their declamations in a public arena, such as a theater. The
audience would frequently interrupt and pose questions to the speaker. The
literary reports often recount how the audience would be divided in their
response to the remarks with some voicing approval and others not. The
Sophist would then move to a more private venue for teaching to a smaller
group.[50] One finds a similar pattern repeated several times in Acts. Each time
Paul arrives in a new town he often preaches in the synagogue, the public
space of the Jewish community. The response is almost invariably mixed with
some approving what he says and others unsure or expressing outrage. Paul
then engages in more private instruction, sometimes in a private home, such
as that of Titius Justus in Corinth, where he taught Crispus, the head of the
synagogue, his household, and many Corinthians (Acts 18:7–8).

Luke-Acts and the Second Sophistic come together once again in a shared
perspective that Greeks, in the case of the Second Sophistic, or Christians, as
presented in Luke-Acts, possess certain knowledge that gives them superiority over Romans and that Roman leaders would be well advised to learn.
Central to the understanding of many of the Second Sophistic is the role of
paideia (education). As Dio has already shown us, the Second Sophistic constructed a discourse world in which true wisdom is the patrimony of Greece
and only through the process of becoming educated, a *pepaideumenos,* can
one, especially Romans, be considered cultured and possess the knowledge
needed to govern properly. The superiority of Greek wisdom gained through
paideia becomes a medium for contesting Roman superiority.[51] Rome may
have its military and magistrates, but Greece has the wisdom requisite for a

---

    49. Loveday Alexander, "Foolishness to the Greeks: Jews and Christians in the Public Life
of the Empire," in Clark and Rajak, *Philosophy and Power in the Graeco-Roman World,* 229–49.
    50. Anderson, "Sophists and Their Outlook," 89–104.
    51. Whitmarsh, *Greek Literature,* 5.

good life and effective rule. Dio particularly represents himself as a "paideutic specialist, an educator of Trajan, and thus as a paradigm of Greek culture as defined against the unlearned but empowered Roman."[52] In Luke-Acts *paideia* gives way to the knowledge and acceptance of the gospel. It is the gospel that distinguishes Christians from Romans and becomes the standard by which Roman magistrates are to be judged. The best Romans, such as Sergius Paulus (Act 13:4–12), are those who recognize and accept what the gospel teaches. The apostle, the one who preaches the gospel and therefore stands in for the *pepaideumenos,* functions as the critic of Rome and hero in Luke-Acts.

The second major theme, the fascination with Rome, permeates both Luke-Acts and the Second Sophistic. Greek writers of the period addressed the reality of Roman power in various ways and in various genres. We have already seen ambivalence in the biographies of Plutarch, direct condemnation in the speeches of Dio, the satirical presentations in the dialogues of Lucian, and resistance expressed through the silences in the geographic catalogue of Pausanias. While message and media differed, Greeks, and the subordinate peoples of the empire in general, invested their writings with images of Rome and responses to Rome's hegemonic discourse. As has already been noted, embedded in the account of the life of Jesus and the apostles are the symbols and structures of Roman power, its emperors, magistrates, and military. Luke's Gospel begins with reference to the first two emperors, Augustus (Luke 2:1) and Tiberius (Luke 3:1). Jesus debates over the question of paying taxes to Rome (Luke 20:25). The first convert to Christianity is a Roman solider. Roman figures, particularly magistrates such as Sergius Paulus, Gallio, Felix, and Festus, occupy important roles in the narrative.

Scholars have long argued whether one can discern in these passages a positive or negative portrayal of Rome, with the majority opting for the former. An advance in understanding this topic begins with the recognition that within the narrative of Luke-Acts Christian figures occupy a clearly subordinate position in relation to the dominant power Rome wields through its economic and administrative structures. Joseph and Mary must travel from Nazareth to Bethlehem to be enrolled in the census. Paul's well-being often rests at the mercy of Roman magistrates. Even Paul's claim to be a Roman citizen affords him limited protection. Recent studies on the relations between dominant and subordinate groups have demonstrated the complex ways they interact. Most important for our purposes, this research has shown that the absence of public acts of resistance, verbal or physical, does not thereby suggest that the "groups endorse the terms of their subordination and are willing,

---

52. Ibid., 201.

even enthusiastic, partners in that subordination."[53] Rather, subordinate groups adopt various, sometimes less obvious forms of resistance. James Scott has argued that prudential concerns lead subordinate groups away from open forms of resistance and toward a discourse of resistance that is subtle, disguised, and safe. The more hidden discourse may assume protean forms, such as anonymity, trickery, gossip, and rumor. He notes that "the least radical step is to criticize some of the dominant stratum for having violated the norms by which they claim to rule; the next most radical step is to accuse the entire stratum of failing to observe the principles of its rule; and the most radical step is to repudiate the very principles by which the dominant stratum justifies its dominance."[54] I wish to suggest that Luke-Acts, like several of its contemporaries in the Second Sophistic, while not creating a hidden transcript in the way Scott describes, nonetheless comes close to taking this final step in its hidden critique of Rome. In Luke-Acts resistance to Roman hegemony comes in the form of transposing various elements of imperial propaganda and applying these terms and images to Jesus and the church. The language of negation appears in several narrative elements, including the identification of Jesus with the title *savior* and as the bringer of peace, the description of Jesus' ascent into heaven, and catalogues of geographic authority.[55]

Luke is unique among the Synoptic Gospels to refer to Jesus as savior (Luke 2:11; Acts 5:31; 13:23) and to associate him with the bringing of peace (Luke 1:79; 2:14; Acts 10:36).[56] By the end of the first century the title of savior and benefaction of peace were almost inextricably bound together with Rome and the emperor. A variety of media, including literary texts, religious altars and shrines, inscriptions, and coins, saturated the Roman world with evocations of and tributes to the emperor as savior as well as testimonies of Rome's ability to establish peace. Augustus himself advertised his role as bringer of

---

53. Scott, *Domination and the Arts of Resistance*, 4.

54. Ibid., 92.

55. For further support of this argument, see Gary Gilbert, "Roman Propaganda and Christian Identity in the Worldview of Luke-Acts," in Penner and Vander Stichele, *Contextualizing Acts*, 233–56. Other passages from Luke-Acts can be adduced in support of this claim. Jesus' birth, reported to have taken place during the universal census in the time of Augustus, "presents an implicit challenge," notes Raymond Brown, "to this imperial propaganda, not by denying the imperial ideals, but by claiming that the real peace of the world was brought about by Jesus" (*The Birth of the Messiah* [Garden City, N.Y.: Doubleday, 1977], 415). Both Rome and Luke envisioned the coming of Augustus and Jesus, respectively, as marking the dawn of a new age. Vergil, for instance, speaks of the age of the time of Augustus as a *magnus ... saeculorum nascitur ordo* (*Ecl.* 4.5). On the Augustan age as a new beginning, see Wolfgang Kirsch, "Die Augusteische Zeit," *Klio* 67 (1985): 43–46.

56. Only John (4:22) uses the term *savior* in reference to Jesus.

peace by recognizing this act in the *Res gestae divi Augusti* and boasting that
on three occasions he shut the doors of the temple of Janus in Rome, sym-
bolizing that peace had been achieved throughout the Roman world, a feat
accomplished only twice in the entire preceding history of Rome (*Res gest.*
13; cf. Vergil, *Aen.* 1.291–296). The emphasis on peace as a salient benefit of
the *imperium Romanum* continued through the first and second centuries.
The doors to the temple of Janus were once again shut during the reigns of
Nero and Vespasian (Suetonius, *Nero* 13.2; Lucan 1.60), the latter also having
erected a temple of peace (Suetonius, *Vesp.* 9.1; Josephus, *J.W.* 7.158; Dio
66.15). As we have already seen, the Greek writers of the Second Sophistic,
even those who were critical of Rome, recognized Rome's achievements in
this regard. Aristides glorifies Rome for having established peace throughout
the entire inhabited world (*Or.* 13.97). Luke knew the ideology that claimed
an inseparable bond between peace and imperial rule very well. When Ter-
tullus addresses the Roman procurator Felix at Paul's trial in Jerusalem, he
begins with customary words of praise: "Because of you we have long enjoyed
peace" (Acts 24:2). Luke-Acts invokes the language used to legitimize imperial authority, but by identifying Jesus as savior and stressing that peace has
been established through him (and therefore not Rome), the narrative negates
Rome's hegemonic claim.

Another example of Luke's contestation of imperial propaganda comes in
Acts 2 and the story of the giving of the Spirit at Pentecost.[57] In the midst of
the narration the reader encounters a list of fifteen peoples or places: Parthia,
Media, Elam, Mesopotamia, Judea, Cappadocia, Pontus, Asia, Phrygia, Pam-
phylia, Egypt, parts of Libya belonging to Cyrene, Rome, Crete, and Arabia
(Acts 2:9–11). Scholars have long pondered the list's source or inspiration.
While the geographic inventory in Acts 2 resembles several similar lists, such
as in Gen 10, it closely mimics contemporary lists that celebrated Rome's
position as ruler over the inhabited world. Roman emperors, general, poets,
and historians compiled numerous lists of nations as a way to give geographic
specificity to the claim to be rulers to the end of the earth. The most famous
Augustan list of nations to illustrate geography's political weight comes to us
in the *Res gestae*. The autobiographical record begins with the words: "the
accomplishments of the deified Augustus by which he subjected the inhabited world under the empire of the Roman people." Much of what follows in
this document records "the direct or indirect completion of the conquest of

---

57. For further support of this argument, see Gary Gilbert, "The List of Nations in Acts 2:
Roman Ideology and the Lucan Response," *JBL* 121 (2002): 497–529.

the world."[58] In chapters 25–33, Augustus tallies fifty-five geographical places conquered, pacified, added, and otherwise dominated by Rome. Claude Nicolet describes the immense political value of this text. "The *Res Gestae* asserts from the very first line that there was Roman control of the inhabited world. And it proves this methodically, without symbolism, by using a series of topographic lists that correspond to precise geographical knowledge."[59] Within the Roman world the listing of nations had far more significance than supplying basic cartographic information. National lists were part of the discourse of Roman power. They promoted the claim of Rome's authority throughout the world. Luke-Acts as well has an understanding of the gospel's authority among all peoples (see Luke 2:10, 30–31; 3:6; 4:25–27; 24:47; Acts 2:17). The giving of the Spirit that takes place in Jerusalem marks the beginning of the gospel's spread among all the nations, even to the end of the earth (Acts 1:8).[60] In the context of Luke-Acts, the list of nations, the well-known trope of imperial propaganda, comes to subvert Rome's claims to universal rule and claims this authority for Jesus and the church. One particular detail in the list seems not only to confirm this analysis but to suggest just how deeply the list means to contest Rome's claim to universal rule. Luke-Acts has not merely aped Roman national lists but has gone Rome one better. By placing Parthia at the head of his list, Luke may be offering a subtle challenge to Rome. Throughout the first century Parthia presented Rome with the most difficult military challenges and stubbornly remained outside of Roman control.[61] The name itself evoked the most significant example of disconfirmation to Rome's claim of universal rule. In the Christian world of Luke-Acts, however, Parthia, the land that Rome could not conquer, is not only a constitutive member but stands at the very head of the list.

The establishment and maintenance of the Roman Empire brought about considerable political and cultural change, particularly for newly subordinate cities and peoples. Rome justified its *imperium* through various mechanisms, among them the claim to be the divinely appointed ruler of the world that had brought peace and other benefactions to its peoples. Many Greeks accepted, if not embraced, Rome's hegemonic discourse and sought ways to advance

---

58. Claude Nicolet, *Space, Geography, and Politics in the Early Roman Empire* (trans. H. Leclerc; Ann Arbor: University of Michigan Press, 1991), 29.

59. Ibid., 23.

60. The expression "to the end of the earth," is generally understood as a generalizing reference to the entire world. See W. C. van Unnik, "Der Ausdruck ὡς εσχάτου της γης (Apostelgeschichte 1:8) und sein alttestamentlicher Hintergrund," in *Sparsa Collecta The Collected Essays of W. C. van Unnik* (3 vols.; NovTSup 29–31; Leiden: Brill, 1973–83), 1:386–401.

61. On Parthia's independence from Rome, see Strabo, *Geogr.* 6.4.2; 11.1.2.1; 11.6.4; 11.9.2–3; 11.13.2; 16.1.28; 17.3.2.

themselves and their cities. Others, however, responded to Rome with resignation, resentment, and resistance. Beginning in the late first century, Greek
authors, through the archaizing of language and admiration for the past
glories of Greece, developed a dialogue with Rome and Roman power. The
Second Sophistic did not speak in a unified voice regarding Rome. Nonetheless, those who wrote within this cultural milieu often sought to redress the
imbalance of power. By reasserting their cultural and intellectual superiority,
often with a highly critical gaze toward Rome, Greek elites found a way of
fashioning their identity as Greeks rather than subordinates of Rome. Simon
Swain offers a helpful understanding of the relation between cultural contestation and identity:

> Most Greek intellectuals viewed that there was only one culture worth
> pursuing in the ancient world—not the modern notion of a unitary Graeco-
> Roman culture, but the Greek idea of Hellenic culture that Greeks were
> more likely to possess than Romans. The Greeks were more than happy if
> Romans adopted their culture. Indeed ... educated Greeks frequently judged
> Romans by their attitudes towards it and toward its exponents.[62]

5. Conclusion

A relatively small number of Greeks advocated, like Monty Python's Reg,
the dismantling of the Roman state. A willingness to coexist with Roman
authority, however, did not foreclose criticism and other less visible forms of
resistance, particularly resistance to Roman hegemonic claims of universal
authority. The Second Sophistic demonstrates how Greek literature of the time
functioned as a means both of negotiating imperial language and thought
and of constructing an identity that claimed both integrity and value.[63] In
most instances, the Second Sophistic saw Rome as unequal to Greece in
terms of intellectual and cultural promise and ability. Greece, understood
usually as a cultural rather than geographic or local entity, remains superior
to Rome. Thinking about Rome among the Second Sophistic had less to do
with promoting or rejecting Roman rule; Roman *imperium* was a given. What
mattered was promoting the continuing importance and value of Greek culture and in the process coming to define what constitutes being Greek under
Roman rule.

Christians faced some of the same concerns that presented themselves
to the wider Greek world. They too experienced Roman power and the dis-

---

62. Swain, *Hellenism and Empire*, 143.

63. Whitmarsh, *Greek Literature*, 34.

course that legitimated that power. Christians responded to both the reality and the rhetoric in different ways. In the case of Luke-Acts, the response itself is complex and variegated. Luke-Acts presents Roman power through the depiction of various Roman officials and instances in which the relation between those officials and Jesus, Paul, and other early Christians garners tacit if not explicit approval. This perspective, however, must be placed alongside another, perhaps more subtle but no less real critique of Rome and its purported imperial claims. As a member of a subordinate group living in the Roman Empire, Luke does not express ideas that directly contradict Roman authority. His work neither condemns Rome nor praises it or its rulers (except when they acknowledge the truth of the gospel). Rather, Luke-Acts appropriates the language of imperial hegemony—savior, peace, ascent, geographic catalogue—and claims it for Jesus and the church. It is precisely through the internalization and negation of the dominant political ideology that Luke-Acts subverts Roman claims of *imperium* and constructs an identity for being Christian under Roman rule. Applying John Barclay's analysis of Josephus, Luke-Acts seeks to "negotiate complex paths of self-expression through the adapted medium of the dominant discourse."[64] Luke-Acts invites its Christian audience to understand itself not only as distinct from but superior to Rome. Knowledge of the gospel allows Christians to reject Rome's imperial claims, which after all are illusory, but not imagine its overthrow. Instead, they should seek to use structures of Roman power, its magistrates, and its emperor to serve the goals of spreading the gospel and preaching it to the nations. Even the longest list of Roman benefactions does not alter the essential understanding of how the gospel speaks truth to Roman power.

---

64. John M. G. Barclay, "The Empire Writes Back: Josephan Rhetoric in Flavian Rome," in *Flavius Josephus and Flavian Rome* (ed. J. Edmondson et al.; Oxford: Oxford University Press, 2005), 318.

THE FALL AND HUMAN DEPRAVITY

John Barton

In 1521 Luther was attacked by the Louvain (Leuven) theologian Jacob Masson, known by his Latin name Latomus, for having put forward the article "Every Good Work is Sin" ("Omne opus bonum est peccatum").[1] Luther's argument was that, because sin remains in the human person even after baptism, everything a person does, even when it is fully righteous, remains tainted with sinfulness and the effects of the fall. Hence every human work, not just those that are overtly evil, falls under God's judgment. The saving good news of the gospel is that God nevertheless has mercy. Although even the good we do is evil in his eyes, yet he loves us and pardons us and makes us righteous in Jesus Christ. A believer is therefore *simul iustus et peccator*, at the same time just and a sinner.

Luther justifies this position by reference to a particular Old Testament text, Isa 64:5–12:

> You meet those who gladly do right, those who remember you in your ways. But you were angry, and we sinned; {in our sins we have been a long time, and we shall be saved [This follows the Vulgate]}. We have all become like one who is unclean, *and all our righteous deeds are like a filthy cloth*. We all fade like a leaf, and our iniquities, like the wind, take us away. There is no one who calls on your name, or attempts to take hold of you; for you have hidden your face from us, and have delivered us into the hand of our iniquity. Yet, O LORD, you are our Father; we are the clay, and you are our potter; we are all the work of your hand. Do not be exceedingly angry, O LORD, and do not remember iniquity forever. Now consider, we are all your people. Your holy cities have become a wilderness, Zion has become a wilderness, Jerusalem a desolation. Our holy and beautiful house, where our

---

1. See Martin Luther, "Rationis Latomianae confutatio (1521)," in *D. Martin Luthers Werke: Kritische Gesamtausgabe* (ed. J. K. F. Knaake et al.; 67 vols.; Weimar: Böhlau, 1883–2000), 8:43–128 (I am following Luther's text on pp. 59–72.) Hereafter referenced with volume, page, and line numbers.

{fathers} praised you, has been burned by fire, and all our pleasant places have become ruins. After all this, will you restrain yourself, O LORD? Will you keep silent, and punish us so severely?[2]

After a preliminary skirmish about the historical reference of this passage, in which Luther shows that it must refer to the Babylonian attack on Jerusalem and not, as Latomus had suggested, to Assyrian or Roman attacks, he moves on to the substance of the argument. Because the passage implies eventual salvation for the speakers—at least it does if we follow the Vulgate in rendering "and we shall be saved" in verse 5—it cannot, according to Luther's understanding, be spoken in the name of the Jews, who are not on the path to salvation, but must have an application to believers: it is in their name that the poet speaks. In his historical context, he was referring not to open sinners but to those whose hearts were right with God and asserting that even they are sinners. And if that is so, then the passage must imply that even the good deeds of the believer are "like a filthy cloth." Luther backs this up with another text, Eccl 7:20, "There is no one on earth so righteous as to do good without ever sinning," which he construes to mean, "no one on earth who does not sin even in doing good," thus making the same point about human depravity. Even the righteous sin in their good works—and so, of course, are thrown on to the mercy of God, who pardons and gives life to undeserving sinners.

Luther's general summary of his argument is worth quoting at length:

> our good works are not good, unless his forgiving mercy reigns over us. Our good works are evil, if the judgment of him who renders to every man threatens us....
>
> This teaching I have confirmed with this text of Isaiah's—and rightly so, as far as I can now see; indeed it is now more firmly established for me than before the wanton mockery of Latomus. Isaiah means to say that God, being angry and having thrust the people into captivity and destruction, does not deal with them in mercy, but in judgment—no, rather in wrath. Even if under this judgment there are just and godly men whose righteousness—apart from judgment and under mercy's rule—could be pure, still nothing of this is now of any use to them, so that they are like the most polluted of those who are even now sinners. God in this wrath does not recognize them, but abandons the godly and ungodly alike. He does not restrain himself. What else, then, does he do but so deal with those that are just that he makes it appear they are not just? Nevertheless, because

---

2. This and all subsequent biblical references are taken from the NRSV. The brackets indicate where Luther's citation of the Vulgate text differs from the NRSV; the italics are mine. Luther cites the Vulgate in "Rationis Latomianae confutatio (1521)," 8:59,25–60,2.

he judges truly and righteously, it must be that those who are under this judgment are at the same time righteous, and yet unclean. In this way he shows that no one ought to rely on his own righteousness, but solely on His mercy. This is also the meaning of Job 9[:22]: "It is all one; therefore I say, he destroys both the blameless and the wicked." This is not said of him whose innocence is counterfeit, and yet he destroys him not unjustly. So also here, Isaiah means the genuinely just and pure, for the Spirit does not speak in the spirit of the godly about the pseudorighteous, nor in the person of the pseudorighteous. Their righteousness is completely genuine and yet it is as if it were unclean, for they suffer everything which the wicked suffer, yet not innocently before a righteous God even if they are guiltless before men and our own conscience. ...

Therefore, if he judges, we all sin before him, and perish if he is angry; and yet if mercy covers us, we are innocent and godly before him and all creatures. This is what Isaiah says here.[3]

I would observe three aspects of Luther's exegesis that are important in understanding how he achieves this degree of scriptural support for his conclusions.

First, following the humanist tradition, Luther places great emphasis on a literal and exact understanding of the biblical text. Latomus had responded to Luther by saying that "all our righteous deeds" should be taken to mean "some of our righteous deeds." In other words, he had appealed to synecdoche, arguing that scripture said "all" when it meant only part of the whole. Luther takes this argument seriously, carefully examining places where synecdoche does indeed occur in the Bible. He points out that the present passage cannot adequately be understood in this way because the assertion that "all our righteous deeds are like a filthy cloth" is linked with the explicit statement that "there is no one who calls on your name." The juxtaposition of "all X" with "no not-X" rules out the possibility of synecdoche and makes it clear that literal universality is implied. This is thus part of Luther's characteristic appeal to the "plain sense" of the scriptural text. For him, Latomus begins with the general doctrinal conviction that there are such things as good works, and he therefore refuses to take at face value a passage that clearly rules such a possibility out; whereas he, Luther, is constrained by the plain sense of the text and forced to the conclusion that even good deeds have the nature of sin in the absence of the forgiving grace of God. We might look slightly askance at that, noting that the alleged "plain sense" of Isa 64 seems quite convenient for Luther and that

---

3. Martin Luther, "Against Latomus (1521)" (trans. G. Lindbeck), in *Luther's Works: American Edition* (ed. J. Pelikan and H. T. Lehmann; 55 vols.; St. Louis: Concordia; Philadelphia: Fortress, 1958–86), 32:172–73.

it is far from obvious that "what Isaiah says here" really is that "if he judges, we all sin before him, and perish if he is angry; yet if his mercy covers us, we are innocent and godly before him and all creatures." A biblical exegete today is likely to see both Luther and Latomus as importing "modern," that is, sixteenth-century, ideas into texts in which they were not actually at home. Nevertheless, the matter is presented in terms of Luther's being constrained by the meaning of the text even against what he might want to believe, while Latomus reads contemporary Roman Catholic doctrine into it.

Second, there is a general hermeneutical problem where a text is in the form of a psalm or hymn, because the speaker is not obviously God but a human person or persons. Luther gets around this by arguing that, where the contents of the psalm are not overtly contradicted elsewhere (as, e.g., in the case of the speeches of Job's friends), then the speaker is to be understood as the Holy Spirit, who speaks in the person of the righteous speaker of the text. Thus the speaker in Isa 64 is the community in exile (their words foreseen, of course, by the prophet Isaiah), and inasmuch as what they say is not contradicted, we must assume that God himself speaks through their words, accommodating himself to their speech. This means that what they say is to be taken as true, and they themselves as righteous—hence the pathos of the fact that they confess the wickedness even of their own righteous deeds, for in doing so they must be understood to be speaking the truth.

Third—and with this we come to our main concern with this whole controversy—it is taken for granted that what is said in the text has a general relevance to human beings as such. To use the terminology of this volume, the text is "fixed" at the level of systematic theology by being taken as a statement about all human beings at all times in relation to the gospel, rather than, as many modern exegetes might assume, as a remark about a particular set of historical circumstances that cannot be generalized beyond them. If I were writing a commentary on Isa 64, for example, I should probably construe the statement "all our righteous deeds are like a polluted rag" as hyperbole, an expression of the extreme despair of the community living in the ruins of Jerusalem (which is where I think the lament in Isa 63–64 comes from), rather than as a claim that can be used in any time and place as an exact theological proposition. But for Luther, part of taking the text seriously and literally, that is, in its plain sense, is to see it as applicable on a universal level. Good people who witness to the fact that in the sight of God even their good deeds are no better than filth show us the true relation of creature to creator *sub specie aeternitatis*. In Luther's hermeneutic, what is said with solemnity in scripture in a particular set of circumstances can legitimately be taken out of those circumstances and applied in a general way. This is in a way the ultimate justification for *dicta probantia*, even though Luther himself is far more nuanced in his use of the Bible than the later practice would become. Anyone who can claim to have "good deeds" comes under the condemnation of the particular people in the captivity in Isa 64.

All that being said, it is not clear that Luther is doing anything very different from what one might do nowadays in writing a biblical theology. Actual exegesis, as practiced in biblical commentaries, concentrates on the particular and time-bound in biblical statements and tries to put them in a specific historical context. But biblical theology looks for the generalizable, for insights arrived at in particular sets of circumstances that are nonetheless more widely applicable. If one were writing an Old Testament theology, one would quite likely want to say something about human moral capacity and the relation between human goodness and divine grace. This would surely include some treatment of the way that God operates sometimes independently of human deserving, both in blessing and in punishment. There are certainly sayings in Proverbs, for example, to which Latomus could have appealed as evidence for the freedom of the human will and the principle that God blesses the righteous and punishes the wicked, apportioning reward appropriately to what human beings merit. At the same time, it would be important not to overlook passages where there is no such equivalence. On the one hand, there are inscrutable divine punishments: the book of Job is filled with reflection on that problem. On the other hand, there are many places where God's blessing falls on those who do not deserve it—that this will happen constitutes a large part of the message of Deutero-Isaiah. The Old Testament is quite generally imbued with the sense that however well people act, they can never act so well that they deserve the riches God lavishes on his people: grace always exceeds deserts.

On the other hand, it is difficult to find places in the Old Testament where Luther's proposition that every good work is sin can really be found. The text from Ecclesiastes makes the point well, for when it says that there is no one on earth who does well and does not sin, it is pretty clearly not saying, as Luther thinks, that one sins even in one's good deeds but rather that everyone, however good, does at times fall into sin. That is, it is denying total human *perfection* or perfectibility, not asserting that good deeds have the nature of sin and thus implying total human *depravity*. The Old Testament is highly realistic about human weakness and moral impotence but not ultimately pessimistic about it to the extent of denying that human beings can ever please God. The endless exhortations to act well in Deuteronomy, for example, make sense only if, as Jesus ben Sira was later to put it, "it was he who created humankind in the beginning, and he left them in the power of their own free choice. If you choose, you can keep the commandments, and to act faithfully is a matter of your own choice. He has placed before you fire and water; stretch out your hand for whichever you choose" (Sir 15:14–16). The idea that humans are unable to act well, or even that when they do, sin is mixed inextricably with their good deeds, does not seem to be an idea at home in the Old Testament, to me at least. To find it there involves reading in doctrinal notions from elsewhere, partly no doubt from Paul and partly from Augustine, and this is what Luther did. The text from Isa 64 only apparently supports his position: it is a cry of despair rather than a dogmatic definition.

This type of distinction, which is related to a distinction of genres within the Bible, does not seem to fall within Luther's horizons but is largely the fruit of a biblical criticism later than his time, although arguably present *in nuce* in his demand for attention to the exact meaning of the text rather than to a dogmatic framework within which it should be read. What has happened, in effect, is that biblical critics have taken to a logical conclusion ideas already developed in outline by him. If we now find it hard to regard Isa 64 as teaching that *omne opus bonum est peccatum*, that is not because we are not heirs of Luther but because we have gone further along a road on which he was already setting out. We have taken further his insight that the biblical text should be interrogated on its terms rather than on ours and, like him, have been willing to believe that it may tell us things we would not have thought of ourselves, rather than merely serving as a useful repository of sayings that can illustrate preexisting dogmatic propositions.

If we wanted to describe in modern terms what Luther was doing, we might put it like this. Luther got his doctrine of the depravity of human conduct without grace from the Bible in the first place, in the sense that it developed out of a particular reading of Paul. It was not a "nonbiblical" doctrine. However, it is a doctrine represented in Paul but almost nowhere else in the Bible. When he came to study other portions of scripture, in particular the Old Testament, he tended to read the Pauline doctrine into those texts in very much the same way that Latomus, and Catholic theologians generally, read into them the doctrinal formulations of their communion. What Luther did was to fix as normative the general thrust of an important argument in Paul, represented of course primarily in Galatians and Romans, and then to take that as the hermeneutical key to other biblical texts. In cases where those texts clearly seemed opposed to the Pauline doctrine of justification, he was prepared to declare himself against their canonicity, as we see in the case of James. But with most texts he was content to read them in the light of his leading doctrine and not to see that the fit was only partial.

If we are to use the Bible for systematic theology, we need a principled theory of what type of hermeneutic is acceptable. Luther's, with hindsight, is a bit ramshackle, working well enough in general but unable to cope with a real lack of correspondence between dogmatic theology and biblical theology. A theology genuinely founded on scripture would look different from Luther's system, just as surely as it would from that of Latomus.

"Who Can Forgive Sins but God Alone?": Jesus, Forgiveness, and Divinity

Stephen T. Davis

1

The present essay is a piece of theological and philosophical exegesis. It concerns the concept of forgiveness of sins, especially Jesus' apparent willingness in the New Testament to offer forgiveness. I will deal primarily with Mark 2:1–12.

Section 2 lays some philosophical groundwork with a brief discussion of the phenomenon of forgiveness of one person by another. Section 3 deals with divine forgiveness and, more specifically, with a recent argument by philosopher Anne C. Minas to the effect that God, a perfect being, *cannot* forgive sins. Then in section 4 we will turn to the Mark text, where Jesus seems to dispense forgiveness to a paralytic. My concerns will be both exegetical and theological; that is, I will try to deal both with the text itself and with its place in the church's theology. In section 5 I will discuss two large ways of interpreting the text christologically, the first of which I will call the traditional reading. The second, which comes in different varieties, I will call a christologically minimalist way of interpreting the text. I will argue that those interpretations are unconvincing. Finally, in section 6 I will argue that Jesus' offer of forgiveness to people is one of the materials from which a coherent Christology should be constructed.

2

In order to forgive, one must have a certain moral standing. If you were to ask me to forgive some offense that you once committed against, say, your brother, I would have to reply that I am unable to do so. I do not have the necessary moral standing. In general, the person who has the moral standing and thus the logical opportunity to forgive is the person against whom the offense was committed. In this case, your brother is the person to whom you should apply for forgiveness.

Forgiveness presupposes that something morally wrong has been done and that the perpetrator is responsible. Forgiveness is inappropriate in cases where the alleged wrongdoer did not really do the deed or cause it to occur or where she did the deed but under the cover, so to speak, of a legitimate excuse or justification. Only those who are truly guilty can be forgiven. So forgiveness is not the same thing as *justification* (which argues for no wrongdoing), *excuse* (which argues for no moral responsibility), *mercy* (which may or may not be involved in forgiveness and which may be granted by those who do not have the moral standing to forgive), or *reconciliation* (which can occur without forgiveness and is often a result of forgiveness).

Forgiveness usually involves the forgiver voluntarily: (1) having a change of heart toward the evildoer, such as giving up anger and resentment toward her; (2) giving up the desire for punishment of the wrongdoer (although forgiveness can be consistent with punishment still being administered); and (3) reconciliation, that is, restoration of the old relationship between the two parties (assuming that there was one). Forgiveness is rarely morally *required*. Since it presupposes the guilt of the wrongdoer, forgiveness also assumes the legitimacy of both the resentment felt by the offended person and the punishment of the wrongdoer. Accordingly, forgiveness is normally morally allowed but not normally required.

Taken to extremes, forgiveness can have an unsavory aspect. Lest forgiveness slide over into servility, condoning of evildoing, or lack of self-respect on the part of the offended person,[1] certain acts are its normal prerequisite. They include contrition (or apology), repentance, and some degree of reparation (where possible) on the part of the wrongdoer.[2] This is not to deny that there can be cases where forgiveness is possible and even desirable quite apart from the satisfaction of some of these prerequisites.

As Jean Hampton argues, forgiving is not the same thing as condoning. Condoning a given act entails accepting it, taking it as morally allowable. Forgiveness, on the other hand, entails that the forgiver continues to hold that the forgiven deed was morally wrong.[3]

In some traditions, for example, the Christian tradition, forgiveness is a virtue. Christians are encouraged to forgive those who commit offenses

---

1. This is a point that is emphasized by Jeffrie Murphy in Jeffrie G. Murphy and Jean Hampton, *Forgiveness and Mercy* (Cambridge: Cambridge University Press, 1988), 17.
2. See Richard Swinburne, *Responsibility and Atonement* (Oxford: Oxford University Press, 1989), 73–92.
3. Murphy and Hampton, *Forgiveness and Mercy*, 40–42, 83.

against them. Harboring grudges instead of forgiving can be damaging to the soul. Indeed, according to scripture (Luke 17:4; Matt 18:22), Christians are to forgive people unlimited amounts of time, since that is how God forgives them. In places in scripture the point is made so strongly as to constitute a virtual prerequisite for receiving forgiveness. "Forgive us our debts," Jesus teaches the disciples to pray, "*as we forgive our debtors*" (Matt 6:12; see also 6:14–15).[4] In other words, those who do not forgive will not be forgiven.

3

Suppose that God exists, and suppose, as Christians hold, that all sins are offenses against God. Then it would seem that, in the case of any sin or offense whatsoever, God has the moral standing to forgive it (of course, so do the people who are harmed by it). If wrongdoing amounts to breaking moral laws, and if God is the author of the moral laws that have been transgressed, then God (unlike most human judges) has the right simply to forgive the guilty sinner.

Christian teaching is that all human beings are guilty before God (Rom 3:23; Jas 2:10). We are called to be obedient to God's command and are accountable to God for our failures to do so. Guilt is simply the moral state of someone who has done something morally wrong. Feeling guilty and being guilty are to a certain extent correlated in normal human beings, but they are not the same thing. It is possible to be guilty without feeling guilty, as we see with people who are unaware of being responsible for an evil deed or unaware of its moral wrongness. It is also possible to feel guilty without being guilty, as we see with people who are overscrupulous, who blame themselves inordinately.

Christianity also teaches that God not only can but does forgive sins: "God for Christ's sake has forgiven you" (Eph 4:32); "Their sins and iniquities I will remember no more" (Heb 10:17). Virtually all human beings are troubled by guilt. There are secular ways of dealing with guilt, but Christianity teaches that in forgiving our sins God makes our guilt disappear, no longer exist. "As far as the east is from the west, so far does he remove our transgressions from us" (Ps 103:12). Accordingly, divine forgiveness is not the same thing as *clemency* (where one is punished more mildly than one deserves) or even *pardon* (where one is not punished at all): in both cases, the person's

---

4. This reference (italics added) and all subsequent references to the Christian Bible are from the NRSV.

guilt remains. In divine forgiveness, on the other hand, sinners are not just pardoned but cleansed (Col 2:13; 1 John 1:9; 2:12).

Let me try to be more precise as to the meaning of "divine forgiveness." Let us say that the statement "God forgives act X committed by Smith" entails the following five statements:

(1) Smith is morally responsible for the occurrence of X.
(2) X is morally wrong.
(3) Accordingly, Smith is guilty and deserves punishment.
(4) Smith sincerely repents and asks God for forgiveness.
(5) God cleanses Smith from the guilt of committing X and does not punish Smith for doing X.

So in forgiveness God sets the sin and guilt aside and restores the old fellowship and friendship between God and the sinner. There is no more enmity between them.

However, philosopher Anne C. Minas has recently argued that God's perfection is logically inconsistent with God's granting forgiveness. God's perfection, she points out, entails that God has "a perfect moral sense, a perfect moral will, perfect knowledge, and perfect benevolence."[5] Minas discusses various possible senses of the word "forgive" and argues in each case that a perfect being cannot offer that sort of forgiveness. Minas is surely correct in several such cases.

(1) She points out that forgiveness sometimes amounts to revising or retracting an adverse moral judgment about an act. She correctly argues that a reversal of moral judgment of that sort is never in order for a perfect being. None of the judgments of a perfect being is subject to reversal. (2) She points out that forgiveness at other times amounts to deciding that a certain moral rule is defective in the special circumstances of a given case (stealing is wrong, to be sure, but perhaps not to feed one's starving children; killing a person is wrong, but maybe not in self-defense). Again, it is hard to see how a perfect being could forgive in this sense; no perfect being will entertain faulty moral rules. (3) She notes that forgiveness sometimes amounts to a decision simply to overlook or condone someone's moral wrong, especially if the offense was minor. But it is hard to see how a morally perfect being can condone anything that is genuinely morally wrong. (5) Minas also argues that forgiveness usually involves giving up a feeling of resentment held against the evildoer

5. Anna C. Minas, "God and Forgiveness," in *Philosophy and Faith: A Philosophy of Religion Reader* (ed. D. Shatz; New York: McGraw-Hill, 2002), 25–34.

because of the harm his evil deeds have done; sometimes this involves an atti-tude of "forgive and forget" or "no longer taking the offense personally" on the part of the injured person. But, she argues, it is hard to see how a perfect being could be harmed or injured, let alone how a perfect being could forget anything.

So far Minas appears to be on firm ground, but she then argues that for-giveness might amount to something akin to (5) clemency exercised by a judge or pardon by a high official. But, she asks, how could a perfect being simply remit justified punishment? Will that not make God something like a practical joker, she asks, assigning punishments that God knows (with perfect foreknowledge) he is going to remit? If the punishment was morally justified, and if a perfect being is perfectly just, she says, no perfect being can forgive in this last sense.[6]

Let me stray from Minas's argument for a moment and ask: Is divine forgiveness *unjust*? In one sense, it is. Christian teaching is that all human beings are guilty of sin and that the just penalty is eternal separation from God. Because of God's grace, however, we can be forgiven. What sinners must hope for, then, is something different from justice. If we were to be treated only according to the canons of justice, we would be condemned. Grace is, so to speak, different from and better than justice. But in another sense God's mercy is not unjust. Since God has certain rights over his creatures, rather than duties to them imposed from the outside, God may compassionately forgive sinners, if God wants to do so, without being accusable of injustice.

To return to Minas, she is correct that a perfect being will never forget a fact that it once knew. It is also true that a perfect being, understood in the broadly Thomistic way that her argument presupposes, cannot be harmed or injured. But the valid point that our sins do not damage or injure God does not entail that they do not do wrong to God. Indeed, that is just what they do. Just as you do me a moral wrong if you tell me a lie (without, let us suppose, the lie harming me in any way), so we do God a wrong whenever we disobey any of his commands, even though God, a perfect being, has not been dam-aged or lessened in any way.

I conclude that the type of divine forgiveness defined above in the fourth paragraph of this section (section 3) of the paper is not refuted by Minas's

---

6. Minas also raises the question of the apparent injustice of God forgiving some sinners but not others. Her discussion of this point (see ibid., 29) turns into an implicit argument for universalism, the theory that all sins will be forgiven and all people will enjoy eternal bliss. But since this point, while important in itself, is quite separate from Minas's main argument that a perfect being cannot forgive at all, I will ignore it.

argument.[7] Divine forgiveness need not involve changing a judgment about a moral issue, need not have anything to do with defective moral rules, need not entail condoning evil deeds, and need not have anything to do with feelings of resentment.

4

Mark 2:1–12, the story of the paralytic who was let down through the roof and was forgiven and then healed by Jesus, is a fascinating text for many reasons. (1) Form critics have discussed the history of this pericope in great detail.[8] (2) With parallels in both the other Synoptic Gospels (Luke 5:17–26; Matt 9:1–8), redaction critics have also mulled it over.[9] (I will not discuss the possibly related but quite different story of the healing in John 5:1–18.) (3) The story plays a crucial narrative role in Mark's Gospel, as the first serious indication in Jesus' ministry of controversy with the religious leaders. (4) The story is dramatic and arresting as a piece of literature. (5) Finally, the story appears to have dogmatic ramifications, or at least so Christians have usually thought.

I will not discuss the interesting question of whether this story really occurred as told by Mark or even largely as told by Mark. That is, I will not offer any arguments on the general historicity of the text or the more specific question of whether the words attributed to Jesus in this pericope constitute the *ipsissima verba* or even capture the *ipsissima vox* of Jesus. I want to ask, rather, what theological implications the story has *as it stands* in Mark (which, of course, Christians have always taken as part of sacred scripture).[10]

The most obvious implication has to do with Jesus' offer of forgiveness to the paralytic. This offer has traditionally been taken as an implicit claim

---

7. Minas burlesques the idea of divine forgiveness by saying, "He did the actions all right, but after God's forgiveness, they are no longer wrong" (ibid., 33). No, the evil deeds of evildoers remain evil; they are just no longer counted against them.

8. Following Bultmann (*The History of the Synoptic Tradition* [2nd ed.; trans. J. Marsh; Oxford: Blackwell, 1966], 12–14, 227), Vincent Taylor reviews the various arguments of the critics and concludes that Mark 2:1–12 is a compilation of various sources. See his *The Gospel according to St. Mark* (London: Macmillan, 1963), 191–201.

9. See, inter alia, Robert H. Gundry, *Matthew: A Commentary on His Literary and Theological Art* (Grand Rapids: Eerdmans, 1982), 161–65.

10. There are several fascinating and controversial points in relation to this text that I will not discuss: the relationship between sin and sickness in first-century Judaism and in Jesus' teachings, the healing of one person because of the faith of other people, the clairvoyance and healing power exhibited by Jesus, and the meaning of "Son of Man." I am interested only in Jesus' apparent ability to forgive sins.

to divinity or at least to divine prerogative on Jesus' part.[11] As we have seen, we all have the right to forgive sins that have been committed against us, but only God has the right to forgive sins *simpliciter*. This point is made clear in the Hebrew Bible (Exod 34:6–7; 2 Sam 12:13; Pss 32:1–5; 51:3–4, 9–11; 103:3; 130:4; Isa 43:25; 44:22; Dan 9:9; Zech 3:4).

Accordingly, the church fathers saw Mark 2:1–12 as proof of Jesus' deity; they pointed to: (1) Jesus' clairvoyant ability to read the thoughts of the scribes (that only God can know the minds and intentions of human beings is attested to in 1 Sam 16:7; 1 Kgs 8:39; 1 Chr 28:9; Ps 139:1–2, 6, 23; Jer 11:20; 17:9–10); (2) his ability to heal the paralytic; and, most important, (3) his forgiveness of the paralytic's sins. On this third point, Irenaeus asks: "How can sins be rightly remitted unless the very One against whom one has sinned grants the pardon?"[12] Novatian declared: "If Christ forgives sins, Christ must be truly God because no one can forgive sins but God alone."[13]

There appears to be no evidence that the Messiah, as most first-century Jews understood that figure, would have had the ability to forgive sins.[14] This is also true of such figures as the Suffering Servant and the eschatological high priest. Carefully surveying the evidence, Robert A. Guelich concludes: "No evidence has emerged to indicate that the Jews expected even the Messiah, regardless of how one defined this expectation, or any other eschatological figure, to have the right to forgive sins."[15] The point, then, is that Jesus was accused of blasphemy because in this text and others he assumed the right to forgive sins that were committed against God rather than personally against him.

5

As noted, there seem to be two possible ways of interpreting Jesus' willingness to offer forgiveness. The traditional interpretation is that Jesus, the incarnation of God in our midst, had as God the full divine authority to forgive sins. Jesus himself was the agent who was dispensing forgiveness of sins.

---

11. See Robert H. Gundry, *Mark: A Commentary on His Apology for the Cross* (Grand Rapids: Eerdmans, 1993), 112–15.

12. Thomas C. Oden and Christopher A. Hall, eds., *Mark* (ACCS 2; Downers Grove, Ill.: InterVarsity Press, 1998), 28 (*Haer.* 5.17).

13. Ibid., 28 (*Trin.* 13).

14. C. S. Mann, *Mark: A New Translation with Introduction and Commentary* (AB 27; Garden City, N.Y.: Doubleday, 1986), 224.

15. Robert A. Guelich, *Mark 1–8:26* (WBC 34A; Dallas: Word, 1989), 87.

But some argue for what I call a christologically minimalist interpretation of the text. There are several ways in which this is done. Some say that in Mark 2:1–12 and similar texts Jesus was not forgiving people (so to speak) on his own initiative but was rather speaking on behalf of God, relaying (as it were) God's own decision to forgive the person. On this reading, Jesus was not explicitly claiming to be divine but to have, so we might say, God's power of attorney. On this theory, Jesus certainly had special status but not necessarily divine status. He was more like God's spokesperson or representative.

Others argue that Jesus was simply conveying the news that God had forgiven the guilty person. Like Nathan in his confrontation with King David (2 Sam 12:1–15), Jesus was simply assuring the guilty party of God's forgiveness. John Hick (following E. P. Sanders) opts for this interpretation. In his *The Metaphor of God Incarnate*, Hick argues that Jesus was not usurping God's prerogative to forgive sins but was only pronouncing forgiveness, "which is not the prerogative of God, but the priesthood."[16] On this interpretation, Jesus had little special status other than that of a passer-on of assurance or good news from God. He certainly did not have divine status. But it seems to me that this second way of interpreting the text cannot be sustained. Let me now make a case for that claim.

It must initially be admitted that there are some texts that can possibly be read in a christologically minimalist way. One would be Luke 7:36–50, where the woman's tears can perhaps be read as contrition for her sins and even repentance; maybe, in this case, Jesus saying, "Your sins are forgiven," amounted to no more than Jesus performing a priestly role, that is, declaring that a sinner who had truly repented would be forgiven by God. But there are problems with this reading: What qualified Jesus to function as a Levitical priest? The central point on this issue is that in Mark 2:1–12 the paralytic is reported as having done *none* of the acts that were normally requisite for receiving divine forgiveness. There is no evidence of sorrow for his sins, confession of them, repentance from them, nor of any sacrificial act at the temple or anywhere else.

It must also be admitted that Mark 2:1–12 may appear to be somewhat anomalous because there is only one other occasion in the Synoptic Gospels where Jesus explicitly pronounced forgiveness: Luke 7:36–50, the text just mentioned. But there are other narratives in the Gospels where forgiveness of a sinner is implicit (Luke 19:1–10; John 8:1–11). Moreover, Jesus had frequent table fellowship with sinners (e.g., Mark 2:15–17; Luke 15:1–2). Finally, Jesus

---

16. John Hick, *The Metaphor of God Incarnate* (Louisville: Westminster John Knox, 1993), 32. See also E. P. Sanders, *Jesus and Judaism* (Philadelphia: Fortress, 1985), 240.

offered many figurative expressions of forgiveness (e.g., Matt 18:27; Luke 7:42; 15:9, 11–32; 18:14). These texts certainly seem to reinforce the idea that Jesus explicitly offered forgiveness.

One theologically minimalist reading of Mark 2:1–12 is provided by the Jesus Seminar. In *The Five Gospels*, the Seminar argues that either Jesus said the words attributed to him assuming the power to forgive or he did not. If he did (which the Seminar raises as a possibility but ultimately rejects), then "v. 10 may represent a bold new claim on Jesus' part that gives authority to forgive sins to all human beings."[17] But if he did not say them, then "the early church was in the process of claiming for itself the right to forgive sins and so would have been inclined to claim that its authorization came directly from Jesus."[18] In either case, so the Seminar seems to be saying, Jesus was claiming no divine prerogative here. Now, as noted, in the present essay I am not interested in debating whether the historical Jesus actually said the words attributed to him in our text. But I think it ought to be rather obvious that the "bold new claim" that the Seminar attributes to Jesus on its first reading of the text is implausible in the extreme.[19]

The crucial point is this: the violent reaction of the scribes in Mark 2:7 ("Why does this fellow speak in this way? It is blasphemy! Who can forgive sins but God alone?") seems to belie minimalist readings. It would hardly amount to blasphemy simply to assure repentant sinners that God had forgiven them. It seems that any priest or any believer in the God of Israel could do that. But suppose the point is pressed that, since the paralytic did *not* repent or offer temple sacrifice for his sins, the charge against Jesus must have been something like falsely assuring a man who did not deserve it of divine forgiveness. But would that charge have amounted to blasphemy? It seems that, if the scribes thought that Jesus was guilty of that offense, what was called for was correction of his error, not execution (the sanction for blasphemy).

Moreover, in 2 Samuel Nathan explicitly names God and attributes the forgiveness of David to God. Jesus did neither. He appears to dispense forgiveness on his own initiative. He did not just assure people that forgiveness

---

17. Robert W. Funk et al., *The Five Gospels: The Search for the Authentic Words of Jesus* (New York: Macmillan, 1993), 44.

18. Ibid.

19. Had the Seminar argued that Jesus was passing on the authority to forgive sins not to all human beings but to a specific group of people, it would have been on firmer ground. Unfortunately, I do not have the space on this occasion to discuss the "keys to the kingdom" and the "binding" and "loosing" authority that Jesus passed on to Peter and the church (Matt 16:19) or the power to forgive or retain sins that Jesus gave to the disciples in John 20:23 and (apparently) Matt 9:8.

had occurred; he seemed to act as the agent of forgiveness. He seemed to the scribes to be blaspheming because he was claiming to be able to do what only God could do. That this is a serious charge indeed (Lev 24:15–16 calls for the death penalty for blasphemy) is revealed by the fact that it was invoked at Jesus' trial (see Mark 14:64).

One point that might be taken in favor of minimalist readings is the claim of Jeremias and others that the words "Your sins are forgiven" (ἀφίενταί σου αἱ ἁμαρτίαι) (Mark 2:5) constitute a "theological passive," which would indicate that the act of forgiving was done by God, not Jesus.[20] If this is true, then perhaps Jesus' declaration was similar to that of a Levitical priest, who makes atonement for the sins of a person, and then "he shall be forgiven" (Lev 4:26; cf. 4:31). The issue, then, is this: Was Jesus in Mark 2:1–12 forgiving sins or declaring on behalf of God that God had forgiven sins?

A point from John Chrysostom seems telling here: "Whenever Christ had to do any of these much greater things [such as forgive sins or make laws], you will not characteristically find him praying or calling on his Father for assistance. All these things, as you discover in the text, he did on his own authority."[21] In short, Jesus seems to be doing more here than simply offering encouragement or assurance to people on the grounds that God has forgiven them or even declaring that God had forgiven them. He certainly seems to be *doing* something, acting as an agent.

That Jesus had authority to forgive sins is consistent with another New Testament notion, that Jesus, the Son of Man, will be the eschatological judge (Matt 25:31–46; Mark 8:38; John 5:22). As Gary Shogren argues, this means that even in advance of the final judgment Jesus is able to pronounce acquittal and judgment (Matt 11:20–24//Luke 10:13–15).[22]

Whether or not Mark 2:5 is a theological passive (and the active voice in 2:7 and 2:10 casts doubt on the idea that Jesus was not acting on his own initiative), it surely seemed to the scribes in the story that Jesus was doing more than simply announcing what God had already done. As Guelich insists:

> Whereas the scribes might have questioned Jesus' right in 2:5b to pronounce forgiveness in God's name apart from the cult and without demanding repentance, or even to pronounce God's forgiveness of sins now rather than in the eschaton, their implicit charge does not arise from the divine pas-

---

20. Joachim Jeremias, *New Testament Theology: The Proclamation of Jesus* (trans. J. Bowden; NTL; London: SCM, 1971), 1:114.

21. Odem and Hall, *Mark*, 28–29 (*On the Incomprehensible Nature of God*, homily 10.19).

22. Gary S. Shogren, "Forgiveness (NT)," *ABD* 2:835.

sive in 2:5b. Rather it focuses on the issue expressed in 2:10, Jesus' usurping God's authority to forgive sins. The answer to the scribes' question, "Who except God…?" is clearly, "the Son of Man" (2:10).[23]

6

It seems, then, that the first and more traditional reading of Mark 2:1–12 is the most sensible. Indeed, the others are hard to reconcile with the climactic statement of our text, "The Son of Man has authority on earth to forgive sins" (Mark 2:10). Of course, Jesus was not going about declaring, "I am God." But he does seem to be claiming to be able to do something that only God has the right to do. Accordingly, the church fathers were right in holding that our text has christological ramifications.

There is nothing in this text that expresses the language of later creedal orthodoxy. There is nothing here about persons or natures or essences or hypostatic unions. Not everything that Christians want to say about Jesus is implicit in this text. Still, it is clear that Mark 2:1–12 is and ought to be one of the texts that Christians take into consideration in doing Christology. In this text, Jesus seems to be giving himself such authority as to be setting himself on a par with God. His willingness to offer forgiveness was surely one of the things about Jesus that made such an impression on early believers that they reached the conclusion that he was divine.[24]

---

23. Guelich, Mark 1–8:26, 87.

24. I relegate to a footnote a final point: the present essay in effect argues against the idea that any attempt to fix the meaning of a biblical text is no more than an act of politics, an exercise of power. I am claiming that it can be cogently argued that the traditional christological interpretation of Mark 2:1–12 is correct.

Worship in Spirit and Truth: Louis-Marie Chauvet's Sacramental Reading of John 4:21–24

Kevin Mongrain

1. Introduction

The purpose of this essay is to argue that the contemporary Roman Catholic liturgist Louis-Marie Chauvet's sacramental theology can be read as an extended interpretation of a conversation between Jesus and the Samaritan woman at Jacob's well in John 4:21–24.[1] The Samaritan woman says to Jesus, "Sir, I can see that you are a prophet. Our ancestors worshiped on this mountain; but you people say that the place to worship is in Jerusalem" (John 4:19–20).[2] Jesus replies in verses 21–24:

> "Believe me woman, the hour is coming when you will worship the Father neither on this mountain nor in Jerusalem. You people worship what you do not understand; we worship what we understand, because salvation is from the Jews. But the hour is coming, and is now here, when true worshipers will worship the Father in spirit and truth; and indeed the Father seeks such people to worship him. God is Spirit, and those who worship him must worship in spirit and truth."

---

1. Chauvet's sacramental theology is primarily presented in *Symbol and Sacrament: A Sacramental Reinterpretation of Christian Existence* (trans. P. Madigan and M. E. Beaumont; Collegeville, Minn.: Liturgical Press, 1995). This book was first published in 1987 in French with the title *Symbole et Sacrement: Une relecture sacramentelle de l'existence chrétienne* (Paris: Cerf, 1987). Chauvet condensed and simplified *Symbol and Sacrament* into a shorter English work, *The Sacraments: The Word of God at the Mercy of the Body* (Collegeville, Minn.: Liturgical Press, 2001).

2. All citations from scripture in this chapter are from the NAB. This English translation is the basis of the English Catholic Lectionary and is the translation that is most similar to the French Bible and lectionary used by Chauvet.

My argument is that Chauvet's theological reading of this passage, particularly the phrase "worship in spirit and truth," seeks to preserve the passage's multivalence, and in so doing resists alternative theological readings ignoring its multivalence, and reducing its complexity. In other words, this chapter contends that, rather than extracting one layer of meaning from a biblical text for theological purposes, as is often common with theological commentaries on scripture, Chauvet formulates a multivalent pneumatic-liturgical theology capable of safeguarding the full multivalence of John 4:21–24 and, by extension, the multivalence of the Fourth Gospel as a whole. This chapter presents an analytical discussion of Chauvet's pneumatic-liturgical theology and its application to John 4:21–24, contending that Chauvet's pneumatic-liturgical interpretation of John identifies and integrates three binary pairs in Johannine theology that other theological commentators either ignore altogether or treat as virulently antithetical. The binary pairs are (1) spiritual and institutional religion; (2) liturgical and ethical religiosity; and (3) Jewish and Christian religious identity. Chauvet's pneumatic-liturgical interpretation allows us to see that in John 4:21–24 each pole in each binary pair exists in a unity-in-tension with its opposite pole. This means that each pole in each pair retains its own distinct character as different from its binary partner, but neither pole seeks to erase the other pole or reduce it to itself; each binary pair exists in a stressful union characterized by mutual correction *and* mutual affirmation.

This essay further contends that Chauvet's purpose in bringing his multivalent pneumatic-liturgical theology to bear on his reading of John 4:21–24 is not simply to preserve the multivalence of this text but also to *reinstate* it in opposition to three simplistic theological misinterpretations of John's Gospel, all of which are rooted in reductive misreadings of these verses, particularly the phrase "worship in spirit and truth." The first misinterpretation Chauvet opposes does not see the unity-in-tension of spiritual and institutional religion in John 4:21–24. Instead it sees only hostility between the two poles and hence reductively reads "worship in spirit and truth" as Christian spirituality's declaration of independence from organized religion, particularly ritual-liturgical religion; this declaration is in almost all cases hostile to Judaism and its supposedly "crude" and "worldly" political-legalistic character. The second misinterpretation opposed by Chauvet's pneumatic-liturgical theology fails to see the unity-in-tension between cultic religiosity and ethical-prophetic religiosity in the text. Instead, it reads the text as setting cultic religiosity and ethical-prophetic religiosity in an absolute dichotomy. The third misinterpretation opposed by Chauvet fails to see the unity-in-tension of Jewish religious identity and Christian religious identity. Instead, it reads John as teaching a crude form of Christian supersessionism in which Christian and

Jewish religious identities are utterly irreconcilable and hence the latter must be destroyed and replaced without remainder by the former. As this essay shows, Chauvet's sophisticated trilevel pneumatic-liturgical theological reading of John 4:21–24 rejects all three misinterpretations and injects some very necessary awareness of complexity into discussions of this extraordinarily multivalent biblical text.

2. Worship in *Spirit* and Truth: Cult as Learning That God Is Not a Thing to Be Understood, Experienced, or Used

This section presents Chauvet's understanding of the binary pair of spiritual and institutional religion and analyzes his use of this first aspect of pneumatic-liturgical theology. Commenting on the meaning of Jesus' saying to the Samaritan woman in verse 24 that "God is spirit, and those who worship him must worship in spirit and truth," Chauvet raises this question:

> Then why not ask: In order to worship the Father what need do we have of all these rites which unfold in a more or less obligatory fashion and make use of antiquated gestures and movements, of pre-programmed formulas, of materials imposed in the name of "tradition," without speaking of the ostentatious and solemn ceremonies with which the church surrounds them? Does not all this run counter to the spirit Jesus speaks of or at least hamper it? And thus we are led to dream of a "truer," therefore necessarily more spare religion in which contact with the pure word of God would at last be possible.[3]

Chauvet's initial response to this kind of thinking seems unequivocally negative: "This is pure imagining!" he rails.[4] For Chauvet the desire to escape sacramental rituals in the hope of thereby having a "direct line" to God and/or Christ is tantamount to Gnosticism.[5] The central problem with Gnosticism is that it "denies the experience of the real" and persists in a perverse desire for the impossible; any hope for a "direct line" to the divine is worse than an illusion and worse than a fantasy; it is "idolatry" because it is "nothing more than the imaginary projection of ourselves into God."[6] However, this critique does not tell the whole story. Chauvet also evidences respect for the intuition behind the antisacramental desire for a pure contact with God:

---

3. Chauvet, *Sacraments*, xi.

4. Ibid.

5. Chauvet, *Symbol and Sacrament*, 172–73; see also 186, 188, 219, 222, 391, 449–50, 488, 493, 539–41.

6. Ibid., 301.

Nevertheless, the question underlying this dream expresses an intuition that deserves to be considered: that the church can never be in serene possession of its liturgical rites, that it must constantly resist the temptation to imprison itself—as well as God—within them. For these rites, which have Christian meaning only if they are filled with the word and in-dwelt by the Spirit, contest the word of God in the very moment they attest it. In this sense, the temptation to do away with them can be salutary.[7]

What does Chauvet mean with his Johannine-sounding claim that liturgical rites should be "in-dwelt by the Spirit"? As we can already surmise, being indwelt by the Spirit cannot mean being detached from organized religion and its liturgical rites. At a more fundamental level, Chauvet's perspective is thoroughly incarnational. He argues for the fundamental corporeality of Christian faith, or in his words, the "arch-sacramentality" of Christian existence.[8] Chauvet asserts:

> the fact that Christian identity cannot be separated from the sacraments (in particular those of initiation) means that faith cannot be lived in any other way, including what is most spiritual in it, than *in the mediation of the body*, the body of a society, of a desire, of a tradition, of a history, of an institution and so on. What is most spiritual always takes place in the most corporeal.[9]

This claim has a vast array of implications, and one of the most important for Chauvet is that it requires a new kind of theology: "Any theology that integrates fully, and *in principle*, the sacramentality of the faith requires a consent to corporality, a consent so complete that it tries to *think about God according to corporality*."[10] This means for him that Christian theology must always have as its point of departure a spirituality of the body in which God "inscribes" (in Jacques Derrida's sense of "arch-writing") Christ's Spirit on the "body" of scripture, the "body" of human "desire," and the "body" of the church's culture, tradition, and institution.[11] For Chauvet, sacramental rituals are God's primary method of inscribing the spirit of Trinitarian love on the body. Chauvet relies on psychoanalytical theory to make this point: ritual practice ("lit-*urgy*" as the work of prayer/worship) is better able to effect conversion from self-righteous egoism to the other-centered attitudes of the Trinitarian

---

7. Chauvet, *The Sacraments*, xi.
8. Chauvet, *Symbol and Sacrament*, 154–55.
9. Chauvet, *The Sacraments*, xii. See also Chauvet, *Symbol and Sacrament*, 146.
10. Chauvet, *Symbol and Sacrament*, 155.
11. See ibid., 141–55, 213–27, 355–76. Chauvet's critical use of "arch-writing" is derived from Derrida's *De la grammatologie* (Paris: Minuit, 1967), especially chs. 1 and 2.

God than conceptual explanation ("theo-*logy*") because rituals are more successful than concepts in reaching and transforming unconscious desires.[12]

We can begin to see, then, that Chauvet's reading of the Johannine phrase "worship in spirit and truth" is quite interested in holding spiritual and institutional religion together. Yet Chauvet is also equally interested in maintaining the healthy tension between them. If the Spirit works in the "hidden order of desire," Chauvet contends in an argument with strong affinities to Augustine's anti-Pelagian writings, then the triune God's life of reconciled love will inscribe itself in human bodiliness beneath the mind's defense mechanisms. Sacramental rituals inscribe the Trinitarian relationships of self-giving/self-receiving in the "hidden order of desire" without the idolatry-prone mind's conscious permission.[13] The nature of these relationships was first inscribed in the body of scripture, which narrates the story of Jesus' completely nondefensive and nonmanipulative worship of the Father. Jesus' life and death is for Chauvet an "antisacrifice," or a pure "spiritual sacrifice" that refuses to set up idolatrous rival alternatives to God's rule (ritual sacrifices, rigid codes of morality, or any other religious ideology that claims for itself the power to take away the sins of the world). The noncoercive love of the Trinity narrated in the body of scripture is then inscribed on the body of the church through sacramental rituals.

Sacramental worship must, however, be "worship in spirit." Chauvet maintains that any discussion of the grace of the sacraments requires a sophisticated pneumatology; "worship in spirit and truth" turns out to be quite different than quasi-gnostic readers of John 4:21–24 assume. The difference is that for Chauvet "worship in spirit and truth" requires a strong institutional locus, namely, formal liturgical rites with a strong christocentric focus and specific attention to the spiritual "lesson" (or better, "antilesson") of the crucifixion.

For Chauvet, the cross makes possible "worship in spirit and truth" in the purest sense. On the cross Jesus reveals God's true identity and hence Christians (unlike the Samaritans of John 4) now "understand" what they worship (John 4:22). However, this means Christians understand that they do not understand. The cross teaches that God is a reality that always exceeds all attempts to understand and grasp God; the cross undermines all tidy and pat theological lessons and reveals the fullness of truth (as divine love) by "crossing out" the supposed "truth" of God as ideology and conceptual mastery.[14] Chauvet's main point here is that "we stop projecting onto Jesus, on

---

12. Chauvet, *Symbol and Sacrament*, 95–98.
13. Ibid., 47–62, 531–37.
14. Ibid., 499.

the basis of his 'divine nature,' our *a priori* notions of what God is; these are precisely the ones that need to be converted."[15] God the Father allows Jesus to be killed in a senseless and meaningless act of violence. Jesus does not use his divinity to save himself. Jesus was emptied of himself by God the Father so that he could be filled by God the Spirit.[16] Here God defines God as the one who gives away fullness, lives in emptiness, and thereby receives fullness from another. But the cross also defines the root meaning of sin: humanity's idolatrous theological tendency to use God to affirm as absolute human-designed religious systems and a priori theological theories.[17] If theology remains focused on the cross, it will learn that God refuses to be a kept idol. Jesus expresses in his dying cry on the cross (Ps 22:1) his true desire to live in perfect obedience to the first commandment. Jesus thereby showed his true relation to the Father as one who manifests his identity as God by with-drawing from our grasp.[18] In his experience of "letting-God-be-God" and of "radical difference" Jesus learns his "likeness" to the Father. On the cross Jesus lets God be God by refusing to "use" God or to "play at being God."[19] This is for Chauvet how we ought to interpret the Johannine phrase "worship the Father in spirit and truth." [20]

From this understanding of "worship in spirit and truth" Chauvet con-structs a properly theological (i.e., not philosophical) antidefinition of God: God is the one who crosses out God. So here then is how Chauvet reads the Johannine phrase "God is Spirit" in verse 24. God comes to us as pure gift of Spirit and not some "thing" to be managed and controlled. Without a theology of the Spirit, the institutional church's liturgical memorial of Jesus crucified becomes only fine-sounding religious propaganda incapable of identifying and rooting out the idols in human hearts. A theology of the Spirit at work in institutionally created and practiced rituals makes it clear that sacramen-tal rituals are rituals of God's radical difference.[21] Indeed, the Spirit's *essence* is to be the one who shows humanity that God is radically Other. Chauvet writes, "The Spirit is God as *ungraspable*, always-surprising, always-elusive; it is the God who cannot be managed, continually spilling over every religious institution."[22] Put differently, the Johannine phrase "God is Spirit, and those

---

15. Ibid., 493.
16. Ibid., 498–99.
17. Ibid., 501.
18. Ibid., 506.
19. Ibid., 506–7.
20. Ibid., 507.
21. Ibid., 511.
22. Ibid., 513.

who worship him must worship in spirit and truth" means for Chauvet a form of learned ignorance that makes possible a nonidolatrous relationship with God. The Spirit's task is to help all sacramental-liturgical rituals remain facilitators of nonidolatrous prayer. This is most especially true in the sacramental rituals of forgiveness and reconciliation, with the Eucharist being the clearest example of this.

Yet if the Eucharist is for Chauvet the clearest example of "worship in spirit and truth," it is so because it brings spiritual and institutional religion into a unity-in-tension. The Eucharist is therefore the most anti-idolatrous sacrament and the sacrament most threatened by idolatry. Christ's eucharistic bodily presence is objective in the sense of arch-writing, so it ought to be the best resistance to the idolatry of the imaginary. The Eucharist ought to be iconic, but it is precisely its radical objectivity that gives rise to idolatrous and fetishistic perversions. The abyss between icon and idol is deep but narrow—one can all too easily step across it. To stay on the icon side of the abyss we need a strong sense of Christ's *absence*, Christ's *absolute difference*.[23] This absence does not negate presence—there is no zero-sum game here. Both presence and absence belong together as "one ambivalent reality."[24] It is the Spirit who makes this holy ambivalence possible. "Worship in spirit and truth," then, means understanding Christ's presence in the eucharistic liturgy not as the presence of a thing but rather as a "coming-into-presence," that is, as a personal Other addressing the hearts of the worshipers. The presence is an elusive presence immune to intellectual manipulation. Hence the Eucharist is for Chauvet the "presence-of-the-absence" of God.[25] Eucharistic worship, therefore, instantiates the true meaning of worshiping the Father "in spirit and truth."

Chauvet's multivalent reading of "worship in spirit and truth" in John 4:21-24 is quite fascinating in itself. However, it is also possible to aver that Chauvet believes the pneumatology of John 4:21-24 is only part of a larger pneumatic-liturgical dimension of Johannine theology as a whole. Indeed, it is quite suggestive that John 6:22-71 (Jesus' discourse on the bread of life) also receives extended attention from Chauvet.[26] Chauvet obviously recognizes that John's presentation of Jesus' teachings in the discourse on the bread of life is christological-eucharistic and not explicitly pneumatological. However, Chauvet is also aware that, unlike the Synoptic Gospel writers, John takes Jesus' teachings on eating his "flesh" and drinking his "blood"

---

23. Ibid., 403–4.
24. Ibid., 404.
25. Ibid., 405.
26. Ibid., 222–26.

(John 6:51, 55–56) out of their Last Supper context and inserts them into the middle of his precrucifixion ministry. In other words, John reflects on the Eucharist outside of what was already at the end of the first century an officially institutionalized ritual. Chauvet reads this displacement as a Johannine statement of the unity-in-tension between spirit and institution in Jesus' imagery of eating and drinking his flesh and blood. The central theological point in the discourse on the bread of life, Chauvet contends, is the crucifixion of the Messiah and its hard-to-swallow implications. The Word of God came down from heaven as a new manna (the eternal word made flesh), only to be killed by the legitimate religious authorities. This was a major scandal. How could God become human, receive the death penalty for blasphemy, and still be God? This scandal was indigestible for many of Jesus' Jewish contemporaries. The issue behind the quarrel in verse 52—"How can this man give us his flesh to eat?"—is the struggle between belief in staid, predictable, institutionally sanctioned religion and belief in something that overturns what counts as religious commonsense. Chauvet believes John thought the eucharistic ritual was an apt metaphorical vehicle for this message. Chauvet reads John as teaching that to have faith in *this crucified Messiah* means "chewing, slowly ruminating over the scandal of the Messiah crucified for the life of the world.... The thoughtful chewing of the Eucharist is precisely the *central symbolic experience* where we encounter this bitter scandal of the faith until it passes through our bodies and becomes assimilated into our everyday actions."[27] Christians need this metaphor of chewing because their necessarily institutionalized faith always tempts them to think they already know exactly what God is and what redemption means independent of the Holy Spirit's work to erase idolatry from their hearts. This chewing gradually liberates them from preconceived idols and enables their institution's liturgies to be truly "worship in *spirit.*"

3. Worship in Spirit and *Truth*: Salvation Is from the Jews

This section of the essay presents Chauvet's understanding of the binary pair of liturgical and ethical religiosity and analyzes how he uses this second aspect of his pneumatic-liturgical theology to preserve theologically the multivalence of John 4:21–24. Recall that the second misinterpretation of this passage that Chauvet opposes fails to see the unity-in-tension between worship and ethics in the text. This misinterpretation takes two forms. The first reads "worship in spirit and truth" as mandating that ethical-prophetic religi-

---

27. Ibid., 225.

osity eclipse cultic religiosity. The assumption behind this mandate is that the only kind of worship that could possibly count as true would be action in the world on behalf of the poor, outcast, and marginalized. The actual ritual activities of the institutional church have minimal, if any, importance because they "are burdened with all the sins of the world—co-optation, alienation, suspect archaisms."[28] The second form of this misinterpretation is the reverse of the first. It reads "worship in spirit and truth" as mandating that cultic religiosity eclipse ethical-prophetic religiosity. The assumption behind this mandate is that the only kind of worship that could possibly count as true would be ritual activity serene in its own sphere of sacred symbolism and untainted by the cares of the profane world.

In arguing for his pneumatic-liturgical theology Chauvet clearly considers the war between these two misinterpretations of John 4:21–24 the source of much contemporary theological and pastoral mischief. He writes,

> it is not self-evident that a religion which proclaims "worship in spirit and truth" (John 4:23–24) should develop ritual forms of worship.... It is easy to simply let oneself forget the evangelical *tension* between ritual practice and ethical practice and, overly confident in the ritual (as well as hierarchical and dogmatic) system of the institution, act as if the rites were natural to Christianity. Was the Church really that healthy when in all serenity it over-did sacramentalization? And is it really that unhealthy, as one sometimes hears today, simply because it conducts its ritual practice in a manner that some find less comfortable? Is it not this uncomfortable tension between the sacramental pole of the institution and the ethical pole of verification that holds the Church evangelically upright and in good health under "the law of the Spirit"?[29]

It is more than plausible to assume that Chauvet believes overlooking the phrase "salvation is from the Jews" in verse 22 is the root problem with misinterpretations of verses 23–24 that disconnect worship and ethics. However, it must be admitted that, when Chauvet himself comments on Jesus' conversation with the Samaritan woman in John's Gospel, he omits explicit reference to this phrase from verse 22. Nevertheless, verse 22 is never far from his mind when thinking about maintaining the necessary tension between worship and ethics.[30] Let us, then, examine his reflections on the unity-in-tension of

---

28. Ibid., 228.

29. Ibid., 228–29. See also Chauvet, *The Sacraments*, 54–66.

30. For example, there is a lengthy section in *Symbol and Sacrament* entitled "The Historic-Prophetic Status of the Jewish Cult" that immediately follows his reflections on misreadings of John 4:23–24 (ibid., 229–39).

worship and ethics in Israelite religion and Judaism as a prelude to his understanding of the phrase "salvation is from the Jews."

Chauvet argues that, in contrast to the timeless myths of pagan religions,
history is central for Judaism. Contrary to the nonbiblical notion of time as
a "spiral" and an "open cycle," the general Israelite notion of time was linear,
with punctuating events and "moments of unexpected newness."[31] Chauvet
further explains that for biblical Judaism God reveals God's own identity
in history, not simply in creation. This is clear from the fact that the biblical Hebrews interpreted the creation of the world in terms of the creation of
Israel (Isa 54:5), and not vice versa.[32] The covenant with the Jews is central
to the unfolding of God's plan, central to the whole creation of time and free
human creatures. There is in biblical Judaism no sense of a fixed ahistorical
fate that dictates its will irrespective of free human efforts. From here Chauvet
explains that, because God intervenes and interrupts history in surprising ways, Judaism knows that history matters and cannot be dismissed as a
fleeting nothing in relation to the eternal. Instead, history has absolute relevance as the arena of God's saving work. This is the basis of cultic *memorial*
in Judaism. Liturgy shapes Israel's identity precisely because it is centered on
the act of collectively remembering God's interruption of the people's lives to
assign them a role in God's plan. As one might expect, Chauvet holds that the
Passover is *the* paradigm of Jewish liturgical memorial. The Israelites are com-
manded in Exod 13:8 always to remember what YHWH did for them in Egypt.
All future generations will have a Jewish identity only insofar as they insert
themselves through memory into their Israelite past. The liturgical memorial
is not paralyzing nostalgia or self-pity but a *commemoration* that regenerates,
re-enlivens, and mobilizes for new action in the present. In this sense, people
have a future only insofar as they have a tradition of memory.[33]

This is clearly illustrated, Chauvet argues, in the future perfect tense
of the theological-literary style of Deut 26:1–11.[34] When read aloud in the

---

31. Ibid., 229.
32. Ibid., 230.
33. Ibid., 232–34.
34. This passage reads, "When you have come into the land which the LORD, your God,
is giving you as a heritage, and have occupied it and settled in it, you shall take some first fruits
of the various products of the soil which you harvest from the land which the LORD, your God,
gives you, and putting them in a basket, you shall go to the place which the LORD, your God,
chooses for the dwelling place of his name. There you shall go to the priest in office at that time
and say to him, 'Today I acknowledge to the LORD, my God, that I have indeed come into the
land which he swore to our fathers he would give us.' The priest shall then receive the basket
from you and shall set it in front of the altar of the LORD, your God. Then you shall declare
before the LORD, your God, 'My father was a wandering Aramean who went down to Egypt

community, Deuteronomy's fictional memory of Moses speaking to Israel yesterday becomes a performance of Moses speaking to it today. In both cases Moses invokes the memory of the exodus and the journey into Canaan to teach the people that land must be "always received" as a gift and never taken for granted.[35] The context, Chauvet explains, is an increasingly "sedentary" Israel on the verge of a reactionary agrarian-paganism because of its historical amnesia.[36] This is why, he contends, the Deuteronomist is unequivocally reminding Jews that their God is a God of history, not a nature-god. The text attempts to repristinate Israel as a religious nation by reminding it of God's interruption of time in the past through liturgically enacting a divine interruption in the present.[37] The ethical injunction of verse 11 demands that Jews verify their past dispossession by acknowledging and ethically dealing with the dispossessed living among them in the present. The text names two classes of dispossessed: aliens and Levites. In the first case of the dispossessed, Jews are reminded of their original status as slaves. In the second case they are reminded that after they possess the land they owe everything every day to YHWH and must continually receive the land with a deep and perpetual sense of gratitude. Once in the land that God gave them, the Israelites were tempted to forget the lesson of the manna: they must live from the grace of God. Hence to remind them of this lesson, and thereby avoid a swerve into paganism, the Deuteronomist speaks in the present tense of the land as a gift given "today," like the manna. Returning the firstfruits is required as a ritual gesture of gratitude that dispossesses Israel of any sense of achievement and "brings home to Israel *its responsibility within history*" to all those in its midst who are also, in some sense, dispossessed.[38] Hence, in its actual ethical practice of justice for the poor, Jews accomplish their liturgy by accomplishing their identity as God's people in the plan of history. Citing Emmanuel Levi-

---

with a small household and lived there as an alien. But there he became a nation great, strong and numerous. When the Egyptians maltreated and oppressed us, imposing hard labor upon us, we cried to the LORD, the God of our fathers, and he heard our cry and saw our affliction, our toil and our oppression. He brought us out of Egypt with his strong hand and outstretched arm, with terrifying power, with signs and wonders; and bringing us into this country, he gave us this land flowing with milk and honey. Therefore, I have now brought you the first fruits of the products of the soil which you, O LORD, have given me.' And having set them before the LORD, your God, you shall bow down in his presence. Then you and your family, together with the Levite and the aliens who live among you, shall make merry over all these good things that the LORD, your God, has given you."

35. Chauvet, *Symbol and Sacrament*, 234.
36. Ibid., 235.
37. Ibid., 236.
38. Ibid., 238.

nas, Chauvet concludes that love of God and love of neighbor are "the very principle of the whole Law."[39]

Yet it is precisely this "liturgy of neighbor" that provokes a "crisis in ritual" in Israel's religion. The temptation to fuse nature worship, such as Baalism of various types, with worship of the God of Moses was strong, and resisting it proved to be a wrenching process. As the great prophets so clearly taught, cult can never be just lip service, never be memory for its own sake.[40] Cult must have ethical consequences in the world, or else it is not true cult; worship is not an end in itself but only the beginning of duty to God. The issue here for Chauvet is not simply an ethical imperative in Judaism but more comprehensively the crisis provoked in Israelite religion as it came to terms with what it meant to be a historical religion as opposed to a nature religion. To explain this crisis and how Israel dealt with it, Chauvet borrows some categories from Paul Ricoeur. Working with Ricoeur's notion of first naïveté,[41] Chauvet argues that in Israel the first naïveté of precritical worship centered on the sacred symbols derived from nature and its cyclical processes. In Chauvet's version of Ricoeur's notion of second naïveté, Jewish worship demythologizes its symbols and critically distances itself from "profane" nature as it integrates prophetic-ethical concerns into its cultic focus on the Lord of history. In place of the first naïveté a second naïveté emerges that resists the iconoclastic trajectory of demythologization and generates a "postcritical" symbolic-metaphorical worldview capable of integrating cultic symbolic rituals and ethics.

When read alongside his commentaries on John 4:21–24 and 6:22–71, Chauvet's commentary on the foot-washing episode in John 13:3–17 demonstrates this point as well as his keen eye for multivalent meaning in John.[42] Indeed, like his reading of John 6:22–71, Chauvet's interpretation of John 13:3–17 also uses the Johannine displacement of the Eucharist from the Last Supper for a theological purpose. Chauvet notes that, just at the moment in the Last Supper when the institution of the Eucharist is expected, John inserts the foot-washing episode. This makes a significant theological point about the meaning of worship, and eucharistic worship in particular. After Jesus completes the washing he tells his disciples, "I have set you an example, that you also should do as [καθὼς] I have done to you" (John 13:15). Chauvet writes,

---

39. Ibid.

40. Ibid. To make this point about the priority of justice over pure cultic ritual, Chauvet cites on this page Amos 5:21–24; Hos 6:6; Isa 1:10–17; Jer 7:1–28; Mic 6:6–8; Pss 50:12–15; 51:18–19; Sir 34:24–35:4.

41. See Paul Ricoeur, *The Symbolism of Evil* (trans. E. Buchanan; Boston: Beacon, 1969), 351–52.

42. See Chauvet, *Symbol and Sacrament*, 260–61.

"This *kathos*, we would say, has the value of a *sacramentum*—that is to say, of a gift on the part of Christ—and not simply of an *exemplum*."[43] Eucharistic worship is only "worship in spirit *and* truth" insofar as it facilitates a passage to ethical living outside the liturgical assembly. "To wash one another's feet is to live existentially the memory of Christ that the Eucharist makes us live ritually."[44] The spiritual truth of worshiping Christ in the symbolism of the liturgical foot-washing ritual is proved in the lives of those who verify the truth of their worship through ethical living.[45]

This outlines the meaning Chauvet finds in Jesus' comment to the Samaritan woman in John 4:22, "You people worship what you do not understand; we worship what we understand, because salvation is from the Jews." What Jesus and his followers understand, Chauvet maintains, is that, because the God of Israel is the Lord of history who commands ethical good works, to be pleasing to God worship must always be "in a constant state of crisis."[46] Far from being eliminated or reduced in Christianity, this state of cultic crisis is exacerbated after Easter and Pentecost.[47] Understanding both the crisis and its exacerbation, Chauvet assumes, is essential for understanding Jesus' assertion in verse 23 that "the hour is coming, and is now here, when true worshipers will worship the Father in spirit and truth; and indeed the Father seeks such people to worship him."

4. Worship in Spirit *and* Truth: Christian Life in a Third Naïveté

This section of the essay presents Chauvet's understanding of the binary pair of Jewish and Christian religious identity and analyzes how he uses this third aspect of his pneumatic-liturgical theology to reinstate the multivalence of John 4:21–24. We have already seen this third aspect emerge in Chauvet's handling of the cultic-ethical question. Now we examine Chauvet's pneumatic-liturgical theological reading of Jesus' words to the Samaritan woman that "the hour is coming when you will worship the Father neither on this mountain nor in Jerusalem" (John 4:21) as his framework for dealing with the question of Jewish and Christian religious identity in 4:21–24.[48]

Granting that it is difficult to know precisely what Jesus believed about the place of ritual in the new covenant, Chauvet makes the following case.

---

43. Ibid., 261.
44. Ibid.
45. Ibid.
46. Chauvet, *The Sacraments*, 59.
47. Ibid., 65.
48. Ibid., x.

First of all, following John the Baptist, Jesus was a critic of "cultic formalism."[49] With John, Jesus stands in a long prophetic tradition. Additionally, neither John nor Jesus was innovative in the Jewish context in summing up the law as love of God and love of neighbor. The best guess we can make, Chauvet speculates, is that Jesus intensified the prophetic criticism of worship detached from ethics and announced a coming new form of worship.[50] Chauvet likely reads "the hour is coming" in verses 21 and 23 as a Johannine announcement of a new post-Easter cultic dispensation, that is, worship in spirit and truth in the senses already described.

The question now is, How does Chauvet read the conjunction "and" in Jesus' announcement of a new cultic order of worship in spirit *and* truth? In other words, what is the connection between the anti-idolatrous institutionally learned ignorance of "worship in *spirit*" and the unity-in-tension of cult and ethics in "worship in *truth*"? The answer is this: it is the same (non)thing that connects the letter of the scriptures to the living body of the church, namely, the Spirit (the "antiname" of God) as the presence-in-absence of the risen Christ.

To begin making sense of this answer, let us return to Chauvet's claim that the tension between cult and ethics in Judaism is "doubled" in Christianity. The difference between biblical Judaism and Christianity is not that the former is less ethically focused than the latter. Rather the difference, Chauvet repeatedly insists, is theological, and specifically pneumatological and eschatological.[51] Christianity still has a cultic dimension, but its cult "is simply *of another order* than the Jewish cult … [because] it is founded entirely upon the rereading of the whole religious system, a rereading imposed by the confession that Jesus is the Christ. Thus, all rests on Easter and Pentecost."[52] Later Chauvet restates this conviction by ingeniously extending Ricoeur's argument about second naïveté into an argument for a third naïveté.

> If for Judaism the cult can be practiced only through a second critical naïveté, in Christianity it may be practiced only with what we can call a

---

49. Like John the Baptist, Jesus was part of the movement against bloody sacrifices at the temple. Yet he also probably attended temple (attested eleven times in the Gospels) and prayed there with his fellow Jews. But he did not participate in the sacrifices of animals. Jesus' attitude, Chauvet believes, is "unclear" to us. Perhaps it was unclear to the earliest Christians who still attended temple but fought among themselves about the prescriptions of the law. The whole subject of Jesus' attitude toward the temple vexed even the Gospel authors. Chauvet, *Symbol and Sacrament*, 244–46.

50. Ibid., 247.

51. Chauvet, *The Sacraments*, 62; idem, *Symbol and Sacrament*, 239, 250–52.

52. Chauvet, *Symbol and Sacrament*, 250.

"third" naiveté. It is still a naiveté, for every symbolic action "embraces" the whole of a subject, rather than directing itself solely to its brain. But it is a naiveté modified by a critical coefficient which, because of Easter and Pentecost, comes to reinforce the prophetic criticism of cult or, according to Christian hermeneutics, to proclaim the fulfillment of this criticism through the gift of the Spirit. Thanks to the gift of the Spirit through the Risen One, the transition from the letter to the body is from now on eschatologically possible.[53]

What is this "critical coefficient"? Perhaps Chauvet's meaning here would be clearer if he had modified "critical" with "self." The (self-)critical coefficient is that which allows Christian worship in spirit to become worship in truth. In a cultic third naiveté Christianity assimilates the critical component of Judaism's second naiveté and stringently applies it to the demythologization of organized religion and the religious self. The third naiveté emerges as a form of cultic religiosity purified by a radical critique of the self-idolatrous delusions of closed religious systems (e.g., the hyper-pious self, the self-obsessed religious authorities, the self-referential legal and cultic structures, the centripetal forces of the tradition). Life in the third naiveté is therefore a "new modality" of faith in the Lord of history, a modality that Chauvet also designates as the "new Christo-pneumatic principle" of faith.[54] Let us examine both ways of describing the third naiveté to clarify how Chauvet interprets the conjunction "and" in Jesus' announcement of a new cultic order of worship in spirit *and* truth.

Life in the third naiveté is a "new modality" because it shares the basic structure of Jewish identity as a religion of faith in the Lord of history. Returning to his analysis of the firstfruits passage in Deut 26:1–11, Chauvet contends that this story epitomizes in a crystal-clear manner the structure of Jewish identity. The structure is tripartite: (1) God initiates contact with Israel by bestowing utterly gratuitous gifts (freedom from slavery and the land of Canaan); (2) Israel recognizes the gifts as gifts—not the reward of their own efforts—and receives them as such; (3) Israel makes a return gift to God in thanksgiving (the fruit of the soil and justice for and joyfulness with the aliens and Levites in their midst).[55] This structure of gift–reception–return gift is, according to Chauvet, foundational for Judaism. He argues that the gift corresponds to God's saving works in history as they are preserved in the scriptures. The reception, Chauvet further argues, corresponds to the ritual-

53. Ibid., 265.
54. Ibid., 252.
55. Ibid., 283–84.

cultic performance of memory in the present where worshipers acknowledge their ongoing status as receivers of a gift that cannot possibly be paid back. Cult is an exercise in spiritual education in which worshipers are schooled in the graciousness and gratuitousness of faith in the Lord of history. In the liturgical pedagogy of grace, the worshipers learn to abandon any notions of religious achievement and become pure receivers who simply open themselves to a gift beyond measure. However, Chauvet maintains, pure receptivity is only the middle step in the process. A liturgy of reception also prepares the worshipers to make a return gift in which they undertake the active work of paying forward God's gift into creation; ethical service to the neighbor is the true firstfruits offered to God. In paying forward the gift (liberation and land) as the return gift (ethical service to the marginalized, poor, and least ones), Jewish worshipers express their cultic schooling in graciousness and gratuitousness. By making cultic rituals of receptivity the "point of passage" from gift to return gift, the worshipers become a people of "symbolic exchange" whose very identity is to live as receivers in a gift-giving network free from any "business exchange" calculations of what is given and what is owed.[56]

Chauvet then applies the category of gift–reception–return gift he derives from his reading of the Hebrew scriptures to Christianity, arguing that Christianity is a "new modality" of Judaism's "symbolic exchange" religiosity. It shares the same tripartite pattern of gift–reception–return gift. Indeed, he argues that the eucharistic ritual is at its core a symbolic exchange rite that follows Judaism's gift–reception–return gift pattern. However, he also sees a substantive difference. Christianity's mode of ritualizing and living this pattern is characterized by "newness" in the sense that the gift originating the process is not liberation from slavery or land or even the law but rather Jesus Christ and his Spirit.[57] To interpret the Johannine phrase "the hour is coming and is now here" (verse 23), Chauvet turns to Paul's theology in the Letter to the Romans. Chauvet argues that Paul's understanding of "newness" ought to be read as teaching that the "Christo-pneumatic principle" is a "new modality of justification" in which the focus is now on "faith in Jesus as Christ" and on the gift of grace, not one's own righteously rigid adherence to "the works of the Law."[58] Chauvet is at pains to make clear that his Pauline distinction between the "oldness" of the law and the "newness" of Christ and Spirit is not a crude form of supersessionism in the sense that Christian religious

---

56. For Chauvet's discussion of the difference between "symbolic exchange" and "market exchange," see ibid., 99–109. For his discussion of worship as the point of passage from gift to return gift, see 281–82.

57. Ibid., 253–54 and 287.

58. Ibid., 252.

identity has totally invalidated and replaced without remainder Jewish religious identity. Rather, the Pauline distinction of "oldness" and "newness" is an assertion about Christian religious identity and its perpetual state of unity-in-tension with the ongoing reality of Jewish religious identity. In a Pauline argument with clear Johannine resonance, Chauvet maintains that "our term *'oldness' does not designate the Old Testament as such, but what led this Testament to become 'old' by condemning the newness in Jesus Christ.* The term refers to whatever led to the smothering of the newness, which ran across it and worked through it."[59] The "oldness" therefore is not the law as the "letter"—Chauvet insists that there can be no Spirit without letter—but rather the law as "imprisoned in the letter" and disconnected from the ethical religiosity advocated by the prophets.[60] The "newness" therefore was even present in Israelite and Jewish religion prior to the coming of Christ. This claim certainly renders discussions of Jewish and Christian identity more rather than less difficult.

To make discussions of Jewish and Christian identity even more complex, Chauvet also makes clear that "newness" is not the New Testament or the church but only Christ and the Spirit. It is perilous to forget this, he warns. "The Church is always in danger of reducing the gospel to the oldness of a document in which the Spirit would be extinguished, of a ritual that would again become a 'good deed' and a 'means of salvation,' of a corps of ministers who would be priestly intermediaries between humans and God."[61] In other words, the great and perennial temptation for Christianity is self-righteous self-idolatry. The herald who only proclaims the love of God but does not receive it as gift and then return the gift in ethical living soon becomes the herald who only proclaims his own righteousness. The once-banished demon of legalism always threatens to return to the house with seven other demons more evil than itself. When properly received, Chauvet believes, the Christo-pneumatic principle both drives Christians into the world to sanctify it with good works and prevents them from becoming either complacent in the knowledge of their own salvation or deluded in undertaking good works with messianic pretensions. Those who worship truly in the Spirit do not become self-idolaters falsifying the Christian cult from within.[62] He insists the Spirit enjoins on the church the labor of an unceasing "pass-over" from the oldness that threatens it to the newness it proclaims accomplished in Christ. This

59. Ibid., 287.
60. Ibid.
61. Ibid.
62. Ibid., 277, 279–80, 311–15, 530.

conversion is a death to oldness and "the violence that it imposes on others and that finds its fundamental alibi in 'God.' "[63]

For Chauvet, therefore, the "newness" of the Christo-pneumatic principle predisposes Christians to worship in spirit *and* truth, which means in part that they must live their Christian identity in both unity and tension with Jewish identity. The new mode of "symbolic exchange" in a self-critical third naïveté is entirely dependent on Jewish religious traditions of the unity-in-tension of both spirit and institution and worship and ethics, and yet it exists in a nonviolent critical tension with the way these traditions are often lived in practice. It is both in unity and in tension with Jewish identity because it shares with and critically applies to it the religious imperative to subvert the idolatrous confusion of liturgical rites and magical manipulation of God and/or ideological manipulation of people. Indeed, Chauvet believes Christianity must be receptive to Jewish critique when its ritual life falls into idolatry. Rituals governed by the new Christo-pneumatic mode of symbolic exchange thinking ought to facilitate demastery and openness to the "scandal" of God's powerlessness on the cross. They ought to challenge the unconscious legalistic desire to buy grace with scrupulously performed rites and good works or, more insidiously, the desire to buy grace by taking on the role of an angel of wrath who performs dirty deeds of violence in God's name. Practiced in the (self-)critical coefficient of the Crucified One's Spirit, Christianity's sacramental rituals ought to undermine the unconscious desire to live "according to a pattern of force and competition" that always excuses its own crucifying violence by puffing itself up with the "megalomaniacal" belief that its ways are God's ways, its truth is God's truth, and its goals are God's goals.[64] Issues of peace, justice, and mercy therefore are at the very core of what it means to "worship in spirit *and* truth."[65] The real test of the spiritual efficacy of the eucharistic *epiclesis* comes in the ethical life of Christians outside the assembly: "go in peace to love and serve the Lord." For Chauvet, it ought to be clear for Christians living in the third naïveté that they must live in the world in a posture of dialogue without rivalry, competition, or enmity of any kind.[66]

5. CONCLUSION

I conclude this chapter with this question: Is it possible to extend Chauvet's pneumatic-liturgical reading of John 4:21–24 to the Fourth Gospel in its

---

63. Ibid., 289.
64. Ibid., 299, 531–37.
65. See ibid., 552–54.
66. Ibid., 522–23.

entirety? Another form of this same question asks: Is the Fourth Gospel in its entirety multivalent in the ways that Chauvet's reading suggests is the case with John 4:21-24? As we have seen already, it does seem plausible to read John 6:22-71 and 13:3-17 as sharing generally the same multivalence as John 4:21-24. It is not unrealistic to think that a close reading of the Fourth Gospel would show that it is at its core a profoundly multivalent text centrally concerned with the unity-in-tension of spiritual and institutional religion, liturgical and ethical religiosity, and Jewish and Christian religious identity. There would be many merits to demonstrating that one could plausibly read John's Gospel in its entirety in this way. It would be particularly important if Chauvet's understanding of the unity-in-tension of Jewish and Christian religious identity in John 4:21-24 could be shown to be pervasive in Johannine theology. For example, if John's Gospel is multivalent on the Jewish-Christian identity question in the way Chauvet's reading suggests, then we would be compelled to seriously rethink many of the indictments against it for being the root cause of the Christian tradition's long and ugly history of violence against Jews. This is the case because the delicate theological negotiations underlying the unity-in-tension of Jewish and Christian religious identity provide the guiding pattern for negotiating the unity-in-tension of liturgical and ethical religiosity, which in turn provides the guiding pattern for negotiating the unity-in-tension of spiritual and institutional religion. A genuinely spiritual and institutional religion practicing an authentic liturgy of the neighbor (i.e., a religion that worships in spirit and truth) would simply not encourage or condone violence of any kind against anyone, nor would it facilitate the types of ecclesiastical-institutional self-idolatry that are sine qua non for religiously motivated hatred and violence.

This does not mean that Chauvet's reading of John clears away all the thorny theological problems inherent to the issue of Jewish and Christian identity. On the contrary, his multivalent reading makes things more complex, not less. For instance, we must grant that, even on Chauvet's reading, John's Gospel remains a supersessionist text; the categories of "oldness" and "newness" necessarily belong to a supersessionist theological paradigm. However, it also must be noted that not all forms of supersessionism are equal. There is a spectrum of possible Christian versions of supersessionism ranging from the crude and demonological (i.e., Christian theologies that are hostile toward Jewish religious identity and treat it as toxic to Christian religious identity) to the qualified and benign. Chauvet's supersessionism obviously falls very much nearer the latter pole: Chauvet's insistence that John is teaching a complex unity-in-tension of spiritual and institutional religion and liturgical and ethical religiosity shows the strong affinities of his theology with Jewish theology both before and after the creation of the biblical canon; this insistence

means also that he reads John as teaching a complex multivalent understanding of the relationship between Jewish and Christian religious identities that
stands in direct contrast to both simplistic dichotomous understandings and
simplistic homogenizing understandings of this relationship. If Chauvet's
reading of John 4:21–24, particularly verse 22, can be plausibly extended to
the entirety of John's Gospel, we would have to conclude that John's supersessionism is also by far more sophisticated than crude, by far more benign
than demonological. Chauvet's reading of John simply will not allow Christians to demonize the Jewish Other or assert a perverse theological notion of
their Christian identity as a religion that replaces Judaism. On the contrary,
Chauvet shows that John teaches Christian identity as a complex project that
must discover itself in a difficult relationship of unity-in-tension with the
ongoing reality of postbiblical Judaism. This conclusion would significantly
challenge increasingly popular and simplistic readings of John's Gospel that
insist it presents Christian and Jewish religious identities as mutually toxic
and therefore that it is a demonological supersessionist text.[67] It would also
lend theological support to those more careful scholarly readings that seek to
do justice to the multivalent set of theological themes at work in the Fourth
Gospel, particularly its presentation of Christian religious identity's complex
negotiations with the spiritual and institutional as well as cultic and ethical
dimensions of Judaism and the Hebrew scriptures.[68]

---

67. See, e.g., Elaine Pagels, *The Origin of Satan* (New York: Vintage, 1995), 89–111; see
also James Carroll, *Constantine's Sword: The Church and the Jews* (New York: Houghton Mifflin,
2002), 92–93.

68. For one particularly admirable example, see Raymond Brown, *An Introduction to the
Gospel of John* (ed. F. J. Moloney; New York: Doubleday, 2003), 132–42, 157–83.

"… Who Proceeds from the Father"—and the Son? The Use of the Bible in the *Filioque* Debate: A Historical and Ecumenical Case Study and Hermeneutical Reflections

Bernd Oberdorfer

It has often been noted that the Christian Bible does not contain an explicit doctrine of the Trinity.[1] There are, of course, numerous references to Jesus Christ's unique relation to God (e.g., Mark 1:11 par.; Luke 10:21–22 par.) and some remarks concerning the Holy Spirit's significant role in preserving the church community (e.g., John 13–16). The New Testament also contains the well-known proto-Trinitarian formulas, such as the Great Commission statement in Matt 28:19 and the closing blessing in 2 Cor 13:13.[2] These allusions to the Trinity are, however, ambiguous. They can be interpreted either in a subordinationist direction, subordinating both Christ and the Spirit to the Father, or in line with the traditional Trinitarian concept of co-equality among the three persons.[3] This ambiguity was not problematized in the early

---

1. For my other treatments of the topic of the Trinity and the *filioque* debate, see Bernd Oberdorfer, *Filioque: Geschichte und Theologie eines ökumenischen Problems* (Forschungen zur systematischen und ökumenischen Theologie 96; Göttingen: Vandenhoeck & Ruprecht, 2001); idem, "Brauchen wir das Filioque? Aspekte des Filioque-Problems in der heutigen Diskussion," *KuD* 49 (2003): 278–92; idem, "Filioque," *RGG* 2:119–21 (part 2, column 120 by Karl Christian Felmy); idem, "The *Filioque* Problem—History and Contemporary Relevance," *Scriptura* 79 (2002): 81–92.

2. "Go therefore and make disciples of all nations, baptizing them in the name of the Father and of the Son and of the Holy Spirit" (Matt 28:19); "The grace of the Lord Jesus Christ, the love of God, and the communion of the Holy Spirit be with all of you" (2 Cor 13:13). These and all subsequent references to the Bible are taken from the NRSV. For details regarding these proto-Trinitarian formulas, see my *Filioque*, 37–58, as well as Michael Theobald, "Trinität II: Neues Testament," *RGG* 8:602.

3. For the history of the doctrine of the Trinity in the early church, see my article, "Trinität III: Dogmengeschichtlich: 1. Alte Kirche," *RGG* 8:602–8.

centuries of Christianity until Arius explicitly denied divine status to Christ, claiming that Christ was a creature created *ex nihilo*. Arius's claim led to the ensuing Trinitarian debates. In the fourth century both the Arians and the Nicene theologians worked out their respective Trinitarian concepts on the basis of the Bible.[4] Both groups attempted to interpret in a coherent way the diverse biblical witnesses to God. These interpretations were inevitably shaped by the intellectual and cultural milieus of late antiquity. Differences in respective Trinitarian concepts resulted from the different ways in which a biblical hermeneutic was reciprocally related to its conceptual-interpretative structure. In the case of the early church's Trinitarian controversies, the differences in Trinitarian conceptions was due to the different conceptual shapings of common biblical witnesses.

The entire history of the Trinitarian doctrine can be read in light of the reciprocal relation between conceptual framework and biblical hermeneutic. More important, this relation is also relevant in systematic-theological claims about the Trinity. Biblical-hermeneutical issues are at the root of Trinitarian explication. The Trinity is not the result of speculative theory; rather, it represents a coherent reading of the biblical witnesses. The biblical root of Trinitarian thinking has often been disregarded in the history of Christianity; yet without an explicit thematization of its relation to the Bible, the doctrine of the Trinity is in danger of becoming irrelevant as a practical expression of Christian faith. It comes as no surprise that in the West the frequent criticism launched against the Trinity is that it has nothing to do either with the Bible or with practical life; it is either merely an example of abstract metaphysics or a paradoxical logic with no practical use.[5]

---

4. Adolf von Harnack (*Die Entwicklung des kirchlichen Dogmas I* [vol. 2 of *Lehrbuch der Dogmengeschichte*; 4th ed.; Tübingen: Mohr Siebeck, 1909], 203, 204 n. 1, and 205 n. 2) lists the biblical references that the Arians and their opponents Alexander and Athanasius used. The Arians explicitly mentioned Deut 6:4; 32:39; Prov 8:22; Ps 45:8; Matt 12:28; 26:39–41; 27:46; 28:18; Mark 13:32; Luke 2:52; 18:19; John 11:34; 12:27; 13:21; 14:28; 17:3; Acts 2:36; 1 Cor 1:24; 15:28; Col 1:15; Phil 2:6; Heb 1:4; 3:2. Alexander and Athanasius alluded to: Pss 2:7; 35:10; 45:2; 110:3; Prov 8:30; Isa 53:8; Mal 3:6; Matt 3:17; 11:27; John 1:1–3; 1:13, 18; 10:15, 30; 14:8–10:28; Rom 1:20; 8:32; 9:5; Col 1:15; Heb 1:2–3; 2:10; 13:8; 1 John 5:1, 20; Rev 1:4. Karlmann Beyschlag correctly points out in his *Grundriss der Dogmengeschichte* ([2nd ed.; Darmstadt: Wissenschaftliche Buchgesellschaft, 1988], 1:277 and n. 147 for a list of biblical references) that Athanasius developed his theology out of a "network" (*Gitternetz*) of biblical arguments.

5. A famous example from Kant: "the doctrine of the Trinity, taken literally, is without any use for practical life" ("Aus der Dreieinigkeitslehre, nach den Buchstaben genommen, läßt sich schlechterdings *nichts fürs Praktische machen*"). See Immanuel Kant, "Der Streit der Fakultäten," in *Werke in Zehn Bänden* (ed. W. Weischedel; Darmstadt: Wissenschaftliche Buchgesellschaft, 1983), 9:303 (translation mine). This philosophical criticism should not obscure the fact that

If the criticism of irrelevance is applied to the doctrine of the Trinity in general, then it must presumably apply even more to the details and subtleties of this doctrine. One of the most intricate subtleties is the *filioque* issue. This topic concerns the relation of the Spirit to the Father and the Son in the eternal life of God. The question is whether the Holy Spirit "proceeds"— according to Greek formulation—"from the Father," "from the Father alone," "from the Father through the Son" or—as the Latin formulation goes—"from the Father *and* the Son (*filioque*)." The one-word *filioque* clause became one of the central church-dividing issues between East and West. The difference is poignantly represented in the two different forms of the Niceno-Constantinopolitan Creed and continues to remain a divisive issue in the global church today. There are contemporary Christians and Christian theologians who would argue that the *filioque* question is not important for understanding the experiences of faith. The technical Trinitarian questions concerning the eternal processions within the Godhead should be left to the historians of the Christian church and to the annals of church dogma. Yet as a church-dividing issue, the *filioque* problem remains a theological responsibility to resolve. It is my aim in this essay to challenge contemporary complacency and to offer a new way of conceiving the Trinity in view of biblical sources.

One way to begin this challenge is to relate the *filioque* question historically to the division between Eastern (Greek) and Western (Latin) Christian churches. This bifurcated history began in the middle of the ninth century when the *filioque* issue emerged as a controversial theme. The history ends up in two very different and even contradictory places of culture, liturgy, and theology while the *filioque* problem continues to dominate discussions and negotiations between the Eastern and Western Christian churches. Some Orthodox theologians argue that the *filioque* clause is the sole reason for the bifurcation between the two traditions, yet this is overstated. There are ecclesiastical and political factors at play as well. Furthermore, the recent climate of ecumenical openness has motivated an intense pursuit of the *filioque* question.[6] All three large confessional families (Orthodox, Protestant, Roman Catholic) accept and use the Niceno-Constantinopolitan Creed as an authentic expression of Christian faith. Hence the ecumenical discussions between the different churches tend to focus on the question of whether agreement can be reached regarding a common text of the Niceno-Constantinopolitan Creed that can function as a shared symbol. The specific debate focuses on the original Greek

---

there is serious *religious* criticism directed against the doctrine of the Trinity in the name of faith in, for example, Pietism or modern liberalism.

6. See Lukas Vischer, ed., *Spirit of God, Spirit of Christ: Ecumenical Reflections on the Filioque Controversy* (Faith and Order Paper 103; Geneva: WCC Publications, 1981).

version of the creed stemming from the Council of Constantinople in 381 C.E. This version does not mention the *filioque*. Hence the question is posed to the Western churches as to their willingness to appropriate this original form of the creed. It is at this point that a whole host of problems arises. The question is not merely the question of interpreting the meaning of the creed. It is more complex, addressing the complicated problem of how the Bible is used to inform the articulation of Trinitarian terms and concepts. The *filioque* problem is neither a matter of keeping or eliminating a term in the creed nor about a mere detail of Trinitarian speculation but strikes at the heart of Christian theology.

My concern in this essay is to identify the complex hermeneutical questions at the bottom of the *filioque* controversy. I show that the key difference between East and West is not simply a matter of prooftexting the Bible; Trinitarian conceptions from both sides of the ecclesial divide appeal to similar biblical texts (e.g., John 15:26; 20:22). The differences in conceptions are related to characteristically different types of neo-Nicene Trinitarian thinking that seem to shape the biblical witnesses in different ways.

I outline in the first part the hermeneutical implications of the Eastern conception of the Trinity as it was developed by Athanasius, Basil of Caesarea, Gregory of Nazianzus, and Gregory of Nyssa. I contrast in the second part the Eastern conception with the Augustinian conception that is foundational for Trinitarian thinking in the West. I argue that the key difference is a biblical-hermeneutical one. Eastern theologians tend to find the eternal relations between the Father and the Son and (the Father and) the Holy Spirit in the simple words of the savior. These words as they are recorded in the New Testament are, for Eastern theologians, the only authentic source of "information" about the incomprehensible being of God. Western theologians tend to see the eternal relations between Father, Son, and Holy Spirit as they are represented in the temporal relations in the history of God's creative, saving, and redeeming self-revelation to and in the world. This Western conception argues on the basis of the Bible but also identifies traces of the Trinity (*vestigia trinitatis*) in the structures of the world. Particularly the human mind is regarded as the analogy of the Trinity in creation par excellence. I argue that this kind of "inductive" understanding of the Bible informs the Western affirmation of the *filioque* clause. Western theology tends to infer Christ's eternal breathing of the Spirit from his temporal sending of the Spirit to or breathing of the Spirit on the disciples (e.g., John 15:26; 20:22; Acts 2:33). Although it has its basis in the Bible, this inference is without explicit biblical warrant.

I turn in the third and final part to twentieth-century Trinitarian theology. I show that contemporary Western theologians such as Jürgen Moltmann and Wolfhart Pannenberg reject this inference by arguing that the Bible reveals a much more complex structure of relations between the Son and the

Spirit in the history of revelation than the *filioque* represents. In conclusion, it is the particularly Western approach to the doctrine of the Trinity—inferring the immanent Trinity from the economic Trinity—that gives new impetus to the ecumenical dialogue with the Orthodox churches.

1. REVEALING WORDS AND THE *APOPHASIS:* THE EASTERN CONCEPTION

Athanasius and the Cappadocians articulated the key conceptual framework for conceiving the doctrine of the Trinity in the East and made key terminological distinctions. Their development of the Trinitarian doctrine was instrumental in overcoming the Arian crisis that had been accelerated rather than resolved by the Council of Nicea in 325 C.E. The council, as I have mentioned above, precipitated the Arian crisis by specifying the term *homoousios* to denote the inner-Trinitarian co-equality between Son and Father: the Son is of the same essence (*ousia*) as the Father. The Arian criticism against the formulation precipitated the theological task of explicating the Christian claim of monotheism under the same conditions as maintaining the claim that Christ is God in a full sense. In defending the Nicene consensus, Athanasius turned to the Bible, basing his defense of the threefold differentiation in the one divine essence as a differentiation revealed by Christ's literal commandment in Matt 28:19 to baptize all people "in the name of the Father and of the Son and of the Holy Spirit."[7] Athanasius did not explore in greater speculative detail the parameters of this differentiation; he rejected as illegitimately inquisitive any attempts to delve more deeply into the inner-Trinitarian mystery.[8] The connection between a strictly biblical basis and an (as it was later called) *apophatic* cautiousness respecting the incomprehensibility of God's very being became the determining characteristic of the Orthodox tradition as a whole. God is known only by what God reveals through Christ in the explicit words of scripture. Every positive *kataphatic* statement about God that is derived from the Bible must be anchored in a negative *apophatic* context. Humans are creatures with very limited cognitive capacity and can only appreciate the most limited of doctrinal determinations.

The Cappadocians followed Athanasius's cautiousness, yet they further developed the Trinitarian doctrine by making specific conceptual distinctions.[9] Basil of Caesarea distinguished between *mia ousia* and *treis*

---

7. See my *Filioque*, 69–75.

8. Athanasius, *Ep. mort. Ar.* 1.18.

9. See my *Filioque*, 75–96. Karl Holl's brilliant study is still important for this question today: *Amphilochius von Ikonium in seinem Verhältnis zu den großen Kappadoziern* (Tübingen: Mohr Siebeck, 1904; repr., Darmstadt: Wissenschaftliche Buchgesellschaft, 1969).

hypostaseis.[10] These terms are, as the history of Trinitarian explication acknowledges, philosophical terms not found in the Bible. Basil, however, understands the content of these terms as the content of the Bible's witness.[11] Basil used the distinction between one essence and three hypostases as a conceptual tool to express the full divinity of each of the three persons—Father, Son, and Holy Spirit—without dividing the divine unity. The "three" are three "modes of being" (hypostases) of the one divine essence. According to Basil, it was not possible to articulate the divine unity of the three hypostases without appealing to the term *ousia*. Basil countered by his conviction the so-called "Homoiists" who proposed in strict biblicist manner that Christ was "like God according to the scriptures" in order to avoid any mixture of theological and philosophical language. Basil represents the Cappadocian conviction that the use of *philosophical* terms is necessary to maintain basic insights of the *biblical* witness.

The Eastern tradition of Trinitarian theology owes to Basil's friend Gregory of Nazianzus a more refined terminology.[12] Gregory of Nazianzus distinguished between the three modes of being in God as *agennesia* (ungeneratedness), *gennesis* (generation), and *ekporeusis* (procession). He adopted biblical terms to articulate the distinctions. This allusion to the Bible is no coincidence. The term *ekporeusis* is taken from John 15:26 and serves to denote the Spirit, who is identified by his origin from the Father (*gennesis* is taken from Ps 2:7, which is quoted with reference to Christ in Acts 13:33; Heb 1:5; 5:5). These two relations of origin from the Father identify the Son and the Holy Spirit, and the Father is defined negatively by his lack of being generated. The Eastern theologians restrict the term relation to the two concrete relations of "generation" and "procession," which constitute the persons of the Son and the Holy Spirit. This use differs from the later Latin tradition that clarifies relation as a general term for the real differentiations in the Godhead; Son and Spirit are not distinguished from each other without the former

---

10. See my *Filioque*, 76–83.

11. The Creed of Nicea (325 c.e.) prescribed the terms *ousia* and *hypostasis* synonymously to denote the unity of God. The rejection of a plurality of *hypostaseis* in God implied a rejection of a plurality of *ousiai* that would destroy the monotheist claim of one divine nature. Origen, however, had already used the term *hypostaseis* (in the plural) to specify the distinct modes of being in God, although he did not restrict these terms to the triad of Father, Son, and Holy Spirit. The Latins suspected that *hypostaseis* was an exact equivalent to *substantia* and only accepted it as an adequate expression for the status of being, attributed respectively to Father, Son, and Holy Spirit, when it became clear that this did not imply tritheism. They preferred instead the term "person."

12. See my *Filioque*, 83–88.

being the origin of the latter.[13] The Orthodox tradition, however, never saw the necessity of defining a difference in the eternal relations of origin between Son and Spirit. Orthodoxy since Photius, the ninth-century Patriarch of Constantinople, explicitly denied the possibility of such a difference because this difference seemed to contradict the fundamental truth of the Father being the only *origin* within God. This emphasis resulted in the strict differentiation between the immanent and the economic Trinity. The Orthodox tradition restricted the explicit term in the Bible that the Spirit is *sent* by the Son (e.g., John 15:26) to the economy of salvation and shied away from applying this relation to the immanent, eternal relation between Son and Spirit.

The task was left to Basil's brother, Gregory of Nyssa, to state with more precision the distinction between Son and Spirit.[14] On the one hand, Gregory of Nyssa concisely identified the Son as the "only one who is being generated" (*monogenes*).[15] On the other hand, he claimed that the Holy Spirit proceeds "from the Father *through the Son*" (*dia tou hyiou*).The first term, *monogenes*, is taken from the Bible, specifically from John, who calls Jesus the *monogenes hyios* (3:16; 3:18) and once even the *monogenes theos* (1:18). The second term, "through the Son," is explicitly taken from the liturgical formula "from the Father through the Son in the Holy Spirit," which, according to Athanasius, summarizes the Trinity's "cooperation" in the creation, salvation, and consummation of the world.[16] The liturgical formula "through the Son," like *monogenes*, is explicitly taken from the Bible (e.g., John 1:3; 1 Cor 8:6). Both Trinitarian specifications of the relations between Son and Spirit demonstrate the characteristic Orthodox use of scripture in theological decision-making.

In short, Gregory's attempt to refine the concept of God's Trinitarian being continues to respect the Eastern hermeneutical rules limiting the knowledge of God's triune being to explicit biblical terms. In a certain sense, the Eastern formula "through the Son" approximates the Western *filioque* ("and the Son"), yet Gregory of Nyssa does not explicitly claim Christ to be the origin of the Spirit. He insists that the only *aition* (origin, cause) in God is the Father. Both the Son and the Spirit are *aitiata* (originated, caused), while the Spirit's origin can be understood to be mediated (*mesiteia*) through the Son.[17]

---

13. Gregory of Nazianzus, *Or. Bas.* 31.9; 9.16.

14. See my *Filioque*, 88–94; see also Werner Jaeger, *Gregor von Nyssas Lehre vom Heiligen Geist: Aus dem Nachlass* (ed. H. Dörries; Leiden: Brill, 1966).

15. Holl, *Amphilocius von Ikonium*, 212.

16. See my *Filioque*, 71.

17. Gregory of Nyssa, *Quod non sint tres dei*, in F. Müller, ed., *Opera dogmatica minora* (4 vols.; Gregorii Nysseni Opera 3; Leiden: Brill, 1958–), 1:56; see also Holl, *Amphilocius von Ikonium*, 214.

2. The History of Revelation and the Analogy: The Western Conception

Augustine is acknowledged to be the father of Western Trinitarian theology.[18] He proposed a specifically Western neo-Nicene conception of the Trinity without explicitly directing a polemic against the Greeks.[19] Augustine's conception differed in some key aspects from the Cappadocian neo-Nicene conception. I will show in this section that these differences have to do with a specific biblical hermeneutic and a particular method of articulating dogmatic-theological claims in view of the Bible. I will frame the hermeneutical and conceptual issues by focusing on three aspects of the Holy Spirit's status in the Trinity.

First, Augustine bases his Trinitarian pneumatology on the formula that the Holy Spirit is the Spirit of the Father and the Son.[20] This formulation is a combination of the biblical words in Matt 10:20 ("the Spirit of your Father") and Gal 4:6 ("the Spirit of his Son"). The Greek theologians did not use or accept this combination because it seemed to erase the difference between the Father and the Son with regard to their respective relations to the Spirit. Augustine also refers his pneumatology to the passages in John's Gospel that mention the Paraclete: in John 15:26 Jesus announces to the disciples that *he himself* will send the Spirit to them after his return to the Father; in 14:26 Jesus claims that *the Father* will send the Spirit. Augustine differs from the characteristic Greek conception by referring the economic relations between Father, Son, and Spirit to their immanent relations in the eternal essence. The Greeks disputed this inference in later controversies by focusing on the verb tense in John 15:26. According to the Greek theologians, Christ deliberately chose the present tense when he spoke about the Spirit's (eternal) *procession* from the Father ("the Spirit of truth who *comes* from the Father") and used the future tense when anticipating the (temporal) *mission* of the Spirit: "whom I *will send* to you from the Father."

Second, Augustine modifies Aristotle's theory of categories when discussing the term *relation*, as is well known in the history of Trinitarian theology. Augustine formalizes the concept of relation as a category between substance and accident. This modification of classical metaphysics results in the claim that there are real (meaning nonaccidental) distinctions in God without threat to the unity of the divine essence. Medieval Western theologians remained

---

18. See my *Filioque*, 107–28.
19. Peter Gemeinhardt, "Lateinischer Neunizänismus bei Augustinus," *ZKG* 110 (1999): 149–69.
20. Augustine, *Trin.* 1.4.7; 1.5.8; 4.20.29; 5.11.12; 15.26.45.

committed to Augustine's terminological and metaphysical development. The only distinguishing mark between Son and Spirit is the respective relation of origin; without this distinction, Son and Spirit are indistinguishable from each other. The following formulation from Anselm of Canterbury became the hermeneutical rule for interpreting biblical statements about the divine persons according to the doctrine of the Trinity: "in divinity, all is the same or one, where the opposition of relation does not stand in the way."[21]

Third, Augustine understands the Holy Spirit as the mutual community of the Father with the Son. The Spirit is the tie of their mutual love and the unity between them (*vinculum caritatis, vinculum unitatis*). Augustine arrives at his understanding of the Spirit by interpreting biblical words and concepts in a Trinitarian-theological way. The inference he draws from the Trinitarian economy to the immanent Trinity is representative of the Western conception. Augustine begins with the Spirit's economic function as the *gift of communion* (e.g., 2 Cor 13:13); the Spirit in her economic Trinitarian function gives herself to Christians and thereby creates their communion of love. Augustine then transfers the Spirit's economic identity in her gift-giving function to the immanent Trinity. In the immanent Trinity, the Spirit is the love constituting the communion between the Father and the Son. The Spirit cannot proceed from the Father alone because the love between Father and Son is mutual.

Augustine's Trinitarian thought paved the way in Western theology for the *filioque*. When all three points mentioned above are taken together, the result is that the Spirit "proceeds from the Father and the Son" (Augustine, *Trin.* 15.26.45), yet this procession is specified to be *principaliter a Patre* (15.26.47). Western theology follows Augustine's path by maintaining the strict correspondence between the economic (temporal) and the immanent (eternal) mutual relations among the divine persons. Furthermore, Western Trinitarian theology defines the divine persons by distinctive eternal *relations of origin* that are revealed in distinctive *causative relations* (*missions*) in the history of revelation. The commitment to the economic Trinitarian revelation that is read back into the immanent Trinity tends toward the *filioque* because it explains how the Spirit's mission follows the Son's mission: the Son sends the Spirit to deepen and complete his mission to the world.

One further addition must be mentioned at this juncture. Augustine invokes an understanding of the "Trinitarian traces," the *vestigia trinitatis*, as traces of the Trinitarian Creator in creation. Particularly the human being

---

21. Anselm of Canterbury, *De processione Spiritus Sancti*, in F. Schmitt, ed., *S. Anselmi Cantuariensis archiepiscopi opera omnia* (6 vols. in 2; Stuttgart: Frommann, 1968), 1.2:181: "in Deo omnia sunt unum ubi non obviat aliqua relationis oppositio."

is the trace of the Trinity par excellence because the human is created in the image of God (*imago dei*); especially it is the human mind as the unity of memory, intellect, and will that depicts the image of the Trinity in the created realm. Augustine does not intend by his understanding of the Trinitarian traces to prove the Trinity in creation. He stresses in his *De Trinitate* that the idea of the *vestigia trinitatis* functions as a second-order argument based on the normative doctrine of the church. Yet Augustine's view proved to be formative for the Western theological imagination. Influential lines of Western thinking about the Trinity privilege a psychological theory of the Trinity. God is the *summus spiritus*; the three persons are God's three modes of consciousness.[22] Such speculative psychological thinking indicates a more constructivist style of interpreting the biblical witnesses against the backdrop of defending biblical monotheism and in the light of a tendency to infer the immanent Trinity from God's economy of salvation. This tendency is already evident in medieval Trinitarian thought and is a central theological reason for the alienation between Western and Eastern churches.

· 3. CLEAR POSITIONS—AND NEW INSIGHTS

Two different theological conceptions of the Trinity developed from the two different approaches to the mystery of the Trinity. The Western tradition claimed that the eternal causative relation between the Son and the Holy Spirit was a necessary relation, while the Eastern tradition claimed this relation to be impossibile. As a result of this difference, the East judged the Western doctrine of the *filioque* to be heretical. Yet the anathema seems to hide important biblical, hermeneutical, and theological issues that might even be deemed, when viewed in a different light, to be complementary. Both conceptions are the result of integrating biblical phrases and concepts into different systematic frameworks. Both conceptions presuppose a different method of articulating doctrinal claims about God's essence in relation to the Bible.

The history of the late Middle Ages and then of the Reformation does not see any substantive changes to the bifurcated trajectory. Attempts to arrive at a mutual understanding of similarities and differences failed.[23] The well-known attempts at reunion at the Councils of Ferrara and Flor-

---

22. The text regarded as being most influential on medieval thinking about the Trinity is Anselm's *Monologion*.

23. According to the West, the Spirit's procession from the Father and the Son is a single act that is executed by the indistinct unity of them both (as Aquinas put it: one *spiratio* with two *spirantes*, but not two *spiratores*). This idea was affirmed at the Fourth Lateran Council in 1215:

ence (1438–39) were never accepted by the Orthodox churches. The Western church insisted upon the Son as *causa* or *aitia* of the Holy Spirit, even though the Greek patristic fathers had never used the term *aitia* with reference to the Son.[24]

The sixteenth-century Reformers affirmed the doctrine of the Trinity, yet changed its hermeneutical context. For them, the doctrine was true because it adequately interpreted the Bible, not because it was ensconced as church dogma. The Reformers accepted the *filioque* without reservation, although they did not polemically insist on a deliberately Western form of Trinitarian theology. In the second half of the sixteenth century, the Lutherans took up the dialogue with the Orthodox. The main record is the correspondence between Lutherans from the University of Tübingen and the Patriarch of Constantinople, Jeremy II.[25] During this debate the Lutherans saw it necessary to defend the *filioque*. They feared that without it the doctrine of the Trinity would lose its epistemological justification in the history of revelation. They argued in distinctive Western manner: the biblical witnesses to Christ's temporal sending of the Spirit could be used to ground the inference to the Spirit's eternal procession from the Son. In the ensuing centuries, Protestant theologians taught the *filioque* as a key part of the doctrine of the Trinity, although it was never historically emphasized as a pillar of Protestant theology.[26] This attitude did not change until the second half of the twentieth century, when, in an atmosphere of new ecumenical openness, new discussions about the *filioque* arose. For this new reflection on the *filioque* doctrine, biblical insights were of greatest relevance.

---

see Heinrich Denzinger, *The Sources of Catholic Dogma* (trans. R. J. Deferrari of the 30th ed. of Denzinger's *Enchiridion Symbolorum*; Fitzwilliam, N.H.: Loreto, 2004), 168–69 (§428).

24. Denzinger, *Sources of Catholic Dogma*, 219 (§691). At the Council of Florence and after long and intense discussions, all the participating Greek theologians with a few notable exceptions, such as Markos Eugenikos, accepted the declaration "Laetentur caeli" (ibid., 219–20 [§§691–94]). The declaration explicitly points to the Latin doctrine of the *filioque* as being equivalent to and a better expression for the Greek *dia tou hyiou*. The Greeks approved of the document, which seemed to correct some misconceptions. The Greeks had been convinced that, on the one hand, the *filioque* was more strongly rooted in the tradition of the Latin fathers than they had previously been aware. Their own patristic tradition, on the other hand, did not entail a strict rejection of the Son's participation in the Spirit's procession, as Photius had led them to believe.

25. See Dorothea Wendebourg, *Reformation und Orthodoxie: Der ökumenische Briefwechsel zwischen der Leitung der Württembergischen Kirche und Patriarch Jeremias II. von Konstantinopel in den Jahren 1573–1581* (Forschungen zur Kirchen- und Dogmengeschichte 37; Göttingen: Vandenhoeck & Ruprecht 1986); and my *Filioque*, 282–95.

26. For an overview of Protestant theology in the seventeenth century, see Bruce D. Marshall, "The Defense of the *Filioque* in Classical Lutheran Theology," *NZSThR* 44 (2002): 154–73.

In order to facilitate an understanding of this discussion, I will summarize the characteristics of the current renaissance of Trinitarian thinking in
Western theology. Karl Barth is usually invoked as the key theologian moti-
vating this revival. One basic conviction of Trinitarian thought since Barth is
that all human knowledge of God's triune being derives from the biblical witnesses to God acting toward and in the world. This conviction is clearly at the
root of Barth's interest in Trinitarian theology. The epistemological question
is one that Barth inherited from the neo-Kantianism of late nineteenth-
century German philosophy and stands as the centerpiece of his prolegom-
ena in *The Church Dogmatics*. Barth introduces the doctrine of the Trinity in
volume 1.1 of this work as a theory of God's self-revelation. Barth views the
biblical narrative of the history of salvation as the sole epistemological source
of any knowledge about God. For Barth, the fact that God is internally triune,
and the way that this is so, is not primarily information revealed by a voice
from heaven; rather, this fact is mirrored by the ways in which the divine
persons relate to each other in the history of salvation. Karl Rahner sums up
what has become a common opinion in twentieth-century Western theology:
the epistemological foundation for any Trinitarian thinking is that "the economic Trinity *is* the immanent Trinity and vice versa."[27]

The implications of Rahner's axiom for the *filioque* are, however, far from
clear. The Bible can be read, on the one hand, to support the *filioque*. This
reading according to a Western conception requires that the inference from
economic to immanent Trinity be rooted in the Spirit's mission beginning
at Pentecost. The Father and the Son are at the origins of the Spirit's mission
and, by following the Western inferential logic, are at the origin of the Spirit's
immanent Trinitarian procession. Karl Barth defended the *filioque* according
to this line of thinking in his *Church Dogmatics*.[28] At second glance, the connection between the biblical witnesses and the inference of their claims to the
immanent Trinity seems to be much more complicated. I will in the following
focus on what I consider to be the two crucial aspects challenging the Western methodological principle of beginning with the economy of salvation.

First, the Bible displays many more options than the *filioque* for conceiving the mutual relations between the Son and the Spirit. The relations between
Son and Spirit are not as one-sided from the biblical perspective as the *fil-*

---

27. Karl Rahner, "Bemerkungen zum dogmatischen Traktat 'de trinitate,'" in *Schriften
zur Theologie* (16 vols.; Einsiedeln: Benziger, 1954–), 4:115 (emphasis added); see also Eber-
hard Jüngel, "Das Verhältnis von 'ökonomischer' und 'immanenter' Theologie," *ZThK* 72 (1975):
353–64; see also my *Filioque*, 371–88.

28. Karl Barth, *Die Lehre vom Wort Gottes* (vol. 1.1 of *Die kirchliche Dogmatik*; Zurich:
Evangelische Buchhandlung, 1932), 496–511; see my *Filioque*, 354–71.

ioque suggests. The Spirit is not only sent by the Son but is also instrumental in the incarnation of the Son (Luke 1:35). The Spirit descends onto the Son after his baptism, guides him, and empowers him to fulfill his earthly mission (Mark 1:10 par.; Matt 12:28). Given these additional biblical witnesses, mutuality must be considered an essential element in the eternal relations between Son and Spirit. The Western tradition unfortunately excluded mutuality by declaring that the three persons of the Trinity are distinguished solely by their relations of origin. These relations of origin cannot, on logical grounds, be mutual. But is this restriction to relations of origin still convincing if it does not sufficiently mirror the complexity of relations between Father, Son, and Spirit depicted in the Bible?

This question can also apply to the Orthodox tradition that grounds the identities of Son and Spirit in their respective origins from the Father. Orthodox theologians since Gregory Kyprios in the thirteenth century and Gregory Palamas in the fourteenth century have answered this question by considering different kinds of eternal relations between the Son and the Spirit. Particular formulations, such as, "The Spirit proceeds from the Father and stays upon the Son" and "The Spirit proceeds from the Father and achieves its eternal manifestation [*ekphansis*] through and by the Son," articulate the mutuality between Son and Spirit. These and other similar expressions are, however, formulated in such a way as to avoid claiming any active participation for the Son in the Spirit's procession and thereby no active role for the Son in constituting the Spirit's identity. But the following question should be asked: How can the claims concerning the distinct types of relations be constitutive for respective personality?

German theologians, Jürgen Moltmann and Wolfhart Pannenberg in particular, have taken up these questions in developing their conceptions of the Trinity. Moltmann distinguishes "giving being" to a person from "giving shape" to the person. Moltmann writes that the Spirit receives her eternal "hypostatic being" (*hypostatisches Dasein*) from the Father alone but receives her concrete shape "from the Father and the Son and their mutual relations."[29] Pannenberg criticizes Moltmann's idea of a "shapeless" hypostatic being and claims that each of the three persons achieves its respective hypostatic identity by a complex set of different mutual relations to each other, of which the

---

29. Jürgen Moltmann, *Der Geist des Lebens: Eine ganzheitliche Pneumatologie* (Munich: Kaiser, 1991), 321. In his *Trinität und Reich Gottes: Zur Gotteslehre* ([Munich: Kaiser, 1980], 199), Moltmann distinguishes between "hypostatic existence (*hypostasis, hyparxis*, Latin *persona*)" and "immanent trinitarian shape (*eidos, prosopon*, Latin *facies*)"; see my *Filioque*, 389–403.

relation of origin is only one.[30] According to Pannenberg, the *filioque* is not a mistaken or even a heretical formulation; rather, it is an incomplete articulation of the immanent relations between Father, Son, and Holy Spirit.[31]

Second, since Augustine the Western tradition has emphasized that the different divine actions toward and in the world cannot be attributed exclusively to a single divine person: *opera trinitatis ad extra sunt indivisa* ("the works of the Trinity toward and in the world are indivisible"). This axiom undergirds the unity of God in every economic Trinitarian operation: creation is not an exclusive work of the Father, incarnation not an exclusive work of the Son, redemption not an exclusive work of the Holy Spirit. Every work *ad extra* is a common work by which the three persons cannot be distinguished. In a strict sense, the history of salvation does not reveal the characteristics of the divine persons and their internal relations; it reveals their concrete community only as the indistinguishable unity of the divine essence. Western theologians since the Middle Ages have recognized that the characteristic Western emphasis on unity instead of community threatens the biblical roots of Trinitarian theology. Hence they sought to show that the Bible displays a *network of concrete cooperation* constituting any acts of the triune God. The theory of appropriations was developed and became a key piece of Western Trinitarian theology. This theory claims that the biblical witnesses suggest a natural relation between creation and the Father, incarnation and the Son, redemption and the Holy Spirit. This natural relation is called an "appropriation," which means that a specific similarity of creation to the eternal characteristics of the Father can be ascertained, although the particular work of creation cannot be taken to be more strongly linked to this person than to the other two. The theory of appropriation is not without its critics, for example, Karl Rahner. In his ingenious treatise on the Trinity, Rahner pushes the strict application of this theory to its unintended and absurd limits, showing it to be an accident as to which of the divine persons has been made man.[32]

If the history of salvation, however, does not disclose the characteristics of the divine persons, then what is the source revealing these characteristics? It turns out that the Western tradition appeals to a very select choice of biblical passages for its picture of the triune God. The Western conception, when viewed as standing on this thin ice of biblical material, veers close to

---

30. Wolfhart Pannenberg, *Systematische Theologie* (3 vols.; Göttingen: Vandenhoeck & Ruprecht, 1988–93), 1:283–364; see my *Filioque*, 404–18.

31. Pannenberg, *Systematische Theologie*, 1:344–47.

32. Karl Rahner, "Der dreifaltige Gott als transzendenter Urgrund der Heilsgeschichte," in *Die Heilsgeschichte vor Christus* (vol. 2 of *Mysterium Salutis*; ed. J. Feiner and M. Löhrer; Einsiedeln: Benziger,1967), 317–401, esp. 320.

the Orthodox conception: knowledge of God's triune being is gleaned from information that reveals only the names of the divine persons and their relations of origin.

The real biblical picture displays interpretative options and possibilities that are a far cry from the usual Western "bottom-up" approach starting with the history of revelation. If Western Trinitarian theologians are to take into consideration a broader range of biblical witnesses, then they must take a serious look at the axiom of the *opera ad extra indivisa*. This axiom seems to be most stifling to an expansive biblical hermeneutic. The axiom, on the one hand, rightly claims that the three persons do all their works toward and in the world in common. They do not, on the other hand, do so indistinguishably; rather, each work betrays a concrete order of community that may differ when another work is considered. Creation, for example, is a work of the Trinity in a different way than the incarnation is the Trinity's work. Such a consideration of the diverse ways in which the Trinitarian order is revealed in its works can help to conceive of diverse mutual relations in God's eternal triune being.

4. CONCLUSION

The contemporary ecumenical dialogue between Eastern and Western Christian churches can serve to inspire theologians to imagine new ways to appeal to biblical witnesses in their conceptions of the Trinity. Trinitarian theology can neither be simply based on its own "speculative" traditions nor have as its only aim the "prooftexting" of that tradition with biblical quotes. Instead, it must take into account a new awareness of the rich and complex possibilities already contained in the Bible. By opening up its exegetical basis to the multiplicity of biblical voices, the doctrine of the Trinity might be seen to be relevant to the practices of Western Christians and might address the many concerns that Christians have in understanding their experiences of faith. Biblical diversity leads to theological relevance. The doctrine of the Trinity might just be exemplary in expanding its dialogical possibilities by expanding its biblical vision.

Recovering the Real: A Case Study of Schleiermacher's Theology

Christine Helmer

Recent and frequent appearances of the adjectival use of "real" connote more than a philosophically naïve tautology, and recent nonphilosophical appearances of the noun "Real" (with a capital R) express a longing in an age that seems to have turned its back at last on an infinite representational regress.[1] Even a recent visitor to the Los Angeles Museum of Contemporary Art can detect a sudden shift from conceptual-subjective art to art that depicts recognizable subjects in identifiable contexts.[2] The interest in reality, in its recovery in text and image, is a sign of the present times. The longing for the real in current intellectual, political, and artistic circles marks a turning point away from postmodern obsession with representation and sociocultural construction. Postmodernism appears to have crashed on the shores of reality, and a new sobering wave of consciousness is surfacing.

This turn to the real is the reappearance of an aspect of the West's own history. The emphasis on evidence as the Enlightenment intended it was to locate truth-telling in the public forum. Empirical study was to be governed by rules concerning reality that were to be displayed for all to see. Not just the sciences but the humanities as well were to be informed by evidence. It was to history, anthropology, and psychology, rather than to metaphysics, that modern theology turned in order to anchor its claims in reality.[3] Even the "linguistic turn" in the early twentieth century could not divorce language from reality, teaching that reality was interpreted through linguistically determined concepts. The empirically real was experienced through conceptual

---

1. See Slavoj Žižek's new book, *Interrogating the Real* (ed. R. Butler and S. Stephens; London: Continuum, 2005).

2. See www.moca.org for an introduction.

3. The representative example of this turn is Friedrich Schleiermacher, the "parent of modern theology."

interpretation. It was perceived through the biases, ideologies, and multiple epistemologies informing the modern subject of knowing.

It is the intention of this essay to recover the real in the distinct discipline of Christian theology and to attempt this recovery in view of the claims expressed in the Christian religion about the saving benefits of the person of Christ. Such claims are more than a cognitive assent to an epistemologically interpreted event. They are the expressions of the many transformative experiences of the encounter with a living reality.

I ask in this essay the question concerning how theology can recover the real in order to anchor its terms in historically and metaphysically determined reality. I will use the example of Friedrich Schleiermacher's theology to show that the real can be grasped both in relation to the text of the New Testament and in the theological categorization of contemporary experience. The real can be recovered in view of the New Testament's expressions concerning Jesus of Nazareth; when the texts are seen as literary records of unique encounters with the person of Jesus, their reality can be extrapolated, compared, and contrasted with the reality expressed in other similar accounts. The real as recounted in the New Testament is multivalent, yet even in this text the beginnings of categorizing multivalent reality can be detected. New Testament topography is the starting point for theological concept formation. In the second section of the essay I argue that theology's process of relating descriptions of reality to theological concepts does not inevitably result in a loss of reality for those concepts. Rather, the method of concept formation that Schleiermacher proposes determines the concepts with predicates gleaned from reality. The application of Schleiermacher's method to theology gives theology the resources to recover the reality of transformative encounters with Jesus for the formation of theological concepts.

1. Recovery of the Real in the New Testament

The linguistic turn characterizing a major philosophical development in the twentieth century gave rise to a fascination with the text. Language exists in texts, it was maintained, and religion also is preoccupied with linguistic-literary studies of the text. The past is presented for contemporary description and analysis by the text, yet is not completely identified with it. The text, produced by a subject or group of subjects, captures in literary form a reality that is available through the text, yet the text neither historically exhausts the reality to which it refers nor can it be metaphysically identified with that reality. Nineteenth-century philosopher and theologian Friedrich Schleiermacher keenly approaches the text as a transcript of the reality of its author and the respective author's encounter with a distinct reality. Schleiermacher recovers the real described in the New Testament by explaining his understanding of how this text expresses the diverse experiences of aspects of a personal reality that its authors have experienced.

The rhetoric of Christian liturgy, preaching, and theology gives the impression of an ongoing rehearsal of the past. Christianity's present-tense existence is permeated with scripture. Maybe not all contemporary preachers and scholars are as well-versed in the living memory of biblical passages and books as were Augustine or Luther, yet even in an age in which the canon has become a "cultural memorial" (*ein kulturelles Gedächtnis*),[4] writings from the Christian religion can hardly be interpreted without appealing to the Bible as a reference work. My question concerning the reason for the sustained representation of ancient texts in contemporary liturgical practices and scholarly works is posed by this actual evidence of use. Why regard the biblical text as the eternal well from which one can continuously draw? Answers to this question range from historical-pragmatic considerations[5] to philosophical-theological[6] explanations, from recognitions of the multivalence of its constitutive texts to longings for a unity as the text spans world history from creation to apocalypse.

But a bit of disentangling is in order here. The "linguistic turn" in some philosophical-theological cases conflates text with reality. When reality is understood in terms of the self-referentiality of language, the text becomes reality.[7] This identification in Christian theology is, as I have argued elsewhere,[8] a development of the neo-Kantian distinction between spirit and

---

4. This is the title of Jan Assmann's book on canon and memory in ancient and modern contexts from a cultural-historical perspective: *Das kulturelle Gedächtnis: Schrift, Erinnerung und politische Identität in frühen Hochkulturen* (C.H. Beck Kulturwissenschaft; Munich: Beck, 1999).

5. Schleiermacher distinguishes between the Christian Bible as the book used by the church throughout its history and the Christian canon as the product of literary-critical, historical, and canon-critical reconstruction. See Friedrich Schleiermacher, *Brief Outline of Theology as a Field of Study* (trans. T. N. Tice; Schleiermacher Studies and Translations 1; Lewiston, N.Y.: Mellen, 1990), §103 (58), §115 (63–64) (page numbers in parentheses).

6. For example, Nicholas Wolterstorff discusses the unity of the Christian canon by using the aesthetic category of a work's completion in "The Unity behind the Canon," in *One Scripture or Many? Canon from Biblical, Theological, and Philosophical Perspectives* (ed. C. Helmer and C. Landmesser; Oxford: Oxford University Press, 2004), 222–32.

7. Frei identifies D. Z. Phillips with the "fifth" type of theology in "Five Types of Theology," in *Types of Christian Theology* (ed. G. Hunsinger and W. C. Placher; New Haven: Yale University Press, 1992), 46–55. This type, Frei argues, asks the question of God's reality as the question concerning the criteria by which talk about God's reality in a specific religious context is meaningful (Frei, "Five Types of Theology," 47).

8. Christine Helmer, "Mysticism and Metaphysics: Schleiermacher and a Historical-Theological Trajectory," *JR* 83 (2003): 517–38.

nature. If the "Word"—in its identification with the risen Christ or in its meaning as the words of the Christian church's proclamation or doctrine—is identified with spirit in opposition to nature, then its reality in language must be its only reality. The Word's spiritual reality in language is contrasted with the reality of the world of nature. The text "absorbs the world." [9]

On metaphysically realist grounds, however, the spiritual reality of the text cannot be said to absorb the world. The text cannot be said to stand as the reality of language's self-referentiality; rather, the text stands *for* a distinct perspective of reality. The text refers to reality by linguistically conceptualizing an aspect of reality that has entered into the work of concept formation. A perspectival categorization of reality both exhibits and occludes dimensions of reality, discloses and hides, grasps and misses aspects of reality that other categorizations may or may not be in a position to see. Multivalence characterizes the perspectival relations of text to reality. This relationship also requires for its plausibility an explanation for the unity of its referent across descriptive difference. Without an account of unity, perspectival difference would lapse into incoherence; there would be no common constraints in reality controlling differences among conceptualizations and therefore no possibility of conversation among different individuals about a common subject.

A starting point for discussing the text's relation to the reality of the real is the historical origin of the text in relation to experience. One site for recovering the real is the site most proximate to an original experience. Some memories fade with time, but the vividness characterizing the early impression of the real cannot be erased. It is to this immediacy of the event in its present tense power that we must turn.

The history of Christianity witnesses to the power of initial impressions. Reformation movements have been born from new experiences with the biblical text. Augustine, Luther, Calvin, and Barth attest to the ongoing fascination with Paul's Letter to the Romans. Christianity can almost be written as a history of rediscovering the power of the Crucified One described in this significant epistle. The documents attesting to the early histories of the Christian tradition—the Old and New Testaments, and in some cases the

---

9. This is my paraphrase of the citation, "A scriptural world is thus able to absorb the universe," by George A. Lindbeck, *The Nature of Doctrine: Religion and Theology in a Postliberal Age* (Philadelphia: Westminster, 1984), 117. The sentences preceding these words suggest an equivocation between text and world: "These same considerations apply even more forcefully to the preeminently authoritative texts that are the canonical writings of religious communities. For those who are steeped in them, no world is more real than the ones they create" (Lindbeck, *Nature of Doctrine,* 117).

deuterocanonical writings—continue to be engaged as these texts are cycled through lectionaries, liturgies, private devotions, and small-group study. The same texts continue to be read for the purpose of recovering the vividness of realities experienced by persons and authors, since those experiences are determinative of Christian traditions. The life in Christian traditions is sustained precisely by the ongoing return to those documents categorizing the early impressions of a distinct aspect of reality.

The text's literary level provides clues identifying the ways in which first impressions took shape. An insight into the literary coherence of a text as the criterion of original liveliness is offered by Schleiermacher's interpretation of John's Gospel. Schleiermacher's special love for John's text consists precisely in his literary appreciation for its coherence. According to Schleiermacher, the liveliness of John's impressions of Jesus of Nazareth is evident in the way in which the Gospel presents Jesus' biography according to the coherence criterion of a single tendency (*Tendenz*) or principle. "The Gospel of John has always given me the impression that in a decisive way it bears the character of a coherent, comprehensive presentation," Schleiermacher writes in *The Life of Jesus.*[10] John has one principle that he uses to describe each different episode in Jesus' life. Schleiermacher continues: "the Gospel of John reveals one and the same tendency from beginning to end. It evidently comes from one who narrates what he himself had experienced."[11] Although Schleiermacher admits that there are gaps in John's chronology and account of Jesus' geographical movement,[12] he evaluates the Gospel's coherence as a literary key unlocking John's proximity to the reality of Jesus.

The literary criterion, however, gets Schleiermacher into some historical trouble. By identifying coherence as the criterion for John's status as an eyewitness, Schleiermacher erroneously proposes an early dating for the Gospel. New Testament consensus regarding John's Gospel, at least since 1820, disagrees with Schleiermacher.[13] Nevertheless, Schleiermacher's interpretation concerning the relation between coherence and first impressions does not require the additional claim of historical accuracy in order to be true. By virtue of Schleiermacher's own claims concerning the identity of

---

10. Friedrich Schleiermacher, *The Life of Jesus* (ed. J. C. Verheyden; trans. S. M. Gilmour; Lives of Jesus Series; Philadelphia: Fortress, 1975; repr., Mifflintown, Penn.: Sigler, 1997), 43.

11. Ibid., 159. John's tendency, according to Schleiermacher, is that he "wishes to make understandable the disaster in Christ's destiny together with the authentic nature of his activity, while—regarding the matter from John's own standpoint—the two conflicted with one another" (ibid.).

12. Ibid., 43.

13. Verheyden refers to Karl Bretschneider's late dating for John's Gospel in 1820 (Verheyden, "Introduction," in ibid., xxxi).

influence emanating from Christ's postmortem and antemortem presence,[14] literary coherence can be applied as a criterion to any expression of experiences of Jesus. The systematic coherence of a doctrinal system, in fact, reflects precisely the relation of systematic coherence to contemporary personal conviction regarding the transformative effect of Jesus.[15] What Schleiermacher means by historical proximity to Jesus is the immediacy of Jesus' presence to every age.

If the text is regarded as the expression of its author's experience with reality, then the interpretation of the text must include, if not presuppose, a psychological mechanism explaining the author's production of the literary work in relation to reality. Authorial intention is a mainstay of Schleiermacher's hermeneutical program.[16] The correct interpretation of a text relies in part on the accurate identification of a subjective authorial unity structuring the work as a whole. This unity is the author's tendency, the theme that is extended throughout the work in order to permit identifying parts of the work to the whole and to order these parts in specific relations to each other. Most important, the tendency expresses the author's psychological grasp of reality. Authorial intention is not just a subjective psychological condition that is presupposed by the text's unity. Rather, it is the psychological site at which the author experiences a reality in terms of a proportion between passive influence from the environment and active contribution to the categorizing of that experience. This hermeneutical insight recalls Schleiermacher's psychological claim in *The Christian Faith*: each of life's moments is constituted by a feeling of dependence and a feeling of freedom that register together mutual reciprocity with the environment.[17] Authorial intention as the psychological unity grasping the reality of an experience is, according to Schleiermacher, the unity between the subjective reality of an author's psychological conditions and the objective reality that is experienced. This unity is a psychological unity of passivity and activity that is evident at the only place at which experiences are expressed: the text, its grammar, choice of terms, syntax, positioning of main to relative clauses, and all other literary evidence. The text is the hermeneutical key for recovering the real of experienced reality from the perspective of its author.

---

14. Friedrich Schleiermacher, *The Christian Faith* (ed. H. R. McKintosh and J. S. Stewart; trans. D. M. Baillie et al.; Edinburgh: T&T Clark 1999), §14.1 (69).

15. See my argument regarding this relation in "Systematic Theology: Beautifully True," in *Truth: Interdisciplinary Dialogues in a Pluralistic Age* (ed. C. Helmer and K. De Troyer, with K. Goetz; Studies in Philosophical Theology 22; Leuven: Peeters, 2003), 34–40.

16. See Friedrich Schleiermacher, *Hermeneutics and Criticism and Other Writings* (ed. and trans. A. Bowie; Cambridge Texts in the History of Philosophy; Cambridge: Cambridge University Press, 1998).

17. Schleiermacher, *Christian Faith*, §4.2 (13–14).

Multiple authorship writes experiential multivalence into the New Testament. The New Testament Gospels, in addition to other Gospels that are
not included in the canonical New Testament, are characterized by plurality.
There are four canonical Gospels, each superscribed by four different names
purporting to be the Gospels' respective authors.[18] The superscription privileges individual authorship at the level of the New Testament's final form, even
though the historical origin of the superscripts might not coincide with the
individual Gospel's composition history. At the level of the canonical whole,
these superscriptions point to four different authors, each presiding over four
different accounts of Jesus' life and passion. Modern literary criticism has
been more insistent than Schleiermacher on the literary integrity of these four
Gospels. Rather than perceiving them as the compiled aggregates of undis-
tinguished writers, modern literary critics concede the literary value of the
Gospels, viewing the authors as literary creators in their own right.[19] Such a
literary appreciation can provide even more helpful evidence than Schleiermacher ascertains for his text theory regarding the recovery of the real through
authorial intention. If the texts are understood in Schleiermacher's terms as
accounts of reality, then their literary quality and features can be related with
hermeneutical precision to the distinct perspectives of experienced reality that
Schleiermacher was unable to claim for Matthew and Luke.[20]

It is an assumption of the New Testament that Jesus is the same referent
in each particular Gospel and epistle. Jesus is designated by different names
that overlap in different texts: Son of Man, Son of God, shepherd, Christ,
the Crucified One, the one raised by the power of the Spirit. The nuances in
the meanings of these names differ according to the semantic fields of individual author's vocabularies. For Paul, the Crucified One is the designation
associated with the unequivocal triumph of grace, whereas for Matthew the
Crucified One is associated with a "secondary conditioning of salvation."[21] In

---

18. David Trobisch uses these superscriptions to argue for an early redaction of a New
Testament codex in *The First Edition of the New Testament* (Oxford: Oxford University Press,
2000), 46–7.

19. See, e.g., David M. Rhoads, *The Challenge of Diversity: The Witness of Paul and the
Gospels* (Minneapolis: Fortress, 1996), 62, 99.

20. Schleiermacher judged Matthew and Luke to be redactions of a third or fourth hand
on the grounds of literary inelegance. See Friedrich Schleiermacher, "Über die Schriften des
Lukas: Ein kritischer Versuch (1817)," in *Exegetische Schriften* (vol. 1.8 of *Kritische Gesamtausgabe*; ed. H. Patsch and D. Schmid; Berlin: de Gruyter, 2001), 19–20.

21. This is Christof Landmesser's terminology (*die sekundäre Konditionierung des Heils*)
in *Jüngerberufung und Zuwendung zu Gott: Ein exegetischer Beitrag zum Konzept der matthäischen Soteriologie im Anschluß an Mt 9,9–13* (WUNT 133; Tübingen: Mohr Siebeck, 2001),
141–49.

all these cases manifesting differences in authorial intentions, the designations identify the same referent. Such an assumption boldly holds together the differences in descriptions, Jesus' life and death, his preexistence and ascension, his postmortem and antemortem existence. There are four Gospels yet one gospel, as Luther summarizes the relation between difference and unity in terms of one common referent.[22]

One reality serves to orient perspectival multivalence in the New Testament. It is this preoccupation that represents the objective side of authorial intention. Authorial intention requires an intentionality that expresses the individual author's perspectival grasp of reality. Without this intentionality, the New Testament authors would have nothing to say. The sameness of the referent in spite of differences in titles and descriptions must be assumed if there is to be complementarity or even disagreement between differing accounts. Each New Testament passage can be investigated as to its contribution to understanding the aspects of personal presence responsible for what is experienced as decisively transformative. From the perspective of its referent, the New Testament already contains its own guides for interpreting its form and content. Without this assumption, there could neither be agreement concerning the genre of the gospel as the "good news of Jesus Christ" (Mark 1:1) nor consensus concerning the intention of the epistles to comfort and exhort communities living under the existing sign of Christ's reign.[23] The assumption furthermore communicates directions regarding how best to interpret a person as the text's referent. The New Testament's personal referent stands under the same anthropological and narrative conditions of interpretation as any human being. The gospel's content is informed by the narrative details of Jesus' life. The four Gospels' common focus on Jesus' ministry and extended accounts of the passion also suggest the significance of these details for an understanding of his person.

The category of person as appropriate for understanding the New Testament's referent is problematized at those sites of description that veer into the realm of theological interpretation. New Testament multivalence poses the problems of historical and chronological gaps, of grammatical and syntactical variation, and of harmonizing different accounts. Theology can help readers engage discrepancies by offering other levels of meaning by which to understand the text. The narrative tracking of Jesus' life and passion in the Gospels, for example, seems to problematize the historical claim that the Gospels were

---

22. Martin Luther, "Preface to the New Testament (1546)" (trans. C. M. Jacobs; rev. E. T. Bachmann), in *Luther's Works: American Edition* (ed. J. Pelikan and H. T. Lehmann; 55 vols.; St. Louis: Concordia; Philadelphia: Fortress, 1958–86), 35:357–58.

23. This and all subsequent references to the Christian Bible are from the NRSV.

written later than Paul's epistles, even though they occur canonically at the beginning of the New Testament. A theological reflection on this historical difficulty interprets the meaning of Jesus' person in terms of his work. The person, whether antemortem or postmortem, is the cause of his saving effect. Salvation is inscribed into the origins of Jesus' life, which are themselves shrouded in mystery. The historical problems of reconstructing Jesus' origins can also be the subject of theological engagement. At the origin of Jesus' life is a signal of his eternal relation to God (John 1:1). This relation of essence explains the power of his work and the divine authority from which he receives this power.

The theological categories of person and work together constitute the conceptual relationship that brings together in a single focus the New Testament's perspectival multivalence. The categories abstract from multivalent accounts of reality, yet as abstractions can be applied as the structural parameter for interpreting the different texts. Different accounts are viewed through this common structural lens so that they can be categorized according to a particular aspect of reality. This aspect of reality remaining the same throughout difference is the attribution of transformative effects to Jesus in each and every case. Schleiermacher captures the attribution of diverse definitive life-transforming effects to their same cause in a sermon:

> But in these conversations there was also something of that other effect—an impression, independent of the subject at hand, that was always the same, although it was manifested in the most various forms and widely divergent conditions throughout his entire association with them. And it was this impression that Christ's whole personality, his distinctive nature however it might express itself, never failed to create.[24]

From new possibilities for living in community to the radical transition from death to life, the varieties of transformative experiences are all predicated of Jesus. From the earliest exorcisms to his resurrection appearances, Jesus is the one from whom all blessings flow. A common reality joins multivalent description to theology.

2. Recovery of the Real in Theology

If theological concepts do not have any corresponding intuitions, this emptiness will result in prescriptive vacuity. This is the danger that haunts

---

24. Friedrich Schleiermacher, "The Effects of Scripture and of the Redeemer," in *Servant of the Word: Selected Sermons of Friedrich Schleiermacher* (trans. D. De Vries; Fortress Texts in Modern Theology; Philadelphia: Fortress, 1987), 103–4.

contemporary Christian theology. This discipline, more than others, seems to be currently preoccupied with canonical questions of geographically limited focus primarily because it has been historically concerned with the historical method as integral to the formation of its concepts. But this does not need to be so. The real can be recovered for theology in a way analogous to what I have described above in section 1 for the New Testament. Here I turn to the possibilities of drawing on the New Testament, on Schleiermacher's epistemology, and on contemporary non-European contextual-theological movements in order to recover the reality of intuitions for theology's concepts.

The multivalence characterizing the New Testament already has a distinct profile; its topography suggests interpretative possibilities. The canonical shape of the Christian Bible, for example, orders the final prophetic books of the Old Testament in proximity to the Gospels and ends with John's eschatological vision in the book of Revelation. This topography leans toward a salvation-historical interpretation. A reception-historical topography privileges Paul's Letter to the Romans, to use another example, and thereby establishes the law-gospel relation as foundational for Western Christian belief. Specific topographical contours function as hermeneutical guides for theological interpretation anchored in the reality shaping the text's presentation.

Theology carries the burden of its own inevitable character. Its nature is to abstract from particulars in order to reach the grand universal; its task is to relate discrete parts in relation to a coherent whole. A coherent comprehension of the whole in view of its parts requires a sufficient degree of abstraction from the particular. Not every particular detail enters into the more abstract concept; rather, bits are integrated into larger wholes through a process of abstracting common elements and determining their interrelations. The comprehension of the whole occurs by grasping common elements through every stage of abstraction. If abstraction proceeds by relegating particulars to an ontologically lesser status than the concepts that allegedly grasp them, the resulting concept will be devoid of determined content. Being devoid of any particular way of being is precisely that, an empty concept alone at the top of Aristotle's chain of being. If abstraction occurs by conveying the particular in the conceptualization of the universal, then the concept grabs hold of reality and more adequately represents it. How the real can be recovered for the theological concept is the serious question in view of theology's burden and challenge.

Theology's burden can also be its joy. Abstraction as a work can be understood for this discipline as seeking precisely to articulate the concepts of religious realities as they are lived, practiced, and thought. In its process of abstraction, theology conceptualizes exactly the radically particular realities of face-to-face encounters, individual stories of personal pain and redemption, and the sacramental centers of real personal presences. If theology is to be about life rather than about the worshipful awe of empty or exhausted concepts, then it must explore ways to retain the determination of its concepts by the real.

The task of topographical design is for the theologian the process of forming concepts. Already in the New Testament, the writers are at work offering topographies for future doctrinal conceptualization; the texts bear the structural imprints of persons who have experienced and schematized reality. Luke's conviction concerning the world-historical significance of the babe in the manger carries his Gospel (Luke 2:1–2). Paul's passion about the universal reconciliation accomplished by the crucified Christ informs his preaching and exhortation (2 Cor 5:18–19). John's Jesus, in the world but not of this world (John 16:16), structures the misunderstood conversations and the death sentence for the one who did not commit a crime. The concepts appear in narrative, expressing tendencies structuring the texts: healing, forgiveness, resurrection. The theological task of interpreting these texts is to determine hermeneutically how the tendencies surface as concepts schematizing reality. Paul's dramatic conversion, the recovery of sight after the blindness with which he was struck on the way to Damascus, is the experience riveting his soul to a new reality (Acts 9), which Paul expresses as he treats different topics in distinct historical circumstances. The Corinthians get a glimpse of this new reality when they are exhorted to temper their spiritual exuberance by obeying the gospel of love (1 Cor 13). The Galatians are exhorted to relinquish their enthusiasm for legalism by entering into the freedom for which Christ has set "us" free (Gal 5:1). By hermeneutically recovering the contours of experience, theology gets to the particular aspect of reality that is schematized by the text.

The theological recovery of the real in the New Testament is the hermeneutical task of describing and analyzing the ways in which concepts focus at the textual surface. The concepts, however, are themselves the products of psychological states and historical events, registering relations between subject and object. They can be described in view of an individual writer's production of her text. Yet the same mechanism of conceptual focus at the surface can also be applied to the New Testament as a whole, albeit without the individuation of the concept to authorial differences. When the New Testament is considered as a theological whole, its conceptual *Tendenz* can be described in view of a distinctive experience. Even though distinctive authorship cannot be applied to the text as a whole,[25] the composite can be read as

---

25. This question (mentioned by Wolterstorff in "Unity behind the Canon," 232) concerns the possibility of God as author of the entire work.

structural agreement concerning the person-work relation. The New Testament is constituted as a whole by a conceptual structure that comes together in its parts. The person-work relation does not imply abstraction from the real by denying its determination by reality. Rather, the abstraction of structural agreement as the person-work relation conveys a key material-theological claim. The unique reality of Christ's person is conveyed by necessarily relating transformative effect to its personal cause. As such, the New Testament topography presents a relation between person and work that the subsequent Christian theological tradition has categorized by the doctrines of Christology and soteriology. The process of abstracting the conceptual relation from the text as a whole presupposes a determination by the unique reality that is conceptualized.

The question regarding the analogy between New Testament theology and contemporary systematic theology can now be formulated. How can the real be recovered for contemporary theology in light of the formation of concepts that are significant to its problem-solving? It is the difference in perspective that Schleiermacher sought to minimize vis-à-vis concept formation at the origins of Christianity and at its present-tense location. For Schleiermacher, there is no qualitative difference in experiencing the person of Christ as a bodily person or as a spiritual presence embodied in the Christian community.[26] The early Christians were at no experiential advantage and, as a result, at no conceptual advantage, by being able to put their hands inside Christ's wounds (John 20:27). The difference in mode of perception, as personal bodily presence or as personal presence communicated by the community, does not presuppose a difference in perceptual apparatus; in both circumstances, the senses are affected. This perceptual difference does not result in a different effect; the same redemptive effect is also guaranteed by the sameness of the person: "Jesus Christ is the same yesterday and today and forever" (Heb 13:8). By underlining the sameness of person and effect, Schleiermacher stabilizes the identity of concept formation for both the New Testament and for any subsequent theology that bases its claims on expressions regarding the reality of Christ's person. The same concepts continue to be formed because they are evoked by the experiences of the same reality.

The challenge to forming the concept in full view of reality becomes a problem when access to reality is hypersaturated with determination. The weight of tradition, its historical span, its experiential comprehensiveness, and its issues of power and authority are factors already playing into concept formation before an individual or community deploys and shapes those

---

26. See n. 14.

concepts to describe reality. Theology in its Western Christian form is particularly burdened by inheritance. Since the incorporation of an explicit history of concept formation as an integral piece of systematic theology, theology itself has been stagnating in its European mold. The history of dogma is a theological tool that is supposed to contextualize contemporary theological questions in the historical light of their intellectual development. It involves, like all other historical descriptions, an abstraction from history, yet its highly reified interpretation of history functions to dislocate intellectual history from the many histories playing into the formation of ideas. Furthermore, the reconstruction of this history itself presupposes an authoritative instance for those doing the reconstruction. Voices are lost, voices are marginalized, and voices are destroyed in the process of abstracting an authoritative canonical connection between past and present. When such a method is coupled with a metaphysic of history, the heavy burden of truth serving power becomes too much even for reality to bear. The real is confused with the rational, and an intellectualized history replaces those living realities that have shaped the concepts in the first place.

Intellectual history as constitutive of theology's concept formation is in contemporary crisis. Theology continues to deploy concepts used by the tradition to schematize reality. Yet it is precisely the assumption concerning the capacity of these concepts to capture contemporary experience that must be reexamined. If these concepts are made to stand as ciphers for a history that is alien, if their truth is presupposed without adequate dialogue, if their empirical determination does not match one's own experience, then the concepts no longer serve the living (Luke 9:60). This difficulty is particularly insistent, given the primarily European history of the concepts' formation. Theological concepts risk becoming the artifacts of a European white male intellectual elite if this historically assumed course is not critically appropriated. A theology that is dead will be preoccupied with the past, canonizing its canon over and over again in every present generation. Theology can live as a conceptual discipline only if its predicates are determined from the contemporary perspective; the past only lives as past in present reality. If intellectual history is to continue to have a formative role to play in assigning concept formation to set up the present, then it must be open to different histories meeting it with regions of experience that cannot be pressed into traditional theological molds. This is the case for the new multibraided accounts of the European reformations and of contextual theologies, both of which are coming up with new empirical determinations for theological concepts.

Schleiermacher offers a useful model to explain how the real can be recovered for a theology that aims to represent ideas living in present Christian experience. The dialectical method can be applied to theology in order to determine theology's concepts by real particulars. According to Schleier-macher, concepts are formed in history, through both individual biography and the transhistory of concepts in a particular historical series. The concept is presupposed as the subject term in a judgment, standing for the unity in reality of a particular comprehending its empirical appearances.[27] As such, it exists in reality, yet the empirical grasp of its existence is assigned to its predicates, and the grasp of its reality is assigned to a conceptual act of reason. Concept formation proceeds by assigning predicates gleaned from reality to the subject term; concept formation proceeds by way of judgment formation. Schleiermacher borrows from a Leibnizian account of intensional logic in order to explain the mechanism of the history of concept formation. A singular concept (conceptus singularis) is permitted on the grounds that it has one predicate. In the language of intensional logic, the concept presupposes the existence of the subject term. As predicates are assigned to the subject term, the concept is formed. Subsequent judgments presuppose earlier predications, whether true or false, so that the historical series of predication can include false predications that need to be revised.

The conceptual grasp of the subject's unity is an achievement of speculative reason working in tandem with empirical reason. While empirical reason investigates the subject's appearances, speculative reason unites those appearances in such a way as to offer a preliminary comprehension of the subject as a whole. By proceeding in this way, the empirical is brought together as a unity by conceptual act. The reality of the conceptual unity of the subject term is informed by the empirical predicates assigned to it. Reality is grasped by the unity of empirical predicates. Schleiermacher's achievement in his understanding of concept formation is both to rid the concept of any psychologically occult unity posited behind appearances and to recover the real by grasping its unity through judgment formation. As a concept, it is fundamentally revisable; as a reality, the appearances of the unity must be available to experience.

A compelling and controversial example of Schleiermacher's method of concept formation is his account of the concept of the Redeemer. Many scholars have noted the similarity of referent between Schleiermacher's reconstruction of the life of Jesus and his conceptual analysis of the Redeemer in The Christian Faith.[28] This structural agreement between exegetical results and theological claims is not the result of a conceptual overriding of his-

---

27. Friedrich Schleiermacher, Vorlesungen über Dialektik (vol. 2.10 of Kritische Gesamtausgabe; ed. Andreas Arndt; 2 vols.; Berlin: de Gruyter, 2004), 2:504–7.

28. See Schleiermacher, Life of Jesus; idem, Christian Faith §§93–100 (377–431).

torical data, as David Friedrich Strauss criticized.[29] Rather, the aim of the reconstructive exegetical work, as Schleiermacher understands it, is to give a "calculus" of Jesus as person.[30] The conceptualization of the person of Jesus is a grasp of his individuality, not as a psychologically occult reality but as his personality becomes available in personal development for viewing. The calculus constituting Jesus is itself the explanation for all his thinking and doing. By the same token, the conceptual delineation of Christ as Redeemer follows from the effects; by virtue of the effects of his person, the predicates can be assigned to their cause. On Schleiermacher's own grounds, the soteriological claims concerning Jesus' effects are attributed to the conceptual grasp of the unity of his person. The determinations of effect and cause are mutually reciprocal, dependent on the recovery of the real through both the empirical and the conceptual.

The multivalent accounts of the reality of Jesus can continue to provide theology with the empirical moorings that it needs. As theology continues to categorize experienced reality, it must work to open up various discourses that point to new areas of religious experience and then strengthen its resources to describe and explain these phenomena. In light of the increased appreciation that the Christian religion is lived out in communities well beyond the bounds of European or European-oriented confines, theologians are drawing increasingly on experiential-contextual resources to determine their concepts. Feminist theologians, for example, privilege experiences particular to women to expose ways in which systems, thought patterns, and behaviors have treated women as less than men. This imperative must change an academic theological environment that seems to place race, class, and gender restrictions on the "universal" reality that it purports to conceptualize.

Yet openness to new discursive regions must not come at the expense of forgetting. Concepts are formed transhistorically, especially those in view of a transhistorical religion such as Christianity. If the concept is to ring true for contemporary use and formation, its historical predicates must also sound as possibilities in the present. There must be agreement that the concept as it has been formed historically is capable of further development precisely because its predicates are possible predicates that might be actualized now. The task of rehearsing the possibility of predicates demands criticism and correction that simultaneously involves making claims to knowledge about the past from the present perspective. The predicates as possibilities undergo transformations

---

29. David Friedrich Strauss, *The Christ of Faith and the Jesus of History: A Critique of Schleiermacher's* Life of Jesus (ed. and trans. L. E. Keck; Lives of Jesus Series; Philadelphia: Fortress, 1977), 36.

30. The term is Schleiermacher's; see Schleiermacher, *Life of Jesus,* 8.

and then, in confrontation with novelty, might even determine the concepts in new ways. True multivalence means recognizing possible predicates together with actual predicates in the concept. This recognition is what makes true liberalism in view of the truth of reality possible.

3. Conclusion

If postmodernism has crashed against a resistant real, then it is the responsibility of theology to restore reality to its proper place for thinking and doing. Thinking about reality is a claim already established in the New Testament; its *raison d'être* is the joyful response to a reality encountered as transformative. Doing also requires the real as the place for moral reasoning and judgment. Without such a temporally and spatially constituted realm, doing would not exist as the concrete actualizations of personal and communal commitment.

The test case of Schleiermacher used in this essay argues for a recovery of the real through the dual application of empirical and conceptual reason. An account of New Testament multivalence showed that a primarily empirical method could glean the diversity of authorial expressions of experiences of Christ, thereby offering possibilities of experience together with an account of the structural parameters of those possibilities. Primarily conceptual reason comprehends the unities of appearances as those unities of authorial intentions are available for interpretation and subsequently for the formation of theological concepts. The conceptual grasp of unity, according to Schleiermacher, is accounted for in such a way that the unity does not remain an abstraction from empirical reality but rather is a specific way of relating the empirical to the conceptual. By this procedure, the empirical can be celebrated rather than repressed as it determines the concepts. The New Testament's multivalence can be an analogy for the reasons why theology should pursue new areas of experiential discourses. By attending deeply and openly to many accounts of experience, theology might become an ethically stronger and materially richer discipline, all the better to convey the reality for which Christian theology is known and for which it exists.

Select Bibliography

Barton, John. *Understanding Old Testament Ethics: Approaches and Explorations*. Louisville: Westminster John Knox, 2003.

———, ed. *The Cambridge Companion to Biblical Interpretation*. Cambridge Companions to Religion. Cambridge: Cambridge University Press, 1998.

Betz, Hans D. *The Sermon on the Mount: A Commentary on the Sermon on the Mount*. Hermeneia. Minneapolis: Fortress, 1995.

Brown, Raymond. *An Introduction to the Gospel of John*. Edited by Francis J. Moloney. New York: Doubleday, 2003.

Carr, David M. *The Erotic Word: Sexuality, Spirituality and the Bible*. New York: Oxford University Press, 2003.

———. "Gender and the Shaping of Desire in the Song of Songs and Its Interpretation." *JBL* 119 (2000): 233–48.

———. "The Song of Songs as a Microcosm of the Canonization and Decanonization Process." Pages 173–89 in *Canonization and Decanonization*. Edited by Arie van der Kooij and Karel van der Toorn. SHR 82. Leiden: Brill, 1998.

Carr, David M., and Colleen Conway. "The Divine-Human Marriage Matrix and Constructions of Gender in the Christian Bible." In *Sacred Marriages in the Biblical World*. Edited by Martti Nissinen and Risto Uru. Winona Lake, Ind.: Eisenbrauns, forthcoming.

Carroll, James. *Constantine's Sword: The Church and the Jews*. New York: Houghton Mifflin, 2002.

Carter, Warren. " 'Solomon in All His Glory': Intertextuality and Matthew 6:29," *JSNT* 65 (1997): 3–25.

Chapman, Stephen, Christine Helmer, and Christof Landmesser, eds. *Biblischer Text und theologische Theoriebildung*. BThSt 44. Neukirchen-Vluyn: Neukirchener, 2001.

Chauvet, Louis-Marie. *The Sacraments: The Word of God at the Mercy of the Body*. Collegeville, Minn.: Liturgical Press, 2001.

———. *Symbol and Sacrament: A Sacramental Reinterpretation of Christian Existence*. Translated by Patrick Madigan and Madeleine E. Beaumont. Collegeville, Minn.: Liturgical Press, 1995.

Childs, Brevard S. *Biblical Theology of the Old and New Testaments: Theological Reflection on the Christian Bible*. Minneapolis: Fortress, 1993.

———. *Isaiah*. OTL. Louisville: Westminster John Knox, 2001.

Clements, R. E. *Isaiah 1–39*. NCBC. Grand Rapids: Eerdmans, 1980.

Cohen, Gershon. "The Song of Songs and the Jewish Religious Mentality." Pages 1–21 in *The Samuel Friedland Lectures, 1960–1966*. Edited by Louis Finkelstein. New York: Jewish Theological Seminary, 1966.

Davis, Ellen F. *Proverbs, Ecclesiastes and the Song of Songs*. Westminster Bible Companion. Louisville: Westminster John Knox, 2000.

Ebeling, Gerhard. "The Meaning of 'Biblical Theology.'" Pages 79–97 in vol. 1 of idem, *Word and Faith*. Translated by James W. Leitch. London: SCM, 1963. Translation of "Was heißt 'Biblische Theologie'? (1955)." Pages 69–89 in vol. 1 of idem, *Wort und Glaube*. 3rd ed. Tübingen: Mohr Siebeck, 1967.

Eberhart, Christian. *Studien zur Bedeutung der Opfer im Alten Testament: Die Signifikanz von Blut- und Verbrennungsriten im kultischen Rahmen*. WMANT 94. Neukirchen-Vluyn: Neukirchener, 2002.

Esler, Philip F. *Community and Gospel in Luke-Acts*. SNTSMS 57. Cambridge: Cambridge University Press, 1987.

Goshen-Gottstein, Alon. "Thinking of/with Scripture: Struggling for the Religious Significance of the Song of Songs." *JSR* 3 (2003). No pages. Cited 3 July 2006. Online: http://etext.lib.virginia.edu/journals/ssr/issues/volume3/number2/ssr03-02-e03.html.

Gundry, Robert H. *Mark: A Commentary on his Apology for the Cross*. Grand Rapids: Eerdmans, 1993.

Helmer, Christine. "Schleiermacher's Exegetical Theology and the New Testament." Pages 229–48 in *Cambridge Companion to Schleiermacher*. Edited by Jacqueline Mariña. Cambridge Companions to Religion. Cambridge: Cambridge University Press, 2005.

Helmer, Christine, and Christof Landmesser, eds. *One Scripture or Many? Canon from Biblical, Theological, and Philosophical Perspectives*. Oxford: Oxford University Press, 2003.

Helmer, Christine, with the assistance of Taylor G. Petrey, eds. *Biblical Interpretation: History, Context, and Reality*. SBLSymS 26. Atlanta: Society of Biblical Literature, 2005.

Hick, John. *The Metaphor of God Incarnate*. Louisville: Westminster John Knox, 1993.

Hubert, Henri, and Marcel Mauss. "Essai sur la Nature et la Fonction du Sacrifice." *Année sociologique* 2 (1899): 29–138.

Jewett, Robert, ed. *Christology and Exegesis: New Approaches*. Semeia 30 (1985).

Kloppenborg Verbin, John S. *Excavating Q: The History and Setting of the Sayings Gospel*. Minneapolis: Fortress, 2000.

Kundert, Lukas. *Gen 22,1–19 im Alten Testament, im Frühjudentum und im Neuen Testament*. Vol. 1 of *Die Opferung/Bindung Isaaks*. WMANT 78. Neukirchen-Vluyn: Neukirchener, 1998.

Luther, Martin. "Against Latomus (1521)." Translated by George A. Lindbeck. Pages 137–260 in vol. 32 of *Luther's Works: American Edition*. Edited by Jaroslav Pelikan and Helmut T. Lehmann. 55 vols. St. Louis: Concordia; Philadelphia: Fortress, 1958–86.

———. "Rationis Latomianae confutatio (1521)." Pages 43–128 in vol. 8 of *D. Martin Luthers Werke: Kritische Gesamtausgabe*. Edited by J. K. F. Knaake et al. 67 vols. Weimar: Böhlau, 1883–2000.

Malina, Bruce J. *The New Testament World: Insights from Cultural Anthropology*. Rev. ed. Atlanta: Knox, 1993.

Milgrom, Jo. *The Binding of Isaac: The Akedah—A Primary Symbol in Jewish Thought and Art*. Berkeley, Calif.: Bibal, 1988.

Moltmann, Jürgen. *Trinität und Reich Gottes: Zur Gotteslehre*. Munich: Kaiser, 1980. Translated as *The Trinity and the Kingdom: The Doctrine of God*. Translated by Margaret Kohl. San Fransisco: Harper & Row, 1981. Repr., Minneapolis: Fortress, 1993.

Murphy, Jeffrie G., and Jean Hampton. *Forgiveness and Mercy*. Cambridge: Cambridge University Press, 1988.

Neyrey, Jerome H. *Honor and Shame in the Gospel of Matthew*. Louisville: Westminster John Knox, 1998.

Nicolet, Claude. *Space, Geography, and Politics in the Early Roman Empire*. Translated by Hélène Leclerc. Ann Arbor: University of Michigan Press, 1991.

Oberdorfer, Bernd. *Filioque: Geschichte und Theologie eines ökumenischen Problems*. Forschungen zur systematischen und ökumenischen Theologie 96. Göttingen: Vandenhoeck & Ruprecht, 2001.

Pagels, Elaine. *The Origin of Satan*. New York: Vintage, 1995.

Pannenberg, Wolfhart. *Systematische Theologie*. Vol. 1. Göttingen: Vandenhoeck & Ruprecht, 1988. Translated as *Systematic Theology*. Vol. 1. Translated by Geoffrey W. Bromiley. Grand Rapids: Eerdmans, 1991.

Rahner, Karl. "Der dreifaltige Gott als transzendenter Urgrund der Heilsgeschichte." Pages 317–401 in *Die Heilsgeschichte vor Christus*. Vol. 2 of *Mysterium Salutis*. Edited by J. Feiner and M. Löhrer. Einsiedeln: Benziger, 1967. Translated as *The Trinity*. Translated by Joseph Donceel. New York: Herder & Herder, 1970. Repr., New York: Crossroad, 1997.

Ricoeur, Paul. *The Symbolism of Evil*. Translated by Emerson Buchanan. Boston: Beacon, 1969.

Robbins, Vernon K. *Exploring the Texture of Texts: A Guide to Socio-rhetorical Interpretation*. Valley Forge, Pa.: Trinity Press International, 1996.

———. *The Tapestry of Early Christian Discourse: Rhetoric, Society and Ideology*. New York: Routledge, 1996.

Schleiermacher, Friedrich. *The Christian Faith*. Edited by H. R. McKintosh and J. S. Stewart. Translated by D. M. Baillie et al. Edinburgh: T&T Clark, 1999.

———. *Exegetische Schriften*. Vol. 1.8 of *Kritische Gesamtausgabe*. Edited by Hermann Patsch and Dirk Schmid. Berlin: de Gruyter, 2001.

———. *Vorlesungen über Dialektik*. Vol. 2.10.1–2 of *Kritische Gesamtausgabe*. Edited by Andreas Arndt. 2 vols. Berlin: de Gruyter, 2004.

Scott, James. *Domination and the Arts of Resistance*. New Haven: Yale University Press, 1990.

Seitz, Christopher R. *Figured Out: Typology and Providence in Christian Scripture*. Louisville: Westminster John Knox, 2001.

———. *Isaiah 1–39*. IBC. Louisville: Knox, 1993.

Smith, Wilfred Cantwell. *What Is Scripture? A Comparative Approach*. Minneapolis: Fortress, 1993.

Stendhal, Krister. "Biblical Theology, Commentary." *IDB* 1:418–32.

Swain, Simon. *Hellenism and Empire: Language, Classicism, and Power in the Greek World, AD 50–250*. Oxford: Oxford University Press, 1996.

Sweeney, Marvin A. *Isaiah 1–39: With an Introduction to Prophetic Literature*. FOTL 16. Grand Rapids: Eerdmans, 1996.

Swinburne, Richard. *Responsibility and Atonement*. Oxford: Oxford University Press, 1989.

Tilborg, Sjef van. *The Sermon on the Mount as an Ideological Intervention*. Wolfeboro, N.H.: Van Gorcum, 1986.

Whitmarsh, Tim. *Greek Literature and the Roman Empire: The Politics of Imitation*. Oxford: Oxford University Press, 2001.

Contributors

John Barton is the Oriel and Laing Professor of the Interpretation of Holy Scripture at the University of Oxford (England).

David Carr is Professor of Old Testament/Hebrew Bible at Union Theological Seminary (New York).

Stephen T. Davis is Russell K. Pitzer Professor of Philosophy at Claremont McKenna College (Claremont, California).

Christian A. Eberhart is Associate Professor of New Testament Studies at Lutheran Theological Seminary in Saskatoon (Saskatchewan, Canada).

Lincoln E. Galloway is Associate Professor of Homiletics at Claremont School of Theology (Claremont, California).

Gary Gilbert is Associate Professor of Religious Studies at Claremont McKenna College (Claremont, California).

Christine Helmer is Senior Scholar in Theology at Harvard Divinity School (Cambridge, Massachusetts).

Charlene T. Higbe is a member of the Faculty Support Team at Harvard Divinity School (Cambridge, Massachusetts).

Kevin Mongrain is Assistant Professor in the Program of Liberal Studies at the University of Notre Dame (South Bend, Indiana).

Bernd Oberdorfer is Professor of Systematic Theology in the Institute of Protestant Theology at the University of Augsburg (Germany).

C. R. Seitz is Professor of Old Testament and Theological Studies in the Faculty of Divinity at the University of St. Andrews (Scotland).

Index of Ancient Sources

Hebrew Bible

New Testament

Index of Names

Abel (and Cain), 50, 61
Abraham (and Isaac), 8, 48–63
Abram, 49
Ackroyd, P. R., 40
Aelius Aristides, 92, 96, 98, 101
Aeneas, 88
Aeschines, 92
Ahasuerus (king), 22
Ahaz (king), 43
Akiba, Rabbi, 11
Alt, Albrecht, 37, 41–42
Anchises, 88
Anselm of Canterbury, 26 fig. 3, 153, 154 n. 22
Apollo, 94
Aponius, 15
Appian of Alexandria, 92
Aquinas, Thomas, 154 n. 23
Aratus, 97
Aristides, 98
Aristotle, 152, 170
Arius, 146
Arrianus, Lucius Flavius, 92
Assmann, Jan, 163 n. 4
Athanasius, 146 n. 4, 148–49, 151
Augustine, 110, 129, 152–54, 158, 163–64
Augustus (emperor), 85, 88–89, 99–102

Barclay, John M. G., 104
Barrett, C. K., 85–86
Barth, Karl, 156, 164
Barton, John, 8–9, 177
Basil of Caesarea, 148–50
Bernard of Clairvaux, 29, 34

Betz, Hans D., 67 n. 3, 177
Bretschneider, Karl, 165 n. 13
Brown, Raymond, 100 n. 55, 144 n. 68, 177
Bultmann, Rudolf, 118 n. 8

Cain (and Abel), 50, 61
Cairns, Francis, 88 n. 16
Calvin, Jean, 164
Carlston, Charles E., 67 n. 2
Carr, David, 6–7, 13 n. 5, 14 n. 8, 15 n. 10, 18 nn. 15–17, 20 n. 19, 21 n. 20, 28 n. 29, 32 n. 34, 177
Carroll, James, 144 n. 67, 177
Carroll R., M. Daniel, 44 n. 19
Carter, Warren, 70 n. 9, 72 n. 11, 180
Chapman, Stephen, 177
Chauvet, Louis-Marie, 9, 125–44, 177
Childs, Brevard S., 4, 8, 38–45, 177–78
Chrysostom, John, 122
Cicero, 87–88
Cleese, John, 83
Clements, R. E., 40, 178
Cohen, Gershon, 31, 178
Conway, Colleen, 32 n. 34, 177
Conzelmann, Hans, 85 n. 5
Cornelius (centurion), 85
Crispus (head of synagogue), 98

Daly, Robert J., 47, 49 n. 3, 57 n. 26, 65 n. 43
David (king), 41–45, 49–50, 120–21
Davis, Ellen F., 31, 178
Davis, Stephen T., 7, 9
Delaney, Carol, 58

INDEX OF SUBJECTS

Printed in the United States
61974LVS00002B/234

9 781589 832213